Lenin's Final Fight

Lenin's Final Fight

Speeches and Writings, 1922-23

PATHFINDER

NEW YORK LONDON MONTREAL SYDNEY

Edited by George Fyson

Copyright © 1995 Pathfinder Press

ISBN 0-87348-807-5 paper; ISBN 0-87348-808-3 cloth
Library of Congress Catalog Card Number 95-68455
Manufactured in the United States of America

First edition, 1995
COVER PICTURE: Leaders of the Bolshevik Party and Communist International, a painting by Malcolm McAllister on the Pathfinder Mural in New York City. From left: Gregory Zinoviev, Nikolai Bukharin, Leon Trotsky, V.I. Lenin, Karl Radek. Courtesy of the Anchor Foundation.
COVER DESIGN by Toni Gorton
BOOK DESIGN by Eric Simpson

Pathfinder
410 West Street, New York, NY 10014, U.S.A.
Fax: (212) 727-0150
CompuServe: 73321,414 • Internet: pathfinder@igc.apc.org

PATHFINDER DISTRIBUTORS AROUND THE WORLD:
Australia (and Asia and the Pacific):
     Pathfinder, 19 Terry St., Surry Hills, Sydney, N.S.W. 2010
     Postal address: P.O. Box K879, Haymarket, N.S.W. 2000
Britain (and Europe, Africa except South Africa, and Middle East):
     Pathfinder, 47 The Cut, London, SE1 8LL
Canada:
     Pathfinder, 4581 rue St-Denis, Montreal, Quebec, H2J 2L4
Iceland:
     Pathfinder, Klapparstíg 26, 2d floor, 101 Reykjavík
     Postal address: P. Box 233, 121 Reykjavík
New Zealand:
     Pathfinder, La Gonda Arcade, 203 Karangahape Road, Auckland
     Postal address: P.O. Box 8730, Auckland
Sweden:
     Pathfinder, Vikingagatan 10, S-113 42, Stockholm
United States (and Caribbean, Latin America, and South Africa):
     Pathfinder, 410 West Street, New York, NY 10014

Contents

1. Communist tasks in the
second year of the New Economic Policy

March 27, 1922

2. The fight opens: the national question and
the voluntary union of Soviet republics

September 24–October 21, 1922

3. The NEP and the world struggle for socialism
November 13–December 10, 1922

4. Defending the state monopoly of foreign trade
December 12–23, 1922

5. Lenin's letter to the party congress
December 23, 1922–January 4, 1923

6. Strengthening the alliance with the peasantry
January 2–6, 1923

7. Socialist revolution, Russia, and the East
January 16–17, 1923

8. The Workers and Peasants Inspection
January 23, 1923

9. Preparing the twelfth party congress
March 2–6, 1923

Appendix 1: Lenin on the fight for Soviet republics in Georgia and the Transcaucasus (1921, 1923)

Appendix 2: The Workers and Peasants Inspection (1919–20, 1923)

Appendix 3: Toward the party congress (1923)

Preface

Five years after the victory of the October 1917 revolution in Russia, Bolshevik leader Vladimir Ilyich Lenin waged his final political fight. The stakes were very high. Against mounting odds Lenin fought to maintain the proletarian internationalist course that had prepared the Communist Party to lead the exploited producers to power over the landlords and capitalists and enabled them to begin building a workers state. He fought for a course to unite the workers and peasants of Russia and of the nations long oppressed under tsarism into a voluntary federation of soviet republics.

This book documents Lenin's battle in his own words.

It is not a history book. The political questions addressed by Lenin deal with the most decisive piece of unfinished business in front of those who produce the wealth of the world and make possible culture: they deal with the worldwide struggle, opened by the Bolshevik-led revolution nearly eighty years ago, to replace the dictatorship of a tiny minority of exploiting capitalist families with the dictatorship of the proletariat—"political power wielded by the *majority* of the population," as Lenin put it in 1919, a "*democracy* for the masses, for the working people, for the factory workers and small peasants."[1] The outcome of this unfinished struggle will determine

Footnotes start on next page

whether the future of the world will be one of capitalist-imposed fascism and war or the transition to a communist society based on human solidarity and collective labor.

How to resolve these bitterly contested issues has been at the center of every modern revolution in which the toilers have toppled the landlords and capitalists from political power and established workers and farmers governments. These questions remain relevant today to the socialist revolution in Cuba—the first revolution since the Bolsheviks to be headed by a communist leadership that consciously uses state power in an effort to defend and advance the interests of the working class.

The revolutionary government that came to power in Russia in October 1917 was based on councils of workers, peasants, and soldiers delegates called soviets, the Russian word for "council." Having overthrown the monarchy and political power of the bourgeoisie, the young Soviet republic immediately acted to negotiate an end to Russia's involvement in the imperialist-organized slaughter of World War I. It encouraged the peasants to expropriate the landlords' estates and distribute the nationalized land to be worked by the tillers themselves. It repudiated tsarist debts to imperialist governments and bankers. It institutionalized separation of church and state. It asserted the full political rights of women, and initiated steps to advance the equality of women in social life.

The Soviet republic organized the working class in Petrograd, Moscow, and elsewhere to take increasing control over the production and distribution of goods and the organization of work in capitalist- and state-owned factories, mines, and mills. The new government set free the peoples subject to Russian oppression in the former tsarist empire and established their right to national self-determi-

1. "The Third International and Its Place in History," Lenin, *Collected Works* (hereafter *CW*) (Moscow: Progress Publishers, 1960–70, based on fourth Russian edition), vol. 29, pp. 305–13. Also in John Riddell, ed., *Founding the Communist International: Proceedings and Documents of the First Congress: March 1919* (New York: Pathfinder, 1987), pp. 31–38, a volume in the series The Communist International in Lenin's Time.

nation. Working people from the Ukraine to Azerbaijan, from Belorussia to Mongolia, were inspired by what workers and peasants in Russia were achieving and rose in revolt to link up with the workers and peasants republic.

By early 1918, forces loyal to the tsar, landlords, and capitalists had launched a civil war to overthrow the revolution. The imperialist powers—from London and Paris to Washington and Tokyo—soon intervened militarily on the side of the counterrevolution.

As the civil war deepened in 1918, the Communist Party and Soviet government backed initiatives by the working class to stop mounting sabotage of production by factory owners and other exploiters, culminating in the expropriation of the big majority of the remaining capitalists by the end of that year. The workers and peasants government also imposed a series of emergency policies that became known as "war communism" to mobilize labor and scarce industrial and agricultural resources to defeat the counterrevolution. These measures included compulsory requisitioning of a surplus portion of peasants' grain in order to feed soldiers at the front and workers in the cities. By the close of 1920 the Soviet government had won the war. But the war had taken a massive, bloody toll on the lives of the most class-conscious workers and devastated the countryside, where the majority of peasants had backed the Soviet government to prevent the return of the landlords.

Given an impulse by the workers and peasants victory in Russia in 1917, a revolutionary wave swept across Europe from 1918 through 1920, and anti-imperialist uprisings were spurred in Asia and elsewhere in the colonial world. In March 1919, in the midst of the civil war and imperialist intervention in Russia, the Communist International (Comintern) was launched under Bolshevik leadership, attracting parties and fighters the world over who sought to emulate the revolutionary accomplishments of workers and peasants in the Soviet republic.

By the end of 1920, however, the revolutionary workers movement had sustained defeats in Germany, Hungary, and Italy. No new soviet republics had been consolidated anywhere outside the boundaries of the old tsarist empire.

When the civil war was over, coal production and rail transport, the sinews of industry, had declined to 30 percent of prewar levels in Russia. Overall factory production in 1920 was a third of the prewar rate, and steel output in 1921 was a mere 5 percent of 1913 production. Agricultural production was also down severely. Grain output in 1920 and 1921 was about 50 percent of the prewar average. In 1921 millions died of starvation.[2]

In a resolution drafted for discussion at the Third Congress of the Communist International in mid-1921, Lenin summed up the revolution's international position by pointing out that "although it is far stronger, imperialism has proved unable to strangle Soviet Russia and has been obliged for the time being to grant her recognition, or semi-recognition, and to conclude trade agreements with her. The result is a state of equilibrium which, although highly unstable and precarious, enables the socialist republic to exist—not for long, of course—within the capitalist encirclement."

As for the alignment of class forces inside Russia at the close of the civil war, Lenin said in the resolution, "The alliance between the small peasants and the proletariat can become a correct and stable one from the socialist standpoint only when the complete restoration of transport and large-scale industry enables the proletariat to give the peasants, in exchange for food, all the goods they need for their own use and for the improvement of their farms."[3]

In face of this situation both internationally and inside the Soviet republic, the Bolsheviks launched the New Economic Policy (NEP) in early 1921. In March the Soviet government decreed the end of requisitioning of peasant grain surpluses and replaced it with a tax

2. A useful summary of the first five years of the Soviet workers and peasants republic is contained in the two-volume series by Farrell Dobbs, *Revolutionary Continuity: The Early Years (1848–1917)* (New York: Pathfinder, 1980) and *Revolutionary Continuity: Birth of the Communist Movement (1918–1922)* (New York: Pathfinder, 1983).

3. Lenin, "Theses for a Report on the Tactics of the R.C.P.," *CW*, vol. 32, pp. 453–61.

in kind. That is, peasants were required to provide the government a percentage of their harvest, fixed by a sliding scale to favor the small peasants as well as those who produced most efficiently. The government authorized a private market, first for farm products and later for other commodities. Privately owned enterprises were permitted in rural and small-scale industry. Foreign capitalists were encouraged to invest in the Soviet republics by acquiring "concessions" that they would operate under strict government control, although very few responded to this offer.

In order to restore production and trade, runaway inflation had to be reined in. The government sharply cut back the minting of rubles, reduced state expenditures, and moved toward the stable currency required for state accounting and planning. State enterprises were increasingly weaned from government subsidies and had to live off revenues from sales and attempt to turn a surplus.

By early 1922 the Soviet working class and revolutionary government had scored modest but important successes through the NEP in regaining the confidence of the peasantry, while increasing overall economic production, and in particular the availability of light industrial products that could be traded for food supplies. These events set the scene for this book, which opens with Lenin's March 1922 political report to the Eleventh Congress of the Russian Communist Party.

The opening rounds of Lenin's final political fight took place in September 1922. This book follows that fight up to the time of the severe stroke in early March 1923 that brought Lenin's political life to an end. Throughout this period, his deteriorating health repeatedly interrupted his activity. After a stroke in late May 1922 that paralyzed his right hand and leg and impaired his speech, and a brief recovery that summer, Lenin suffered several relapses in the closing months of 1922 and early 1923. He died a year later in January 1924.

The chapters in this book present, chronologically, the articles, letters, speeches, resolutions, and memos by Lenin that were part of this fight. From December 21, 1922, until his last letter of March 6,

1923, everything that Lenin is known to have written is included here. In addition, writings by other Bolshevik leaders have been included to the degree these documents figured prominently in the battle and help the reader follow its evolution. The editor has provided chapter titles highlighting an aspect of the struggle during a particular time period, but each chapter contains material by Lenin on not just that aspect but on the range of questions central to the communist course he was fighting to defend and advance.

Over the years following Lenin's death, an increasingly privileged bureaucratic caste consolidated its brutal hold on the state and party apparatus and carried out a political counterrevolution against the proletarian internationalist policies around which Lenin had organized the Bolshevik leadership of the Soviet workers and peasants republic, Communist Party, and Communist International. Joseph Stalin emerged as the despotic arbiter for that petty-bourgeois social layer, and his murderous regime suppressed many of Lenin's writings contained in these pages for more than three decades.

A few years after Stalin's death in 1953 a section of his heirs, for whom Soviet premier Nikita Khrushchev was the spokesman, sought to distance themselves from some of the Stalin regime's most infamous crimes. Only then were many of these writings by Lenin acknowledged and published in the Soviet Union. Some had not been available anywhere since the mid-1920s.

As long-suppressed items were finally translated and printed in the English-language edition of Lenin's *Collected Works,* published in Moscow between 1960 and 1970, however, they were broken up and scattered in volumes 33, 36, 42, and 45. Most of the material by Lenin in this collection has been taken from that Moscow edition, but it is presented here chronologically as the fight actually unfolded.

In addition, a few items by Lenin from this period have never before been published in English and appear for the first time in this collection. One item—the March 1923 report prepared for Lenin on the Dzerzhinsky commission investigation into events in the republic of Georgia—was kept secret by Moscow until the collapse of the

Stalinist apparatus in the former USSR in 1991. The final section of that report, "On the Conclusions of the Dzerzhinsky Commission," is published in appendix 1 of this volume for the first time in any language.

Footnotes about events referred to in the text have been included. For each item the source and related information appear as the first footnote. A glossary containing names of individuals, organizations, and publications has been compiled. A list of abbreviations and initials used in the book and a chronology of important events are also included.

In items by Lenin taken from the English-language edition of his *Collected Works*, spelling and punctuation have been changed to conform with current U.S. usage. A few translation changes have been made on the basis of a comparison with the fifth Russian-language edition of Lenin's writings.

Translations from Russian for this volume are by Sonja Franeta, Jeff Hamill, Doug Hord, Brian Pearce, John Riddell, and Andrew Rodomar. John Riddell did much of the research and editorial preparation on this book before its final compilation and editing.

Chapter divisions, titles, and footnotes were prepared by the editor.

George Fyson
April 3, 1995

Abbreviations and initials

CC	Central Committee
CEC	Central Executive Committee
CLD	Council of Labor and Defense
COMINTERN	Communist International
CP	Communist Party
CPC	Council of People's Commissars
NEP	New Economic Policy
POLITBURO	Political Bureau
RCP	Russian Communist Party
RSDLP	Russian Social Democratic Labor Party
RSFSR	Russian Soviet Federated Socialist Republic
USSR	Union of Soviet Socialist Republics
WPI	Workers and Peasants Inspection

Chronology

1917

November 7 Russian revolution establishes workers and
peasants government based on soviets.
According to calendar then in use, date was
October 25, and event is universally known as
October revolution.

1918

March 3 Brest-Litovsk treaty ends war between
Germany and Soviet government.

May Czech divisions in Siberia revolt against Soviet
rule, opening civil war in Russia.

early November Revolutions in Germany and Austria-Hungary
overthrow monarchies, ending World War I.

1919

early January Workers' uprising in Berlin crushed.

March 4 Communist International founded.

1920

November White forces in Crimea routed, ending civil
war.

1921

February	Workers and peasants government established in Georgia.
March 8–16	Tenth party congress inaugurates first measures of New Economic Policy.
December 6	Lenin takes first of several sick leaves that continue through March 1922.

1922

March 12	Transcaucasian Soviet Federation launched.
March 27–April 2	Lenin participates in eleventh party congress.
April 3	Stalin named general secretary of RCP.
April 10–May 19	Genoa conference.
late May	Lenin on sick leave; is partly paralyzed by stroke and unable to speak; health recovers over summer.
September 26	Criticizes Stalin's proposal to incorporate independent Soviet republics into RSFSR.
October 2	Returns to Moscow and resumes regular duties.
October 6	Central Committee (Lenin absent) decides to weaken foreign trade monopoly. Central Committee adopts revised plan for USSR federation.
October 13	Lenin writes Stalin opposing October 6 decision on trade monopoly.
October 22	Nine of eleven Georgian Central Committee members resign to protest Stalin and Ordzhonikidze's policies on national question.
October 31	Fascists take power in Italy, marking retreat of European revolutionary wave.
November 13	Lenin speaks at fourth Comintern congress.
November 20	Last public speech.
late November	Ordzhonikidze strikes Kobakhidze, one of dissident Georgian Communists.

December 7–12	Lenin on sick leave.
December 10–15	International Peace Congress in The Hague.
December 12	Lenin returns to Moscow.
December 13	Proposes that Trotsky defend their common position on foreign trade monopoly.
December 18	Central Committee rescinds decision of October 6, reaffirms foreign trade monopoly.
December 22	Stalin assails Krupskaya for writing letter dictated by Lenin.
December 22–23	Lenin again partially paralyzed.
December 23–31	Dictates "Letter to the Congress," including notes on State Planning Commission and nationalities question.
December 24	Decree by doctors and Political Bureau limits Lenin's access to information.
December 30	Congress of Soviets forms USSR.

1923

January 1–2	Lenin dictates "Pages from a Diary."
January 4	Dictates postscript to "Letter to the Congress" proposing that Stalin be removed as general secretary.
January 4, 6	Dictates "On Cooperation."
January 9, 13	Dictates first draft of "How We Should Reorganize the Workers and Peasants Inspection."
January 16–17	Dictates "Our Revolution."
January 19–23	Dictates second draft of "How We Should Reorganize the Workers and Peasants Inspection."
January 24	Unsuccessfully requests files of Dzerzhinsky commission on Georgia.
January 25	Political Bureau endorses Dzerzhinsky commission findings.
February 1	Political Bureau yields to Lenin's demand for

	Dzerzhinsky commission files.
February 2–9	Lenin dictates "Better Fewer, but Better."
March 3	Lenin's private investigating committee submits findings on Georgian affair.
March 4	"Better Fewer, but Better" appears in *Pravda*.
March 5	Lenin writes Trotsky asking that he defend dissident Georgian Communist leaders. Writes Stalin attacking his abuse of Krupskaya and threatening to break relations.
March 6	Writes to Georgian Communist leaders pledging support.
March 10	Another stroke incapacitates Lenin, ending his political life.
April 17	Twelfth party congress opens.

1924

| January 21 | Lenin dies. |

I

Communist Tasks in the Second Year of the New Economic Policy

Political report to eleventh party congress

MARCH 27, 1922

(*Applause*) Comrades, permit me to start the political report of the Central Committee from the end and not from the beginning of the year.[1] The political question most discussed today is Genoa.[2] But since a great deal has already been said on the subject in our press, and since I have already said what is most essential to it in my speech on March 6, which has been published,[3] I would ask you to permit me to refrain from going into details unless you particularly wish me to do so.

On the whole you know everything about Genoa, because much has been written about it in the newspapers—in my opinion too much, to the detriment of the real, practical, and urgent require-ments of our work of construction in general and of our economic development in particular. In Europe, in all bourgeois countries, of course, they like to occupy people's minds, or stuff their heads, with all sorts of trash about Genoa. On this occasion (I would say not only on this occasion) we are copying them, and copying them far too much.

I must say that in the Central Committee we have taken very great pains to appoint a delegation of our best diplomats (we now have a fair number of Soviet diplomats, which was not the case in

Footnotes start on next page

the early period of the Soviet republic). The Central Committee has
drawn up sufficiently detailed instructions for our diplomats at the
Genoa conference; we spent a long time discussing these instructions
and considered and reconsidered them several times.[4] It goes without saying that the question here is, I shall not say of war, because
that term is likely to be misunderstood, but at all events one of rivalry.

In the bourgeois camp there is a very strong trend that wants to
convene the Genoa conference, much stronger than the one that
wants to wreck it. There are trends that greatly favor the Genoa conference and want it to meet at all costs. The latter have now gained the
upper hand. Lastly, in all bourgeois countries there are trends that
might be called pacifist trends, among which should be included the
entire Second and Two-and-a-Half Internationals.[5] It is this section of

1. Lenin, "Political Report of the Central Committee of the R.C.P.(B.)," in
CW, vol. 33, pp. 263–309.

2. At a conference held in Genoa, Italy, April 10–May 19, 1922, Soviet
delegates offered the Allied powers economic concessions, including recognition of a portion of the tsar's debts. In return, the Soviet government
asked for cancellation of Russian war debts, compensation for damage
done during the civil war by Allied interventionist armies, and loans to
speed the resumption of trade.

The conference foundered over the issue of restoring to foreign capitalists all property they had held in Russia under the tsars. During the conference the Soviet delegation concluded the Treaty of Rapallo for economic, political, and military cooperation with Germany.

3. See Lenin's speech to the All-Russia Congress of Metalworkers,
"The International and Domestic Situation of the Soviet Republic," in
CW, vol. 33, pp. 212–26.

4. See in particular Lenin's draft directives to the Soviet delegation to
Genoa in CW, vol. 42, pp. 390–93 and 396–98, and his letter to Chicherin in CW, vol. 45, pp. 506–12.

5. The Second International, founded in 1889 as an international association of workers parties, collapsed at the outbreak of World War I
when leaders of most of its constituent parties supported the interests of
their own bourgeoisies. The right wing formed the Labor and Socialist International in 1923.

Two-and-a-Half International was the derogatory name applied to the
International Association of Socialist Parties that was formed in 1921 by

the bourgeoisie that is advocating a number of pacifist proposals and is trying to concoct something in the nature of a pacifist policy. As Communists we have definite views about this pacifism, which it would be superfluous to expound here. Needless to say, we are going to Genoa not as Communists, but as merchants. We must trade, and they must trade. We want the trade to benefit us, they want it to benefit them. The course of the issue will be determined, if only to a small degree, by the skill of our diplomats.

Insofar as we are going to Genoa as merchants it is obviously by no means a matter of indifference to us whether we deal with those people from the bourgeois camp who are inclined to settle the problem by war or with those who are inclined toward pacifism, even the worst kind of pacifism, which from the communist viewpoint will not stand the slightest criticism. It would be a bad merchant indeed who was unable to appreciate this distinction and (by shaping his tactics accordingly) to achieve practical aims.

We are going to Genoa for the practical purpose of expanding trade and of creating the most favorable conditions for its successful development on the widest scale. But we cannot guarantee the success of the Genoa conference. It would be ridiculous and absurd to give any guarantees on that score. I must say, however, that, weighing up the present possibilities of Genoa in the most sober and cautious manner, I think that it will not be an exaggeration to say that we shall achieve our object.

Through Genoa, if the other parties in the negotiations are sufficiently shrewd and not too stubborn; bypassing Genoa, if they take it into their heads to be stubborn. But we shall achieve our goal!

The fact of the matter is that the most urgent, pressing, and practical interests that have been sharply revealed in all the capitalist countries during the past few years call for the development, regulation, and expansion of trade with Russia. Since such interests exist,

centrist parties that opposed Soviet power but had left the Second International. The two formations reunited in 1923.

we may argue, we may quarrel, we may disagree on specific combinations—it is highly probable that we shall have to disagree. This fundamental economic necessity will, nevertheless, after all is said and done, make a way for itself. I think we can rest assured of that. I cannot vouch for the date; I cannot vouch for success; but at this gathering we can say with a fair amount of certainty that regular trade relations between the Soviet republic and all the capitalist countries in the world are certain to continue developing. When I come to it in another part of my report I shall mention the hitches that may possibly occur; but I think that this is all that need be said on the question of Genoa.

Needless to say, the comrades who desire to study the question in greater detail and who are not content with the list of delegates published in the newspapers may set up a commission, or a section, and acquaint themselves with all the material of the Central Committee, and all the correspondence and instructions. Of course, the details we have outlined are provisional, for no one up to now knows exactly who will sit round the table at Genoa and what terms, or preliminary terms or provisions, will be announced. It would be highly inexpedient, and I think practically impossible, to discuss all this here. I repeat, this congress, through the medium of a section, or a commission, has every opportunity to collect all the documents on this question—both the published documents and those in the possession of the Central Committee.

I shall not say any more, for I am sure that it is not here that our greatest difficulties lie. This is not the question on which the attention of the whole party should be focused. The European bourgeois press is artificially and deliberately inflating and exaggerating the importance of this conference in order to deceive the masses of the working people (as nine-tenths of the bourgeois press in all these free democratic countries and republics always does). We have succumbed to the influence of this press to some extent. As usual, our press still yields to the old bourgeois habits; it refuses to adopt new, socialist methods, and we have made a greater fuss about this subject than it deserves.

In fact, for Communists, especially for those who have lived through such stern years as we have lived through since 1917 and witnessed the formidable political combinations that have appeared in that period, Genoa does not present any great difficulties. I cannot recall any disagreement or controversy on this question either in the Central Committee or in the ranks of the party. This is natural, for there is nothing controversial here from the point of view of Communists, even bearing in mind the various shades of opinion among them. I repeat: we are going to Genoa as merchants for the purpose of securing the most favorable terms for promoting the trade which has started, which is being carried on, and which—even if someone succeeded in forcibly interrupting it for a time—would inevitably continue to develop after the interruption.

Hence, confining myself to these brief remarks about Genoa, I shall now proceed to deal with the issues which, in my opinion, have been the major political questions of the past year and which will be such in the ensuing year. It seems to me that the political report of the Central Committee should not merely deal with the events of the year under review, but also point out (that, at any rate, is what I usually do) the main, fundamental political lessons of the events of that year, so that we may learn something for the ensuing year and be in a position to correctly determine our policy for that year.

The NEP and the link with the peasant economy[6]

The New Economic Policy is, of course, the major question. This has been the dominant question throughout the year under review. If we have any important, serious, and irrevocable gain to record for this year (and I am not so very sure that we have), it is that we have learned something from the launching of this New Economic Policy. If we have learned even a little, then, during the past year, we have learned a great deal in this field. And the test of whether we have really learned anything, and to what extent, will probably be made by subsequent events of a kind that we ourselves can do little to de-

6. All headings in this speech have been supplied by the editor.

termine, as for example the impending financial crisis.[7] It seems to me that in connection with the New Economic Policy, the most important things to keep in mind as a basis for all our arguments, as a means of testing our experience during the past year and of learning practical lessons for the ensuing year, are contained in the following three points.

First, the New Economic Policy is important for us primarily as a means of testing whether we are really establishing a link with the peasant economy. In the preceding period of development of our revolution, when all our attention and all our efforts were concentrated mainly on—or almost entirely absorbed by—the task of repelling invasion, we could not devote the necessary attention to this link. We had other things to think about. To some extent we could and had to ignore this bond when we were confronted by the absolutely urgent and overshadowing task of warding off the danger of being immediately crushed by the gigantic forces of world imperialism.

The turn toward the New Economic Policy was decided on at the last congress with exceptional unanimity, with even greater unanimity than other questions have been decided by our party (which, it must be admitted, is generally distinguished for its unanimity). This unanimity showed that the need for a new approach to socialist economy had fully matured. People who differed on many questions and who assessed the situation from different angles unanimously, very quickly, and unhesitatingly agreed that we lacked a real approach to socialist economy, to the task of building its foundation; that the only means of finding this approach was the New Economic Policy.

Owing to the course taken by the development of war events, by the development of political events, by the development of capital-

7. Despite far-reaching measures taken during 1921 to reduce state expenditure and increase income, the budget for 1922 projected that state revenue would cover only 60 percent of expenses. The ruble, whose decline had slowed during the summer of 1921, resumed its precipitous fall in late 1921 and 1922.

ism in the old civilized West, and owing also to the social and political conditions that developed in the colonies, we were the first to make a breach in the old bourgeois world at a time when our country was economically, if not the most backward, at any rate one of the most backward countries in the world. The vast majority of the peasants in our country are engaged in small individual farming. The items of our program of building a communist society that we could apply immediately, were to some extent outside the sphere of activity of the broad mass of the peasantry, upon whom we imposed very heavy obligations, which we justified on the grounds that war permitted no wavering in this matter.

Taken as a whole, this was accepted as justification by the peasantry, notwithstanding the mistakes we could not avoid. On the whole, the mass of the peasantry realized and understood that the enormous burdens imposed upon them were necessary in order to save the workers and peasants rule from the landowners and prevent it from being strangled by capitalist invasion, which threatened to wrest away all the gains of the revolution. But there was no link between the peasant economy and the economy that was being built up in the nationalized, socialized factories and on state farms.

We saw this clearly at the last party congress. We saw it so clearly that there was no hesitation whatever in the party on the question as to whether the New Economic Policy was inevitable or not.

It is amusing to read what is said about our decision in the numerous publications of the various Russian parties abroad. There are only trifling differences in the opinions they express. Living with memories of the past, they still continue to reiterate that to this day the Left Communists are opposed to the New Economic Policy. In 1921 they remembered what had occurred in 1918 and what our Left Communists themselves have forgotten, and they go on chewing this over and over again, assuring the world that these Bolsheviks are a sly and false lot, and that they are concealing from Europe that they have disagreements in their ranks. Reading this, one says to oneself, "Let them go on fooling themselves." If this is what they imagine is going on in this country, we can judge the degree of intelligence of these allegedly highly educated old fogies who have fled abroad. We know that there have been no disagreements in our ranks, and the reason for this is that the practical necessity of a different approach to the task of building the foundation of socialist economy was clear to all.

There was no link between the peasant economy and the new economy we tried to create. Does it exist now? Not yet. We are only approaching it. The whole significance of the New Economic Policy—which our press still often searches for everywhere except where it should search—the whole purpose of this policy is to find a way of establishing a link between the new economy, which we are creating with such enormous effort, and the peasant economy. That is what stands to our credit; without it we would not be communist revolutionaries.

We began to develop the new economy in an entirely new way, brushing aside everything old. Had we not begun to develop it we would have been utterly defeated in the very first months, in the very first years. But the fact that we began to develop this new economy with such splendid audacity does not mean that we must necessarily continue in the same way. Why should we? There is no reason.

From the very beginning we said that we had to undertake an entirely new task, and that unless we received speedy assistance from our comrades, the workers in the capitalistically more developed countries, we should encounter incredible difficulties and certainly make a number of mistakes. The main thing is to be able dispassionately to examine where such mistakes have been made and to start again from the beginning. If we begin from the beginning, not twice, but many times, it will show that we are not bound by prejudice and that we are approaching our task, which is the greatest the world has ever seen, with a sober outlook.

Today, as far as the New Economic Policy is concerned, the main thing is to assimilate the experience of the past year correctly. That must be done, and we want to do it. And if we want to do it, come what may (and we do want to do it and shall do it!), we must know that the problem of the New Economic Policy, the fundamental, decisive, and overriding problem, is to establish a link between the new economy that we have begun to create (very badly, very clumsily, but have nevertheless begun to create on the basis of an entirely new, socialist economy, of a new system of production and distribution) and the peasant economy, by which millions and millions of peasants obtain their livelihood.

This link has been lacking, and we must create it before anything else. Everything else must be subordinated to this. We have still to ascertain the extent to which the New Economic Policy has succeeded in creating this link without destroying what we have begun so clumsily to build.

We are developing our economy together with the peasantry. We shall have to alter it many times and organize it in such a way that it will provide a link between our socialist work on large-scale industry and agriculture and the work every peasant is doing as best he can, struggling out of poverty, without philosophizing (for how can philosophizing help him to extricate himself from his position and save him from the very real danger of a painful death from starvation?).

We must reveal this link so that we may see it clearly, so that all the people may see it, and so that the whole mass of the peasantry may see that there is a connection between their present severe, incredibly ruined, incredibly impoverished and painful existence and the work which is being done for the sake of remote socialist ideals. We must bring about a situation where the ordinary, rank-and-file working man realizes that he has obtained some improvement, and that he has obtained it not in the way a few peasants obtained improvements under the rule of landowners and capitalists, when every improvement (undoubtedly there were improvements and very big ones) was accompanied by insult, derision, and humiliation for the muzhik [peasant], by violence against the masses, which not a single peasant has forgotten, and which will not be forgotten in Russia for decades.

Our aim is to restore the link, to prove to the peasant by deeds that we are beginning with what is intelligible, familiar, and immediately accessible to him, in spite of his poverty, and not with something remote and fantastic from the peasant's point of view. We must prove that we can help him and that in this period, when the small peasant is in a state of appalling ruin, impoverishment, and starvation, the Communists are really helping him. Either we prove that, or he will send us to the devil. That is absolutely inevitable.

Such is the significance of the New Economic Policy; it is the basis of our entire policy; it is the major lesson taught by the whole of the past year's experience in applying the New Economic Policy, and, so to speak, our main political rule for the coming year. The peasant is allowing us credit, and, of course, after what he has lived through, he cannot do otherwise. Taken in the mass, the peasants go on saying, "Well, if you are not able to do it yet, we shall wait; perhaps you will learn." But this credit cannot go on forever.

This we must know; and having obtained credit we must hurry. We must know that the time is approaching when this peasant country will no longer give us credit, when it will demand cash, to use a commercial term. It will say, "You have postponed payment for so many months, so many years. But by this time, dear rulers, you must have learned the most sound and reliable method of helping us free ourselves from poverty, want, starvation, and ruin. You can do it, you have proved it." This is the test that we shall inevitably have to face; and, in the last analysis, this test will decide everything: the fate of NEP and the fate of communist rule in Russia.

From retreat to renewed advance

Shall we accomplish our immediate task or not? Is this NEP fit for anything or not? If the retreat turns out to be correct tactics, we must link up with the peasant masses while we are in retreat and subsequently march forward with them a hundred times more slowly, but firmly and unswervingly, in a way that will always make it apparent to them that we are really marching forward. Then our cause will be absolutely invincible, and no power on earth can vanquish us. We did not accomplish this in the first year. We must say this frankly. And I am profoundly convinced (and our New Economic Policy enables us to draw this conclusion quite definitely and firmly) that if we appreciate the enormous danger harbored by the NEP and concentrate all our forces on its weak points, we shall solve this problem.

Link up with the peasant masses, with the rank-and-file working peasants, and begin to move forward immeasurably, infinitely more slowly than we expected, but in such a way that the entire mass will actually move forward with us. If we do that we shall in time progress much more quickly than we even dream of today. This, in my opinion, is the first fundamental political lesson of the New Economic Policy.

The second, more specific lesson is the test through competition between state and capitalist enterprises. We are now forming mixed companies—I shall have something to say about these later on—which, like our state trade and our New Economic Policy as a whole, mean that we Communists are resorting to commercial, capitalist methods. These mixed companies are also important because through them practical competition is created between capitalist methods and our methods.

Consider it practically. Up to now we have been writing a program and making promises. In its time this was absolutely necessary. It is impossible to launch on a world revolution without a program and without promises. If the White Guards, including the Mensheviks, jeer at us for this, it shows only that the Mensheviks and the Socialists of the Second and Two-and-a-Half Internationals have no idea, in general, of the way a revolution develops. We could proceed in no other way.

Now, however, the position is that we must put our work to a serious test, and not the sort of test that is made by control institutions set up by the Communists themselves—even though these control institutions are magnificent, even though they are almost the ideal control institutions in the Soviet system and the party; such a test may be mockery from the point of view of the actual requirements of the peasant economy, but it is certainly no mockery from the standpoint of our construction. We are now setting up these control institutions, but I am referring not to this test but to the test from the point of view of the entire economy.

The capitalist was able to supply things. He did it inefficiently, charged exorbitant prices, insulted and robbed us. The ordinary workers and peasants, who do not argue about communism because they do not know what it is, are well aware of this.

"But the capitalists were, after all, able to supply things. Are you? You are not able to do it." That is what we heard last spring; though not always clearly audible, it was the undertone of the whole of last spring's crisis. "As people you are splendid, but you cannot cope with the economic task you have undertaken." This is the simple and withering criticism which the peasantry—and through the peasantry, some sections of workers—leveled at the Communist Party last year. That is why in the NEP question, this old point acquires such significance.

We need a real test. The capitalists are operating alongside us. They are operating like robbers; they make profit; but they know how to do things. But you—you are trying to do it in a new way: you make no profit, your principles are communist, your ideals are splendid; they are written out so beautifully that you seem to be saints, that you should go to heaven while you are still alive. But can you get things done? We need a test, a real test, not the kind the Central Control Commission makes when it censures somebody and the All-Russia Central Executive Committee imposes some penalty. Yes, we want a real test from the viewpoint of the national economy.

We Communists have received numerous deferments, and more credit has been allowed us than any other government has ever been given. Of course, we Communists helped to get rid of the capitalists and landowners. The peasants appreciate this and have given us an extension of time, longer credit, but only for a certain period. After that comes the test: can you run the economy as well as the others? The old capitalist can; you cannot.

That is the first lesson, the first main part of the political report of the Central Committee. We cannot run the economy. This has been proved in the past year. I would like very much to quote the example of several *gostrests* [state trusts] (if I may express myself in the beautiful Russian language that Turgenev praised so highly)[8] to show how we run the economy.

Unfortunately, for a number of reasons, and largely owing to ill health, I have been unable to elaborate this part of my report and so I must confine myself to expressing my convictions, which are based on my observations of what is going on. During the past year we showed quite clearly that we cannot run the economy. That is the fundamental lesson. Either we prove the opposite in the coming year, or Soviet power will not be able to exist. And the greatest danger is that not everybody realizes this. If all of us Communists, the responsible officials, clearly realize that we lack the ability to run the economy, that we must learn from the very beginning, then we shall win—that, in my opinion, is the fundamental conclusion that should be drawn. But many of us do not appreciate this and believe that if there are people who do think that way, it can only be the ignorant, who have not studied communism; perhaps they will some day learn and understand. No, excuse me, the point is not that the peasant or the nonparty worker has not studied communism, but that the time has passed when the job was to draft a program and call upon the people to carry out this great program. That time has passed. Today you must prove that you can give practical economic assistance to the workers and to the peasants under the present difficult conditions, and thus demonstrate to them that you have stood the test of competition.

The mixed companies that we have begun to form, in which private capitalists, Russian and foreign, and Communists participate, provide one of the means by which we can learn to organize competition properly and show that we are no less able to establish a link with the peasant economy than the capitalists; that we can meet

---

8. Lenin is poking fun here at the acronyms, like "gostrest," that proliferated in the Soviet administration.

its requirements; that we can help the peasant make progress even at his present level, in spite of his backwardness—for it is impossible to change him in a brief space of time.

That is the sort of competition confronting us as an absolutely urgent task. It is the pivot of the New Economic Policy and, in my opinion, the quintessence of the party's policy. We are faced with any number of purely political problems and difficulties. You know what they are: Genoa and the danger of intervention. The difficulties are enormous, but they are nothing compared with this economic difficulty. We know how things are done in the political field; we have gained considerable experience; we have learned a lot about bourgeois diplomacy. It is the sort of thing the Mensheviks taught us for fifteen years, and we got something useful out of it. This is not new.

But here is something we must do now in the economic field. We must win the competition against the ordinary shop assistant, the ordinary capitalist, the merchant, who will go to the peasant without arguing about communism. Just imagine, he will not begin to argue about communism, but will argue in this way: if you want to obtain something, or carry on trade properly, or if you want to build, I will do the building at a high price; the Communists will, perhaps, build at a higher price, perhaps even ten times higher. It is this kind of agitation that is now the crux of the matter; herein lies the root of economics.

I repeat, thanks to our correct policy, the people allowed us a deferment of payment and credit, and this, to put it in terms of the NEP, is a promissory note. But this promissory note is undated, and you cannot learn from the wording when it will be presented for redemption. Therein lies the danger; this is the specific feature that distinguishes these political promissory notes from ordinary, commercial promissory notes. We must concentrate all our attention on this and not rest content with the fact that there are responsible and good Communists in all the state trusts and mixed companies. That is of no use, because these Communists do not know how to run the economy. In that respect, they are inferior to the ordinary capitalist salesmen, who have received their training in big factories and big firms. But we refuse to admit this; in this field communist conceit—*komchvanstvo,*[9] to use the great Russian language again—still persists.

Communists must learn to trade

The whole point is that the responsible Communists, even the best of them, who are unquestionably honest and loyal, who in the old days suffered penal servitude and did not fear death, do not know how to trade, because they are not businessmen, have not learned to trade, do not want to learn, and do not understand that they must start learning from the beginning. Communists, revolutionaries who have accomplished the greatest revolution in the world, on whom the eyes of, if not forty pyramids, then at all events forty European countries are turned in the hope of emancipation from capitalism, must learn from ordinary salesmen. But these ordinary salesmen have had ten years' warehouse experience and know the business, whereas the responsible Communists and devoted revolutionaries do not know the business and do not even realize that they do not know it.

And so, comrades, if we do away with at least this elementary ignorance we shall achieve a tremendous victory. We must leave this congress with the conviction that we are ignorant of this business and with the resolve to start learning it from the bottom. After all, we have not ceased to be revolutionaries (although many say, and not altogether without foundation, that we have become bureaucrats) and can understand this simple thing, that in a new and unusually difficult undertaking we must be prepared to start from the beginning over and over again. If after starting you find yourselves at a dead end, start again, and go on doing it ten times if necessary, until you attain your object. Do not put on airs, do not be conceited because you are a Communist while there is some nonparty salesman, perhaps a White Guard—and very likely he is a White Guard

9. Literally, "comconceit."

—who can do things that economically must be done at all costs, but that you cannot do. If you, responsible Communists, who have hundreds of ranks and titles and wear communist and Soviet orders, realize this, you will attain your object, because this is something that can be learned.

We have some successes, even if only very tiny ones, to record for the past year, but they are insignificant. The main thing is that there is no realization nor widespread conviction among all Communists that at the present time the responsible and most devoted Russian Communist is less able to perform these functions than any salesman of the old school. I repeat, we must start learning from the very beginning. If we realize this, we shall pass our test, and the test is a serious one that the impending financial crisis will set—the test set by the Russian and international market to which we are subordinated, with which we are connected, and from which we cannot isolate ourselves. The test is a crucial one, for here we may be beaten economically and politically.

That is how the question stands, and it cannot be otherwise, for the competition will be very severe, and it will be decisive. We had many outlets and loopholes that enabled us to escape from our political and economic difficulties. We can proudly say that up to now we have been able to utilize these outlets and loopholes in various combinations corresponding to the varying circumstances. But now we have no other outlets.

Permit me to say this to you without exaggeration, because in this respect it is really "the last and decisive battle," not against international capitalism—against that we shall yet have many "last and decisive battles"—but against Russian capitalism, against the capitalism that is growing out of the small-peasant economy, the capitalism that is fostered by the latter. Here we shall have a fight on our hands in the immediate future, and the date of it cannot be fixed exactly.

Here the "last and decisive battle" is impending; here there are no political or any other flanking movements that we can undertake, because this is a test in competition with private capital. Either we pass this test in competition with private capital, or we fail completely. To help us pass it we have political power and a host of economic and other resources; we have everything you want except ability. We lack ability. And if we learn this simple lesson from the experience of last year and take it as our guiding line for the whole of 1922, we shall conquer this difficulty too, in spite of the fact that it is much greater than the previous difficulty, for it rests upon ourselves. It is not like some external enemy.

The difficulty is that we ourselves refuse to admit the unpleasant truth forced upon us. We refuse to undertake the unpleasant duty that the situation demands of us, namely, to start learning from the beginning. That, in my opinion, is the second lesson that we must learn from the New Economic Policy.

The third, supplementary lesson is on the question of state capitalism. It is a pity Comrade Bukharin is not present at the congress.[10] I should have liked to argue with him a little, but that had better be postponed to the next congress. On the question of state capitalism, I think that generally our press and our party make the mistake of dropping into intellectualism, into liberalism. We philosophize about how state capitalism is to be interpreted and look into old books. But in those old books you will not find what we are discussing. They deal with the state capitalism that exists under capitalism. Not a single book has been written about state capitalism under communism. It did not occur even to Marx to write a word on this subject, and he died without leaving a single precise statement or definite instruction on it. That is why we must overcome the difficulty entirely by ourselves. And if we make a general mental survey of our press and see what has been written about state capitalism, as I tried to do when I was preparing this report, we shall be convinced that it is missing the target, that it is looking in an entirely wrong direction.

10. Nikolai Bukharin, while in accord with the measures that made up the NEP, argued that use of the term state capitalism in the context of Soviet society was an "absurdity."

The state capitalism discussed in all books on economics is that which exists under the capitalist system, where the state brings under its direct control certain capitalist enterprises. But ours is a proletarian state; it rests on the proletariat; it gives the proletariat all political privileges; and through the medium of the proletariat it attracts to itself the lower ranks of the peasantry (you remember that we began this work through the poor peasants committees). That is why very many people are misled by the term state capitalism. To avoid this we must remember the fundamental thing that state capitalism in the form we have here is not dealt with in any theory or in any books, for the simple reason that all the usual concepts connected with this term are associated with bourgeois rule in capitalist society.

Our society is one that has left the rails of capitalism but has not yet got onto new rails. The state in this society is ruled not by the bourgeoisie but by the proletariat. We refuse to understand that when we say "state," we mean ourselves, the proletariat, the vanguard of the working class. State capitalism is capitalism that we shall be able to restrain, and the limits of which we shall be able to fix. This state capitalism is connected with the state, and the state is the workers, the advanced section of the workers, the vanguard. We are the state.

State capitalism is capitalism that we must confine within certain bounds, but we have not yet learned to confine it within those bounds. That is the whole point. And it rests with us to determine what this state capitalism is to be. We have sufficient, quite sufficient political power; we also have sufficient economic resources at our command, but the vanguard of the working class that has been brought to the forefront to directly supervise, to determine the boundaries, to demarcate, to subordinate and not be subordinated itself, lacks sufficient ability for it. All that is needed here is ability, and that is what we do not have.

Never before in history has there been a situation in which the proletariat, the revolutionary vanguard, possessed sufficient political power and had state capitalism existing alongside it. The whole question turns on our understanding that this is the capitalism that we can and must permit, that we can and must confine within certain bounds; for this capitalism is essential for the broad masses of the peasantry and for private capital, which must trade in such a way as to satisfy the needs of the peasantry. We must organize things in such a way as to make possible the customary operation of capitalist economy and capitalist exchange, because this is essential for the people. Without it, existence is impossible. All the rest is not an absolutely vital matter to this camp. They can resign themselves to all that. You Communists, you workers, you, the politically enlightened section of the proletariat, which undertook to administer the state, must be able to arrange it so that the state, which you have taken into your hands, shall function the way you want it to.

The car refuses to obey the driver

Well, we have lived through a year, the state is in our hands; but has it operated the New Economic Policy in the way we wanted in this past year? No. But we refuse to admit that it did not operate in the way we wanted. How did it operate? The machine refused to obey the hand that guided it. It was like a car that was going not in the direction the driver desired, but in the direction someone else desired; as if it were being driven by some mysterious, lawless hand, God knows whose, perhaps of a profiteer, or of a private capitalist, or of both. Be that as it may, the car is not going quite in the direction the man at the wheel imagines, and often it goes in an altogether different direction. This is the main thing that must be remembered in regard to state capitalism. In this main field we must start learning from the very beginning, and only when we have thoroughly understood and appreciated this can we be sure that we shall learn.

Now I come to the question of halting the retreat, a question I dealt with in my speech at the congress of metalworkers. Since then I have not heard any objection, not in the party press, in private letters from comrades, nor in the Central Committee. The Central Committee approved my plan, which was that in the report of the

Central Committee to the present congress strong emphasis should be laid on calling a halt to this retreat and that the congress should give binding instructions on behalf of the whole party accordingly.

For a year we have been retreating. On behalf of the party we must now call a halt. The purpose pursued by the retreat has been achieved. This period is drawing, or has drawn, to a close. We now have a different objective, that of regrouping our forces. We have reached a new line; on the whole, we have conducted the retreat in fairly good order. True, not a few voices were heard from various sides that tried to convert this retreat into a stampede. Some—for example, several members of the group which bore the name of Workers Opposition (I don't think they had any right to that name)—argued that we were not retreating properly in some sector or other.[11] Owing to their excessive zeal they found themselves at the wrong door, and now they realize it. At that time they did not see that their activities did not help us to correct our movement, but merely had the effect of spreading panic and hindering our effort to beat a disciplined retreat.

Retreat is a difficult matter, especially for revolutionaries who are accustomed to advancing; especially when they have been accustomed to advancing with enormous success for several years; especially if they are surrounded by revolutionaries in other countries who are longing for the time when they can launch an offensive. Seeing that we were retreating, several of them burst into tears in a disgraceful and childish manner, as was the case at the last extended plenary meeting of the Executive Committee of the Communist International. Moved by the best communist sentiments and communist aspirations, several of the comrades burst into tears because— oh horror!—the good Russian Communists were retreating.

Perhaps it is now difficult for me to understand this western

11. The Workers Opposition, an ultraleft syndicalist current formed within the Russian Communist Party in 1920, demanded the transfer of management of the Soviet economy to the trade unions. Several of its leaders later strongly criticized the measures enacted to introduce the NEP.

European mentality, although I lived for quite a number of years in those marvelous democratic countries as an exile. Perhaps from their point of view this is such a difficult matter to understand that it is enough to make one weep. We, at any rate, have no time for sentiment. It was clear to us that because we had advanced so successfully for many years and had achieved so many extraordinary victories (and all this in a country that was in an appalling state of ruin and lacked the material resources!) to consolidate that advance, since we had gained so much, it was absolutely essential for us to retreat.

We could not hold all the positions we had captured in the first onslaught. On the other hand, it was because we had captured so much in the first onslaught, on the crest of the wave of enthusiasm displayed by the workers and peasants, that we had room enough to retreat a long distance and can retreat still further now, without losing our main and fundamental positions.

On the whole, the retreat was fairly orderly, although certain panic-stricken voices, among them that of the Workers Opposition (this was the tremendous harm it did!) caused losses in our ranks, caused a relaxation of discipline, and disturbed the proper order of retreat. The most dangerous thing during a retreat is panic. When a whole army (I speak in the figurative sense) is in retreat, it cannot have the same morale as when it is advancing. At every step you find a certain mood of depression. We even had poets who wrote that people were cold and starving in Moscow, that "everything before was bright and beautiful, but now trade and profiteering abound." We have had quite a number of poetic effusions of this sort.

Of course, retreat breeds all this. That is where the serious danger lies; it is terribly difficult to retreat after a great victorious advance, for the relations are entirely different. During a victorious advance, even if discipline is relaxed, everybody presses forward on his own accord. During a retreat, however, discipline must be more conscious and is a hundred times more necessary because, when the entire army is in retreat, it does not know or see where it should halt. It sees only retreat. Under such circumstances a few panic-stricken voices are, at times, enough to cause a stampede. The danger here is enormous. When a real army is in retreat, machine guns are kept ready, and when an orderly retreat degenerates into a disorderly one, the command to fire is given, and quite rightly, too.

If, during an incredibly difficult retreat when everything depends on preserving proper order, anyone spreads panic—even from the best of motives—the slightest breach of discipline must be punished severely, sternly, ruthlessly, and this applies not only to certain of our internal party affairs but also, and to a greater extent, to such gentry as the Mensheviks and to all the gentry of the Two-and-a-Half International.

The other day I read an article by Comrade Rákosi in number 20 of the *Communist International* on a new book by Otto Bauer, from whom at one time we all learned, but who, like Kautsky, became a miserable petty bourgeois after the war. Bauer now writes, "There, they are now retreating to capitalism! We have always said that it was a bourgeois revolution."

And the Mensheviks and Socialist Revolutionaries, all of whom preach this sort of thing, are astonished when we declare that we shall shoot people for such things. They are amazed, but surely it is clear. When an army is in retreat a hundred times more discipline is required than when it is advancing, because during an advance everybody presses forward. If everybody started rushing back now, it would spell immediate and inevitable disaster.

The most important thing at such a moment is to retreat in good order, to fix the precise limits of the retreat, and not to give way to panic. And when a Menshevik says, "You are now retreating. I have been advocating retreat all the time, I agree with you, I am your man, let us retreat together," we say in reply, "For the public manifestations of Menshevism our revolutionary courts must pass the death sentence, otherwise they are not our courts, but God knows what."

They cannot understand this and exclaim, "What dictatorial manners these people have!" They still think we are persecuting the Mensheviks because they fought us in Geneva.[12] But had we done

12. The reference is to the congress of the Second International held in

that we would have been unable to hold power even for two months. Indeed, the sermons that Otto Bauer, the leaders of the Second and Two-and-a-Half Internationals, the Mensheviks and Socialist Revolutionaries preach express their true nature, "The revolution has gone too far. What you are saying now we have been saying all the time; permit us to say it again." But we say in reply, "Permit us to put you before a firing squad for saying that. Either you refrain from expressing your views, or—if you insist on expressing your political views publicly in the present circumstances, when our position is far more difficult than it was when the White Guards were directly attacking us—then you will have only yourselves to blame if we treat you as the worst and most pernicious White Guard elements." We must never forget this.

When I speak about halting the retreat I do not mean that we have learned to trade. On the contrary, I am of the opposite opinion, and if my speech were to create that impression it would show that I had been misunderstood and that I am unable to express my thoughts properly.

The point, however, is that we must put a stop to the nervousness and fuss that have arisen with the introduction of the NEP—the desire to do everything in a new way and to adapt everything.

We now have a number of mixed companies. True, we have only very few. There are nine companies formed in conjunction with foreign capitalists and sanctioned by the Commissariat of Foreign Trade. The Sokolnikov commission has sanctioned six,[13] and the Northern Timber Trust has sanctioned two. Thus we now have seventeen companies with an aggregate capital amounting to many millions, sanctioned by several government departments (of course, there is plenty of confusion with all these departments, so that some slip here is also possible). At any rate, we have formed companies

---

Geneva in July–August 1920.

13. The Commission for Mixed Companies, chaired by G.Y. Sokolnikov, was set up by a decision of the Council of Labor and Defense on February 15, 1922.

jointly with Russian and foreign capitalists. There are only a few of them. But this small but practical start shows that the Communists have been judged by what they do. They have not been judged by such high institutions as the Central Control Commission and the All-Russia Central Executive Committee. The Central Control Commission is a splendid institution, of course, and we shall now give it more power. For all that, the judgment these institutions pass on Communists is not—just imagine—recognized on the international market. (*Laughter*)

But now that ordinary Russian and foreign capitalists are joining the Communists in forming mixed companies, we say, "We can do things after all; bad as it is, meager as it is, we have got something for a start." True, it is not very much. Just think of it: a year has passed since we declared that we would devote all our energy (and it is said that we have a great deal of energy) to this matter, and in this year we have managed to form only seventeen companies.

This shows how devilishly clumsy and inept we are; how much Oblomovism still remains,[14] for which we shall inevitably get a good thrashing. For all that, I repeat, a start, a reconnaissance has been made. The capitalists would not agree to have dealings with us if the elementary conditions for their operations did not exist. Even if only a very small section of them has agreed to this, it shows that we have scored a partial victory.

Of course, they will cheat us in these companies, cheat us so that it will take several years before matters are straightened out. But that does not matter. I do not say that that is a victory; it is a reconnaissance, which shows that we have an arena, we have a terrain, and can now stop the retreat.

The reconnaissance has revealed that we have concluded an insignificant number of agreements with capitalists; but we have con-

---

14. Oblomov, an indolent nobleman, was the main character of a novel of that name by I.A. Goncharov, published in 1858. The word *Oblomovism* was coined to describe narrow-mindedness, stagnation, and indecision.

cluded them nevertheless. We must learn from that and continue our operations. In this sense we must put a stop to nervousness, screaming, and fuss. We received notes and telephone messages, one after another asking, "Now that we have the NEP, may we be reorganized too?" Everybody is bustling, and we get utter confusion; nobody is doing any practical work; everybody is continuously arguing about how to adapt oneself to the NEP, but no practical results are forthcoming.

The merchants are laughing at us Communists, and in all probability are saying, "Formerly there were Persuaders-in-Chief,[15] now we have Talkers-in-Chief." That the capitalists gloated over the fact that we started late, that we were not sharp enough—of that there need not be the slightest doubt. In this sense, I say, these instructions must be endorsed in the name of the congress.

The retreat is at an end. The principal methods of operation, of how we are to work with the capitalists, are outlined. We have examples, even if an insignificant number.

Stop philosophizing and arguing about the NEP. Let the poets write verses, that is what they are poets for. But you economists, you stop arguing about the NEP and get more companies formed. Check up on how many Communists we have who can organize successful competition with the capitalists.

The retreat has come to an end; it is now a matter of regrouping our forces. These are the instructions that the congress must pass so as to put an end to fuss and bustle. Calm down, do not philosophize; if you do, it will be counted as a black mark against you. Show by your practical efforts that you can work no less efficiently than the capitalists. The capitalists create an economic link with the peasants in order to amass wealth; you must create a link with the peasant economy in order to strengthen the economic power of our

15. "Persuader-in-Chief" was the nickname given by soldiers in 1917 to Aleksandr Kerensky, then war minister of the Provisional Government, when he toured the front trying to rally support among the ranks for an offensive.

proletarian state. You have the advantage over the capitalists in that political power is in your hands; you have a number of economic weapons at your command; the only trouble is that you cannot make proper use of them. Look at things more soberly. Cast off the tinsel, the festive communist garments, learn a simple thing simply, and we shall beat the private capitalist. We possess political power; we possess a host of economic weapons. If we beat capitalism and create a link with peasant farming, we shall become an absolutely invincible power. Then the building of socialism will not be the task of that drop in the ocean called the Communist Party, but the task of the entire mass of the working people. Then the rank-and-file peasants will see that we are helping them, and they will follow our lead. Consequently, even if the pace is a hundred times slower, it will be a million times more certain and more sure.

NEP—a tactic, not a new direction

It is in this sense that we must speak of halting the retreat, and the proper thing to do is, in one way or another, to make this slogan a congress decision.

In this connection, I should like to deal with the question: What is the Bolsheviks' New Economic Policy—evolution or tactics? This question has been raised by the *Smena vekh*[16] people who, as you know, are a trend that has arisen among Russian émigrés; it is a socio-political trend led by some of the most prominent Constitutional Democrats, several ministers of the former Kolchak government,[17] people who have come to the conclusion that the Soviet government is building up the Russian state and therefore should be supported. They argue as follows: "What sort of state is the Soviet government building? The Communists say they are building a communist state

16. *Smena vekh* (Changing landmarks) was the name of a collection of articles published in Prague in 1921, and then of a journal published in Paris from October 1921 to March 1922.

17. Admiral A.V. Kolchak headed a regime in Siberia based on the White armies that, with British backing, held sway from November 1918 to January 1920.

and assure us that the new policy is a matter of tactics. The Bolsheviks say they are making use of the private capitalists in a difficult situation and will later get the upper hand. The Bolsheviks may do what they like; as a matter of fact it is not tactics but evolution, internal regeneration. They will arrive at the ordinary, bourgeois state, and we must support them. History proceeds in devious ways."

Some of them pretend to be Communists; but there are others who are more straightforward. One of these is Ustryalov. I think he was a minister in Kolchak's government. He does not agree with his colleagues and says, "You can think what you like about communism, but I maintain that it is not a matter of tactics but of evolution." I think that by being straightforward like this, Ustryalov is rendering us a great service. We, and I particularly, because of my position, hear a lot of sentimental communist lies, "communist fibbing," every day, and sometimes we get sick to death of them. But now instead of these "communist fibs" I get a copy of *Smena vekh,* which says quite plainly, "Things are by no means what you imagine them to be. As a matter of fact, you are slipping into the ordinary bourgeois morass with communist flags inscribed with catchwords stuck all over the place." This is very useful. It is not a repetition of what we are constantly hearing around us, but the plain class truth uttered by the class enemy.

It is very useful to read this sort of thing, and it was written not because the communist state allows you to write some things and not others, but because it really is the class truth, bluntly and frankly uttered by the class enemy. "I am in favor of supporting the Soviet government," says Ustryalov, although he was a Constitutional Democrat, a bourgeois, and supported intervention. "I am in favor of supporting Soviet power because it has taken the road that will lead it to the ordinary bourgeois state."

This is very useful, and I think that we must keep it in mind. It is much better for us if the *Smena vekh* people write in that strain than if some of them pretend to be almost Communists, so that from a distance one cannot tell whether they believe in God or in the communist revolution. We must say frankly that such candid enemies are useful. We must say frankly that the things Ustryalov speaks about are possible. History knows all sorts of metamorphoses. Relying on firmness of convictions, loyalty, and other splendid moral qualities is anything but a serious attitude in politics. A few people may be endowed with splendid moral qualities, but historical issues are decided by vast masses, which, if the few do not suit them, may at times treat them none too politely.

There have been many cases of this kind; that is why we must welcome this frank utterance of the *Smena vekh* people. The enemy is speaking the class truth and is pointing to the danger that confronts us and that the enemy is striving to make inevitable. *Smena vekh* adherents express the sentiments of thousands and tens of thousands of bourgeois or of Soviet employees whose function it is to operate our New Economic Policy. This is the real and main danger.

And that is why attention must be concentrated mainly on the question, "Who will win?" I have spoken about competition. No direct onslaught is being made on us now; nobody is clutching us by the throat. True, we have yet to see what will happen tomorrow; but today we are not being subjected to armed attack. Nevertheless, the fight against capitalist society has become a hundred times more fierce and perilous, because we are not always able to tell enemies from friends.

When I spoke about communist competition, what I had in mind were not communist sympathies but the development of economic forms and social systems. This is not competition but, if not the last, then nearly the last, desperate, furious, life-and-death struggle between capitalism and communism.

And here we must squarely put the question: Wherein lies our strength and what do we lack? We have quite enough political power. I hardly think there is anyone here who will assert that on such-and-such a practical question, in such-and-such a business institution, the Communists, the Communist Party, lack sufficient power. There are people who think only of this, but these people are hopelessly looking backward and cannot understand that one must look ahead. The main economic power is in our hands. The number of leased enterprises, although considerable in places, is on the whole insignificant; altogether it is infinitesimal compared with the rest. The economic power in the hands of the proletarian state of Russia is quite adequate to ensure the transition to communism. What then is lacking? Obviously, what is lacking is culture among the stratum of the Communists who perform administrative functions.

Will the vanquished impose their culture on the conquerors?

If we take Moscow with its 4,700 Communists in responsible positions, and if we take that huge bureaucratic machine, that gigantic heap, we must ask: Who is directing whom? I doubt very much whether it can truthfully be said that the Communists are directing that heap. To tell the truth, they are not directing, they are being directed. Something analogous happened here to what we were told in our history lessons when we were children: sometimes one nation conquers another; the nation that conquers is the conqueror and that nation that is vanquished is the conquered nation. This is simple and intelligible to all. But what happens to the culture of these nations? Here things are not so simple. If the conquering nation is more cultured than the vanquished nation, the former imposes its culture upon the latter; but if the opposite is the case, the vanquished nation imposes its culture upon the conqueror.

Has not something like this happened in the capital of the RSFSR? Have the 4,700 Communists (nearly a whole army division, and all of them the very best) come under the influence of an alien culture? True, there may be the impression that the vanquished have a high level of culture. But that is not the case at all. Their culture is miserable, insignificant, but it is still at a higher level than ours. Miserable and low as it is, it is higher than that of our responsible Communist administrators, for the latter lack administrative ability. Communists who are put at the head of departments—and sometimes artful saboteurs deliberately put them in these positions in order to use them as a shield—are often fooled. This is a very unpleasant admission to make, or, at any rate, not a very pleasant one; but I think we must admit it, for at present this is the salient problem. I think that this is the political lesson of the past year, and it is around this that the struggle will rage in 1922.

Will the responsible Communists of the RSFSR and of the Russian Communist Party realize that they cannot administer; that they only imagine they are directing but are, actually, being directed? If they realize this they will learn, of course, for this business can be learned. But one must study hard to learn it, and our people are not doing this. They scatter orders and decrees right and left, but the result is quite different from what they want.

The competition and rivalry that we have placed on the order of the day by proclaiming the NEP is a serious business. It appears to be going on in all government offices, but as a matter of fact it is one more form of the struggle between two irreconcilably hostile classes. It is another form of the struggle between the bourgeoisie and the proletariat. It is a struggle that has not yet been brought to a head, and culturally it has not yet been resolved even in the central government departments in Moscow. Very often the bourgeois officials know the business better than our best Communists, who are invested with authority and have every opportunity, but who cannot make the slightest use of their rights and authority.

I should like to quote a passage from a pamphlet by Aleksandr Todorsky. It was published in Vesyegonsk (there is a district town of that name in the province of Tver) on the first anniversary of the Soviet revolution in Russia, on November 7, 1918, a long, long time ago. Evidently this Vesyegonsk comrade is a member of the party—I read the pamphlet a long time ago and cannot say for certain. He describes how he set to work to equip two Soviet factories and for this purpose enlisted the services of two bourgeois. He did this in the way these things were done at that time—threatened to imprison them and to confiscate all their property. They were enlisted for the task of restoring the factories. We know how the services of the bourgeoisie were enlisted in 1918, (*laughter*) so there is no need for me to go into details. The methods we are now using to enlist the bourgeoisie are different. But here is the conclusion he arrived at: "This is only half the job. It is not enough to defeat the bourgeoisie, to overpower them; they must be compelled to work for us."

Now these are remarkable words. They are remarkable for they show that even in the town of Vesyegonsk, even in 1918, there were people who had a correct understanding of the relationship between the victorious proletariat and the vanquished bourgeoisie.

When we rap the exploiters' knuckles, render them innocuous, overpower them, it is only half the job. In Moscow, however, ninety out of a hundred responsible officials imagine that all we have to do is to overpower, render innocuous, and rap knuckles. What I have said about the Mensheviks, Socialist Revolutionaries, and White Guards is very often interpreted solely as rendering innocuous, rapping knuckles (and, perhaps, not only the knuckles, but some other place), and overpowering. But that is only half the job. It was only half the job even in 1918, when this was written by the Vesyegonsk comrade; now it is less even than one-fourth. We must make these hands work for us, and not have responsible Communists at the head of departments, enjoying rank and title, but actually swimming with the stream together with the bourgeoisie. That is the whole point.

The idea of building communist society exclusively with the hands of the Communists is childish, absolutely childish. We Communists are but a drop in the ocean, a drop in the ocean of the people. We shall be able to lead the people along the road we have chosen only if we correctly determine it not only from the standpoint of its direction in world history. From that point of view we have determined the road quite correctly, and this is corroborated by the situation in every country. We must also determine it correctly for our own native land, for our country. But the direction in world history is not the only factor. Other factors are whether there will be intervention or not, and whether we shall be able to supply the peasants with goods in exchange for their grain. The peasants will say, "You are splendid fellows; you defended our country. That is why we obeyed you. But if you cannot run the show, get out!" Yes, that is what the peasants will say.

We Communists shall be able to direct our economy if we succeed in utilizing the hands of the bourgeoisie in building up this economy of ours and in the meantime learn from these bourgeois and guide them along the road we want them to travel. But when a Communist imagines that he knows everything, when he says, "I am a responsible Communist, I have beaten enemies far more formidable than any salesman. We have fought at the front and have beaten far more formidable enemies," it is this prevailing mood that is doing us great harm.

Rendering the exploiters innocuous, rapping them over the knuckles, clipping their wings is the least important part of the job. That must be done, and our State Political Administration [GPU] and our courts must do it more vigorously than they have up to now. They must remember that they are proletarian courts surrounded by enemies the world over. This is not difficult, and in the main we have learned to do it. Here a certain amount of pressure must be exercised, but that is easy.

To win the second part of the victory, i.e., to build communism with the hands of non-Communists, to acquire the practical ability to do what is economically necessary, we must establish a link with peasant farming. We must satisfy the peasant so that he will say, "Hard, bitter, and painful as starvation is, I see a government that is an unusual one, is no ordinary one, but is doing something practically useful, something tangible." We must see to it that the numerous elements with whom we are cooperating, and who far exceed us in number, work in such a way as to enable us to supervise them. We must learn to understand this work and direct their hands so that they do something useful for communism. This is the key point of the present situation; for although individual Communists have understood and realized that it is necessary to enlist the nonparty people for this work, the rank-and-file of our party have not. Many circulars have been written, much has been said about this, but has anything been accomplished during the past year? Nothing. Not five party committees out of a hundred can show practical results. This shows how much we lag behind the requirements of the present time, how much we are still living in the traditions of 1918 and 1919. Those were great years, a great historical task was then accomplished. But if we only look back on those years and do not see the task that now confronts us, we shall be doomed, certainly and absolutely. And the whole point is that we refuse to admit it.

I should now like to give two practical examples to illustrate how we administer. I have said already that it would be more correct to take one of the state trusts as an example, but I must ask you to excuse me for not being able to apply this proper method, for to do so it would have been necessary to study the concrete material concerning at least one state trust. Unfortunately, I have been unable to do that, and so I will take two small examples. One example is the accusation of bureaucracy leveled at the People's Commissariat of Foreign Trade by the Moscow Consumers Cooperative Society. The other example I will take from the Donets Basin.

Why was Political Bureau needed to buy canned meat?

The first example is not quite relevant—I am unable to find a better—but it will serve to illustrate my main point. As you know from the newspapers, I have been unable to deal with affairs directly during these past few months. I have not been attending the Council of People's Commissars or the Central Committee. During the short and rare visits I made to Moscow I was struck by the desperate and terrible complaints leveled at the People's Commissariat of Foreign Trade. I have never doubted for a moment that the People's Commissariat of Foreign Trade functions badly and that it is tied up with red tape. But when the complaints became particularly bitter I tried to investigate the matter, to take a concrete example and for once get to the bottom of it; to ascertain the cause, to ascertain why the machine was not working properly.

The Moscow Consumers Cooperative Society wanted to purchase a quantity of canned goods. A French citizen appeared and offered some. I do not know whether he did it in the interests of the international policy and with the knowledge of the leadership of the Entente countries, or with the approval of Poincaré and other enemies of the Soviet government (I think our historians will investigate and make this clear after the Genoa conference), but the fact is that the French bourgeoisie took not only a theoretical, but also a practical interest in this business, as a French bourgeois turned up in Moscow with an offer of canned goods. Moscow is starving; in the summer the situation will be worse; no meat has been delivered, and knowing the merits of our People's Commissariat of Railways, probably none will be delivered.

An offer is made to sell canned meat for Soviet currency (whether or not the meat is entirely bad will be established by a future investigation). What could be simpler? But if the matter is approached in the Soviet way, it turns out to be not so simple after all. I was unable to go into the matter personally, but I ordered an investigation and I have before me the report which shows how this celebrated case developed.

It started with the decision adopted on February 11 by the Political Bureau of the Central Committee of the Russian Communist Party on the report of Comrade Kamenev concerning the desirability of purchasing food abroad. Of course, how could a Russian citizen decide such a question without the consent of the Political Bureau of the party! Think of it! How could 4,700 responsible officials (and this is only according to the census) decide a matter like purchasing food abroad without the consent of the Political Bureau of the Central Committee? This would be something supernatural, of course.

Evidently, Comrade Kamenev understands our policy and the realities of our position perfectly well, and therefore, he did not place too much reliance on the numerous responsible officials. He started by taking the bull by the horns—if not the bull, at all events the Political Bureau—and without any difficulty (I did not hear that there was any discussion over the matter) obtained a resolution stating, "To call the attention of the People's Commissariat of Foreign Trade to the desirability of importing food from abroad; further, the import duties," etc. The attention of the People's Commissariat of Foreign Trade was drawn to this.

Things started moving. This was on February 11. I remember that I had occasion to be in Moscow at the very end of February, or about that time, and what did I find? The complaints, the despairing complaints of the Moscow comrades.

"What's the matter?" I ask. "There is no way we can buy these provisions."

"Why?" "Because of the red tape of the People's Commissariat of Foreign Trade."

I had not been taking part in affairs for a long time and I did not know that the Political Bureau had adopted a decision on the matter. I merely ordered the executive secretary of our council to investigate, procure the relevant documents, and show them to me. The matter was settled when Krasin arrived. Kamenev discussed the matter with him; the transaction was arranged, and the canned meat was purchased. All's well that ends well.

I have not the least doubt that Kamenev and Krasin can come to an understanding and correctly determine the political line desired by the Political Bureau of the Central Committee of the Russian Communist Party. If the political line on commercial matters were decided by Kamenev and Krasin, ours would be the best Soviet republic in the world. But Kamenev, a member of the Political Bureau, and Krasin—the latter is busy with diplomatic affairs connected with Genoa, affairs which have entailed an enormous and excessive amount of labor—cannot be dragged into every transaction, dragged into the business of buying canned goods from a French citizen. That is not the way to work. This is not new, not economic, and not a policy, but sheer mockery.

Now I have the report of the investigation into this matter. In fact, I have two reports: one, the report of the investigation made by Gorbunov, the executive secretary of the Council of People's Commissars, and his assistant, Miroshnikov; and the other, the report of the investigation made by the State Political Administration. I do not know why the latter interested itself in the matter, and I am not quite sure whether it was proper for it to do so; but I will not go into that now, because I am afraid this might entail another investigation. The important thing is that material on the matter has been collected, and I now have it before me.

On arriving in Moscow at the end of February I heard bitter complaints, "We cannot buy canned goods," although in Libau [Liepaja] there was a ship with a cargo of canned goods and the owners were prepared to take Soviet currency for real canned goods! (*Laughter*) If these canned goods are not entirely bad (and I now emphasize the "if," because I am not sure that I shall not call for another investigation, the results of which, however, we shall have to report at the next congress) if, I say, these goods are not entirely bad and they have been purchased, I ask, Why could not this matter have been settled without Kamenev and Krasin?

From the report I have before me I gather that one responsible Communist sent another responsible Communist to the devil. I also gather from this report that one responsible Communist said to another responsible Communist, "From now on I shall not talk to you except in the presence of a lawyer."

Reading this report I recalled the time when I was in exile in Siberia, twenty-five years ago, and had occasion to act in the capacity of a lawyer. I was not a certified lawyer because, being summarily exiled, I was not allowed to practice, but as there was no other lawyer in the region, people came and confided their troubles to me. But sometimes I had the greatest difficulty in understanding what the trouble was.

A woman would come and, of course, start telling me a long story about her relatives, and it was incredibly difficult to get from her what she really wanted. I said to her, "Bring me a copy." She went on with her endless and pointless story. When I repeated, "Bring me a copy," she left, complaining, "He won't hear what I have to say unless I bring a copy." In our colony we had a hearty laugh over this copy. I was able, however, to make some progress. People came to me, brought copies of the necessary documents, and I was able to gather what their trouble was, what they complained of, what ailed them. This was twenty-five years ago, in Siberia, in a place many hundreds of versts[18]

18. A verst is 0.66 miles or 1.07 kilometers.

from the nearest railway station.

But why was it necessary, three years after the revolution, in the capital of the Soviet republic, to have two investigations, the intervention of Kamenev and Krasin, and the instructions of the Political Bureau to purchase canned goods? What was lacking? Political power? No. The money was forthcoming, so they had economic as well as political power. All the necessary institutions were available. What was lacking then? Culture. Ninety-nine out of every hundred officials of the Moscow Consumers Cooperative Society—against whom I have no complaint to make whatever, and whom I regard as excellent Communists—and of the Commissariat of Foreign Trade lack culture. They were unable to approach the matter in a cultured manner.

When I first heard of the matter I sent the following written proposal to the Central Committee: "All the officials concerned of the Moscow government departments—except the members of the All-Russia Central Executive Committee, who as you know enjoy immunity—should be put in the worst prison in Moscow for six hours, and those of the People's Commissariat of Foreign Trade for thirty-six hours." And then it turned out that no one could say who the culprits were, (*laughter*) and from what I have told you it is evident that the culprits will never be discovered.

It is simply the usual inability of the Russian intellectuals to get things done—inefficiency and slovenliness. First they rush at a job, do a little bit, and then think about it, and when nothing comes of it, they run to complain to Kamenev and want the matter to be brought before the Political Bureau. Of course, all difficult state problems should be brought before the Political Bureau—I shall have to say something about that later on—but one should think first and then act.

If you want to bring up a case, submit the appropriate documents. First send a telegram, and in Moscow we also have telephones, send a telephone message to the competent department and a copy to Tsyurupa saying, "I regard the transaction as urgent and will take proceedings against anyone guilty of red tape." One must think of this elementary culture, one must approach things in a thoughtful manner. If the business is not settled in the course of a few minutes, by telephone, collect the documents and say, "If you start any of your red tape I shall have you clapped in jail." But not a moment's thought is given to the matter, there is no preparation, the usual bustle, several commissions, everybody is tired out, exhausted, run down, and things begin to move only when Kamenev is put in touch with Krasin.

All this is typical of what goes on not only in the capital, Moscow, but also in the other capitals, in the capitals of all independent republics and regions. And the same thing, even a hundred times worse, constantly goes on in the provincial towns.

In our struggle we must remember that Communists must be able to reason. They may be perfectly familiar with the revolutionary struggle and with the state of the revolutionary movement all over the world, but if we are to extricate ourselves from desperate poverty and want, we need culture, integrity, and an ability to reason. Many lack these qualities. It would be unfair to say that the responsible Communists do not fulfill their functions conscientiously. The overwhelming majority of them, ninety-nine out of a hundred, are not only conscientious—they proved their devotion to the revolution under the most difficult conditions before the fall of tsarism and after the revolution; they were ready to lay down their lives. Therefore, it would be radically wrong to attribute the trouble to lack of conscientiousness. We need a cultured approach to the simplest affairs of state. We must all understand that this is a matter of state, a business matter; and if obstacles arise we must be able to overcome them and take proceedings against those who are guilty of red tape.

We have proletarian courts in Moscow; they must bring to account the persons who are to blame for the failure to effect the purchase of several tens of thousands of poods[19] of canned food. I think the proletarian courts will be able to punish the guilty, but in order to punish, the culprits must be found. I assure you that in this case no culprits will be found. I want you all to look into this business; no one is guilty; all we see is a lot of fuss and bustle and nonsense. Nobody has the ability to approach the business properly; nobody

19. The pood, a unit of weight, is equal to 36.1 pounds or 16.38 kilograms.

understands that affairs of state must not be tackled in this way.

And all the White Guards and saboteurs take advantage of this. At one time we waged a fierce struggle against the saboteurs; that struggle confronts us even now. There are saboteurs today, of course, and they must be fought. But can we fight them when the position is as I have just described it? This is worse than any sabotage. The saboteur could wish for nothing better than that two Communists should argue over the question of when to appeal to the Political Bureau for instructions on principles in buying food, and of course he would soon slip in between them and egg them on. If any intelligent saboteur were to stand behind these Communists, or behind each of them in turn, and encourage them, that would be the end. The matter would be doomed forever. Who is to blame? Nobody, because two responsible Communists, devoted revolutionaries, are arguing over last year's snow, are arguing over the question of when to appeal to the Political Bureau for instructions on principles in buying food.

That is how the matter stands and that is the difficulty that confronts us. Any salesman trained in a large capitalist enterprise knows how to settle a matter like that, but ninety-nine responsible Communists out of a hundred do not. And they refuse to understand that they do not know how and that they must learn the ABC of this business. Unless we realize this, unless we sit down in the preparatory class again, we shall never be able to solve the economic problem that now lies at the basis of our entire policy.

The other example I wanted to give you is that of the Donets Basin. You know that this is the center, the real basis of our entire economy. It will be utterly impossible to restore large-scale industry in Russia, to really build socialism—for it can be built only on the basis of large-scale industry—unless we restore the Donets Basin and bring it up to the proper level. The Central Committee is closely watching developments there.[20]

20. The Donets Basin (Donbas) in the Ukraine was the source of close to 90 percent of the coal mined in Soviet territory, production of which had fallen by 1921 to less than a third the prewar level. During 1921 a

As regards this region there was no unjustified, ridiculous, or absurd raising of minor questions in the Political Bureau; real, absolutely urgent business was discussed.

The Central Committee ought to see to it that in such real centers, bases, and foundations of our entire economy, work is carried on in a truly businesslike manner. At the head of the Central Coal Industry Board we had not only undoubtedly devoted, but really educated and very capable people. I would not be wrong even if I said talented people. That is why the Central Committee has concentrated its attention on it. The Ukraine is an independent republic. That is quite all right. But in party matters it sometimes—what is the politest way of saying it?—takes a roundabout course, and we shall have to get at them. For the people in charge there are sly, and their Central Committee I shall not say deceives us, but somehow edges away from us. To obtain a general view of the whole business, we discussed it in the Central Committee here and discovered that friction and disagreement exist. There is a Commission for the Utilization of Small Mines there and, of course, severe friction between it and the Central Coal Industry Board.

Still we, the Central Committee, have a certain amount of experience, and we unanimously decided not to remove the leading people, but if there was any friction it was to be reported to us, down to the smallest detail. For since we have not only devoted but capable people in the region, we must back them up and enable them to complete their training, assuming that they have not done so.

In the end, a party congress was held in the Ukraine—I do not know what happened there; all sorts of things happened. I asked for information from the Ukrainian comrades, and I asked Comrade Ordzhonikidze particularly—and the Central Committee did the same—to go down there and ascertain what had happened. Evidently, there was some intrigue and an awful mess, which the

---

vigorous campaign was launched to restore Donbas coal production under the leadership of Pyatakov, head of the Donbas Central Coal Industry Board.

Commission on Party History would not be able to clear up in ten years should it undertake to do so. But the upshot of it all was that contrary to the unanimous instructions of the Central Committee, this group was superseded by another group.

Danger of total absorption in administration

What was the matter? In the main, notwithstanding all its good qualities, a section of the group made a mistake. They were overzealous in their methods of administration. There we have to deal with workers. Very often the word *workers* is taken to mean the factory proletariat. But it does not mean that at all. During the war people who were by no means proletarians went into the factories; they went into the factories to dodge the war. Are the social and economic conditions in our country today such as to induce real proletarians to go into the factories? No. It would be true according to Marx; but Marx did not write about Russia; he wrote about capitalism as a whole, beginning with the fifteenth century. It held true over a period of six hundred years, but it is not true for present-day Russia. Very often those who go into the factories are not proletarians; they are casual elements of every description.

The task is to learn to organize the work properly, not to lag behind, to remove friction in time, not to separate administration from politics. For our administration and our politics rest on the ability of the entire vanguard to maintain contact with the entire mass of the proletariat and with the entire mass of the peasantry. If anybody forgets these cogs and becomes wholly absorbed in administration, the result will be a disastrous one. The mistake the Donets Basin officials made is insignificant compared with other mistakes of ours, but this example is a typical one. The Central Committee unanimously ordered, "Allow this group to remain; bring all conflicts, even minor ones, before the Central Committee, for the Donets Basin is not an ordinary district, but a vital one, without which socialist construction would remain simply a pious wish." But all our political power, all the authority of the Central Committee proved of no avail.

This time there was a mistake in administration, of course; in addition, a host of other mistakes were made.

This instance shows that it is not a matter of possessing political power, but of administrative ability, the ability to put the right man in the right place, the ability to avoid petty conflicts, so that state economic work may be carried on without interruption. This is what we lack; this is the root of the mistake.

I think that in discussing our revolution and weighing up its prospects, we must carefully single out the problems that the revolution has solved completely and that have irrevocably gone down in history as an epoch-making departure from capitalism. Our revolution has such solutions to its credit. Let the Mensheviks and Otto Bauer of the Two-and-a-Half International shout, "Theirs is a bourgeois revolution." We say that our task was to consummate the bourgeois revolution. As a certain White Guard newspaper expressed it: Dung had accumulated in our state institutions for four hundred years, but we cleaned it all out in four years. This is the great service we rendered. What have the Mensheviks and Socialist Revolutionaries done? Nothing. The dung of medievalism has not been cleared out either in our country, or even in advanced, enlightened Germany. Yet they reproach us for doing what stands very much to our credit. The fact that we have consummated the revolution is an achievement that can never be expunged from our record.

War is now in the air. The trade unions, for example, the reformist trade unions, are passing resolutions against war and are threatening to call strikes in opposition to war. Recently, if I am not mistaken, I read a report in the newspapers to the effect that a certain very good Communist delivered an antiwar speech in the French Chamber of Deputies in the course of which he stated that the workers would prefer to rise in revolt rather than go to war. This question cannot be formulated in the way we formulated it in 1912, when the Basel Manifesto was issued.[21] The Russian revolution

21. The 1912 Basel Congress of the Second International called on socialists of all countries to wage a vigorous struggle against war. The manifesto emphasized the theme that the imperialist rulers could be dissuaded from go-

alone has shown how it is possible to emerge from war, and what effort this entails. It showed what emerging from a reactionary war by revolutionary methods means. Reactionary imperialist wars are inevitable in all parts of the world, and in solving problems of this sort mankind cannot and will not forget that tens of millions were slaughtered then and will be slaughtered again if war breaks out.

We are living in the twentieth century, and the only nation that emerged from a reactionary war by revolutionary methods—not for the benefit of a particular government, but by overthrowing it—was the Russian nation, and it was the Russian revolution that extricated it. What has been won by the Russian revolution is irrevocable. No power on earth can erase that, nor can any power on earth erase the fact that the Soviet state has been created. This is a historic victory. For hundreds of years, states have been built according to the bourgeois model, and for the first time a nonbourgeois form of state has been discovered. Our machinery of government may be faulty, but it is said that the first steam engine that was invented was also faulty. No one even knows whether it worked or not, but that is not the important point; the important point is that it was invented. Even assuming that the first steam engine was of no use, the fact is that we now have steam engines.

Even if our machinery of government is very faulty, the fact remains that it has been created; the greatest invention in history has been made; a proletarian type of state has been created. Therefore, let all Europe, let thousands of bourgeois newspapers broadcast news about the horrors and poverty that prevail in our country, about suffering being the sole lot of the working people in our country; the workers all over the world are still drawn towards the Soviet state. These are the great and irrevocable gains that we have achieved.

But for us, members of the Communist Party, this meant only

---

ing to war through fear of possible resulting revolutions. For the text of the Basel Manifesto, see John Riddell, ed., *Lenin's Struggle for a Revolutionary International* (New York: Pathfinder, 1986), pp. 88–90.

opening the door. We are now confronted with the task of laying the foundations of socialist economy. Has this been done? No, it has not. We still lack the socialist foundation. Those Communists who imagine that we have it are greatly mistaken. The whole point is to distinguish firmly, clearly, and dispassionately what constitutes the historic service rendered by the Russian revolution from what we do very badly, from what has not yet been created, and what we shall have to redo many times yet.

Political events are always very confused and complicated. They can be compared with a chain. To hold the whole chain you must grasp the main link. Not a link chosen at random. What was the central event in 1917? Withdrawal from the war. The entire nation demanded this, and it overshadowed everything. Revolutionary Russia accomplished this withdrawal from the war. It cost tremendous effort, but the major demand of the people was satisfied, and that brought us victory for many years. The people realized, the peasants saw, every soldier returning from the front understood perfectly well that the Soviet government was a more democratic government, one that stood closer to the working people. No matter how many outrageous and absurd things we may have done in other spheres, the fact that we realized what the main task was proved that everything was right.

What was the key feature of 1919 and 1920? Military resistance. The all-powerful Entente was marching against us, was at our throats. No propaganda was required there. Every nonparty peasant understood what was going on. The landowners were coming back. The Communists knew how to fight them. That is why, taken in the mass, the peasants followed the lead of the Communists; that is why we were victorious.

In 1921, the key feature was an orderly retreat. This required stern discipline. The Workers Opposition said, "You are underrating the workers; the workers should display greater initiative." But initiative had to be displayed then by retreating in good order and by maintaining strict discipline. Anyone who introduced an undertone of panic or insubordination would have doomed the revolution to defeat, for there is nothing more difficult than retreating with people who have been accustomed to victory, who are imbued with revolutionary views and ideals, and who, in their hearts, regard every retreat as a disgraceful matter. The greatest danger was the violation of good order and the greatest task was to maintain good order.

And what is the key feature now? The key feature now—and I would like to sum up my report with this—is not that we have changed our line of policy. An incredible lot of nonsense is being talked about this in connection with NEP. It is all hot air, pernicious twaddle. In connection with NEP, some people are beginning to fuss around, proposing to reorganize our government departments and to form new ones. All this is pernicious twaddle. In the present situation the key feature is people, the proper choice of people. A revolutionary who is accustomed to struggle against petty reformists and uplift educators finds it hard to understand this. Soberly weighed up, the political conclusion to be drawn from the present situation is that we have advanced so far that we cannot hold all the positions, and we need not hold them all.

Internationally our position has improved vastly these last few years. The Soviet type of state is our achievement, it is a step forward in human progress, and the information the Communist International receives from every country every day corroborates this. Nobody has the slightest doubt about that. From the point of view of practical work, however, the position is that unless the Communists render the masses of the peasants practical assistance they will lose their support. Passing laws, passing better decrees, etc., is not now the main object of our attention. There was a time when the passing of decrees was a form of propaganda. People used to laugh at us and say that the Bolsheviks do not realize that their decrees are not being carried out; the entire White Guard press was full of jeers on that score.

But at that period this passing of decrees was quite justified. We Bolsheviks had just taken power, and we said to the peasant, to the worker, "Here is a decree; this is how we would like to have the state administered. Try it!" From the very outset we gave the ordi-

nary workers and peasants an idea of our policy in the form of decrees. The result was the enormous confidence we enjoyed and now
enjoy among the masses of the people. This was an essential period
at the beginning of the revolution; without it we would not have
risen on the crest of the revolutionary wave, we would have wal-
lowed in its trough. Without it we would not have won the
confidence of all the workers and peasants who wanted to build
their lives on new lines.

But this period has passed, and we refuse to understand this. Now
the peasants and workers will laugh at us if we order this or that
government department to be formed or reorganized. The ordinary
workers and peasants will display no interest in this now, and they
will be right, because this is not the central task today. This is not
the sort of thing with which we Communists should now go to the
people. Although we who are engaged in government departments
are always overwhelmed with so many petty affairs, this is not the
link that we must grasp, this is not the key feature.

Choose the right persons and introduce controls
The key feature is that we have not got the right persons in the right
places, that responsible Communists who acquitted themselves
magnificently during the revolution have been given commercial and
industrial functions about which they know nothing, and they prevent
us from seeing the truth, for rogues and rascals hide magnificently
behind their backs. The trouble is that we have no such thing as practical control of how things have been done. This is a prosaic job, a
small job; these are petty affairs. But after the greatest political change
in history, bearing in mind that for a time we shall have to live in the
midst of the capitalist system, the key feature now is not politics in the
narrow sense of the word (what we read in the newspapers is just political fireworks; there is nothing socialist in it at all) the key feature is
not resolutions, not departments, and not reorganization. As long as
these things are necessary we shall do them, but don't go to the people
with them. Choose the proper individuals and introduce practical control. That is what the people will appreciate.

In the sea of people, we are after all but a drop in the ocean, and we can administer only when we express correctly what the people are conscious of. Unless we do this, the Communist Party will not lead the proletariat, the proletariat will not lead the masses, and the whole machine will collapse. The chief thing the people, all the working people, want today is nothing but help in their desperate hunger and need; they want to be shown that the improvement needed by the peasants is really taking place in the form they are accustomed to. The peasant knows and is accustomed to the market and trade. We were unable to introduce direct communist distribution. We lacked the factories and their equipment for this. That being the case, we must provide the peasants with what they need through the medium of trade and provide it as well as the capitalist did, otherwise the people will not tolerate such an administration. This is the key to the situation, and—unless something unexpected arises—this, given three conditions, should be the central feature of our activities in 1922.

The first condition is that there shall be no intervention. We are doing all we can in the diplomatic field to avoid it; nevertheless, it may occur any day. We must really be on the alert and we must agree to make certain big sacrifices for the sake of the Red Army, within definite limits, of course. We are confronted by the entire bourgeois world, which is seeking only a way in which to strangle us. Our Mensheviks and Socialist Revolutionaries are nothing more nor less than the agents of this bourgeoisie. Such is their political status.

The second condition is that the financial crisis shall not be too severe. The crisis is approaching. You will hear about that when we discuss financial policy. If it is too severe and rigorous we shall have to revise many things again and concentrate all efforts on one thing. If it is not too severe it may even be useful; it will give the Communists in all the state trusts a good shaking; only we must not forget to do it. The financial crisis will shake up government departments and industrial enterprises, and those that are not equal to their task will be the first to burst; only we must take care that all the blame for this is not thrown on the specialists while the responsible Communists are praised for being very good fellows who have fought at the fronts and have always worked well. Thus, if the financial crisis is not too severe we can derive some benefit from it and comb the ranks of the responsible Communists engaged in the business departments not in the way the Central Control Commission and the Central Verification Commission comb them, but very thoroughly.

The third condition is that we shall make no political mistakes in this period. Of course, if we do make political mistakes, all our work of economic construction will be disrupted and we shall land ourselves in controversies about how to rectify them and what direction to pursue. But if we make no sad mistakes, the key feature in the near future will be not decrees and politics in the narrow sense of the word, not departments and their organization—the responsible Communists and the Soviet institutions will deal with these things whenever necessary—the main thing in all our activities will be choosing the right people and making sure that decisions are carried out. If, in this respect, we learn something practical, if we do something practically useful, we shall again overcome all difficulties.

In conclusion I must mention the practical side of the question of our Soviet institutions, the higher government bodies, and the party's relation to them. The relations between the party and the Soviet government bodies are not what they ought to be. On this point we are quite unanimous. I have given one example of how minor matters are dragged before the Political Bureau. It is extremely difficult to get out of this by formal means, for there is only one governing party in our country, and a member of the party cannot be prohibited from lodging complaints. That is why everything that comes up on the Council of People's Commissars is dragged before the Political Bureau.

I, too, am greatly to blame for this, for to a large extent contact between the Council of People's Commissars and the Political Bureau was maintained through me.[22] When I was obliged to retire

22. The Council of People's Commissars (CPC) was the day-to-day government of the workers and peasants republic, responsible to the All-Russia

from work, it was found that the two wheels were not working in unison, and Kamenev had to bear a treble load to maintain this contact. Inasmuch as it is hardly likely that I shall return to work in the near future, all hope devolves on the fact that there are two other deputies: Comrade Tsyurupa, who has been cleansed by the Germans, and Comrade Rykov, whom they have splendidly cleansed. It seems that even Wilhelm, the German emperor, has stood us in good stead—I never expected it. He had a surgeon, who happened to be the doctor treating Comrade Rykov, and he removed his worst part, keeping it in Germany, and left the best part intact, sending that part of Comrade Rykov thoroughly cleansed to us. If that method continues to be used it will be a really good thing.

Joking aside, a word or two about the main instructions. On this point there is complete unanimity on the Central Committee, and I hope that the congress will pay the closest attention to it and endorse the instructions that the Political Bureau and the Central Committee be relieved of minor matters and that more should be shifted to the responsible officials. The people's commissars must be responsible for their work and should not bring these matters up first on the Council of People's Commissars and then on the Political Bureau. Formally, we cannot abolish the right to lodge complaints with the Central Committee, for our party is the only governing party in the country. But we must put a stop to the habit of bringing every petty matter before the Central Committee; we must raise the prestige of the Council of People's Commissars. The meetings of the council must be mainly attended by the commissars, not the deputy commissars. The functions of the council must be changed in the direction in which I have not succeeded in changing them during the

---

Congress of Soviets and its Central Executive Committee. Lenin was the chairman of the CPC from its establishment in 1917 until his death in 1924; he was a member of the Political Bureau of the Communist Party throughout this period, as well.

From 1921, A.I. Rykov and A.D. Tsyurupa were deputy chairmen of the CPC; L.B. Kamenev was added as a third deputy in the latter half of 1922.

past year, that is, it must pay much more attention to executive control.

We will still have two deputies—Rykov and Tsyurupa. When Rykov was in the Extraordinary Authorized Council of Workers and Peasants Defense for the Supply of the Red Army and Navy, he tightened things up and the work went well.[23] Tsyurupa organized one of the most efficient people's commissariats. If together they make the maximum effort to improve the people's commissariats in the sense of efficiency and responsibility, we shall make some, even if a little, progress here. We have eighteen people's commissariats of which not less than fifteen are of no use at all—efficient people's commissars cannot be found everywhere, and I certainly hope that people give this more of their attention. Comrade Rykov must be a member of the Central Committee Bureau and of the Presidium of the All-Russia Central Executive Committee because there must be a link between these two bodies, for without this link the main wheels sometimes spin in the air.

In this connection, we must see to it that the number of commissions of the Council of People's Commissars and of the Council of Labor and Defense is reduced. These bodies must know and settle their own affairs and not split up into an infinite number of commissions. A few days ago the commissions were overhauled. It was found that there were one hundred and twenty of them. How many were necessary? Sixteen. And this is not the first cut. Instead of accepting responsibility for their work, preparing a decision for the Council of People's Commissars, and knowing that they bear responsibility for this decision, there is a tendency to take shelter behind commissions. The devil himself would lose his way in this maze of commissions. Nobody knows what is going on, who is responsible; everything is mixed up, and finally a decision is passed for

23. The Council of Workers and Peasants Defense became the Council of Labor and Defense in 1920, following the end of the civil war. It oversaw government economic policy and was responsible to the Council of People's Commissars.

which everybody is held responsible.

In this connection, reference must be made to the need for extending and developing the autonomy and activities of the regional economic conferences. The administrative division of Russia has now been drawn up on scientific lines; the economic and climatic conditions, the way of life, the conditions of obtaining fuel, of local industry, etc., have all been taken into account. On the basis of this division, district and regional economic conferences have been instituted. Changes may be made here and there, of course, but the prestige of these economic conferences must be enhanced.

Then we must see to it that the All-Russia Central Executive Committee works more energetically, meets in session more regularly, and for longer periods. The sessions of the All-Russia Central Executive Committee should discuss bills which sometimes are hastily brought before the Council of People's Commissars when there is no need to do so. It would be better to postpone such bills and give the local workers an opportunity to study them carefully. Stricter demands should be made upon those who draft the bills. This is not done.

If the sessions of the All-Russia Central Executive Committee last longer, they can split up into sections and subcommissions and thus will be able to verify the work more strictly and strive to achieve what in my opinion is the key, the quintessence of the present political situation: to concentrate attention on choosing the right people and on verifying how decisions are carried out.

It must be admitted, and we must not be afraid to admit, that in ninety-nine cases out of a hundred the responsible Communists are not in the jobs they are now fit for, that they are unable to perform their duties, and that they must sit down to learn. If this is admitted, and since we have the opportunity to learn—judging by the general international situation we shall have time to do so—we must do it, come what may. (*Stormy applause*)

2

The Fight Opens: The National Question and the Voluntary Union of Soviet Republics

The 'Autonomization' resolution: On relations between the RSFSR and the independent republics

by Joseph Stalin

SEPTEMBER 24, 1922

1. It is considered advisable that treaties be concluded between the Soviet republics of the Ukraine, Belorussia, Azerbaijan, Georgia, Armenia, and the RSFSR for their formal entry into the RSFSR.[1] The question of Bukhara, Khorezm, and the Far Eastern Republic is left open and confined to agreements with them on customs arrangements, foreign trade, foreign and military affairs, and so on.

NOTE: Corresponding changes in the constitutions of the republics mentioned in point 1 and of the RSFSR are to be made after enactment by Soviet procedure.

2. In accordance with this, the decisions of the All-Russia Central Executive Committee of the RSFSR shall be considered binding upon the central bodies of the republics mentioned in point 1, while the decisions of the Council of People's Commissars and the Council of Labor and Defense of the RSFSR shall be binding upon the unified commissariats of these republics.

NOTE: These republics are to be represented on the Presidium of the All-Russia CEC of the RSFSR.

3. External affairs (foreign affairs and foreign trade), military affairs, ways of communication (with the exception of local transport)

Footnotes start on next page

and the people's commissariat of posts and telegraphs of the republics mentioned in point 1 shall be merged with those of the RSFSR. The corresponding commissariats of the RSFSR shall have their agents and a small staff in the republics.

The agents are appointed by the people's commissars of the RSFSR by arrangement with the central executive committees of the republics.

It is considered desirable that the republics concerned be represented on the corresponding foreign agencies of the People's Commissariat of Foreign Affairs and the People's Commissariat of Foreign Trade.

4. The commissariats of finance, food, labor, and the national

---

1. Printed in the notes to Lenin, *CW,* vol. 42, pp. 602–3.

The right of the subject peoples of the old tsarist empire to national self-determination was asserted by one of the first decrees of the newly established Soviet government in November 1917 and codified by the third Soviet congress in January 1918. That congress declined to specify the geographic extent or constitutional form of the Russian Soviet Federated Socialist Republic (RSFSR), "leaving it to the workers and peasants of each nation to decide independently at their own authoritative congress of soviets whether they wish to participate in the federal government and in the other federal Soviet institutions, and on what terms." Within the Soviet republic of Russia itself, minority peoples were encouraged to form autonomous republics and regions, twenty-one of which had been established by the end of 1922.

Stalin's draft resolution was approved September 24, 1922, by a commission established by the party's Organization Bureau in August to make proposals on relations between the RSFSR and the various independent republics. The commission then submitted the resolution for action by the October 5–7 Central Committee plenum.

Prior to the commission vote, the resolution had been submitted to the regional Communist Party central committees in the five independent republics proposed for entry into the RSFSR as "autonomous" republics— Armenia, Azerbaijan, Belorussia, Georgia, and the Ukraine. Only the bodies in Azerbaijan and Armenia approved it.

The commission's plan, which became known as "autonomization," also provoked sharp disagreements within the commission itself. A motion to refer the draft back for further consideration by the leaderships of the Communist organizations in each republic was defeated by a vote of five to four.

economy of the republics shall be formally subject to the directives of the corresponding RSFSR commissariats.

5. The remaining commissariats of the republics mentioned in point 1, namely, the commissariats of justice, education, internal affairs, agriculture, Workers and Peasants Inspection, public health, and social security, shall be considered independent.

NOTE 1: The agencies fighting counterrevolution in the aforementioned republics shall be subject to the directives of the State Political Administration of the RSFSR.

NOTE 2: The central executive committees of the republics shall be granted the right of amnesty only in civil cases.

6. This decision, if approved by the CC of the RCP, shall not be published, but shall be passed on to the national central committees as a circular directive to be enacted through the central executive committee or the congress of soviets of the aforementioned republics pending the convocation of the All-Russia Congress of Soviets, at which it is to be declared as the desire of these republics.

On the establishment of the USSR

LETTER TO KAMENEV FOR MEMBERS OF THE POLITICAL BUREAU

SEPTEMBER 26, 1922

Comrade Kamenev, Stalin has probably already sent you the resolution of his commission on the entry of the independent republics into the RSFSR.[2]

If he has not, please take it from the secretary at once and read it. I spoke about it with Sokolnikov yesterday and with Stalin today. Tomorrow I shall see Mdivani (the Georgian Communist suspected of "independent" sentiments).

In my opinion the matter is of utmost importance. Stalin tends to be somewhat hasty. Give the matter good thought (you once intended to deal with it and even had a bit to do with it); Zinoviev too.

Stalin has already consented to make one concession: in clause 1, instead of "entry" into the RSFSR, to put:

"Formal unification with the RSFSR in a union of Soviet republics of Europe and Asia."

I hope the purport of this concession is clear: we consider ourselves, the Ukrainian SSR[3], and others equal and enter with them on an equal basis into a new union, a new federation, the Union of the Soviet Republics of Europe and Asia.

Clause 2 needs to be amended as well. What is needed besides the sessions of the All-Russia Central Executive Committee of the RSFSR is a:

"Federal All-Union Central Executive Committee of the Union of the Soviet Republics of Europe and Asia."

If the former should hold sessions once a week and the latter once a week (or once a fortnight even), this may be easily arranged.

The important thing is not to provide material for the "pro-independence" people, not to destroy their *independence,* but to create another *new level,* a federation of *equal* republics.

The second part of clause 2 could stand: the dissatisfied will appeal (against decisions of the Council of Labor and Defense, and the Council of People's Commissars) to the Federal All-Union Central Executive Committee, *without thereby suspending* implementation (just as in the RSFSR).

Clause 3 could stand, but its wording should be: "amalgamate in *federal* people's commissariats whose seat shall be in Moscow, with the proviso that the respective people's commissariats of the RSFSR have their authorized representatives with a small staff in all the republics *that have joined the union of republics of Europe and Asia.*"

Part 2 of clause 3 remains; perhaps it could be said to emphasize equality: "by agreement of the *central executive committees* of the member republics of the Union of the Soviet Republics of Europe and Asia."

Let's think about part 3: perhaps we had better substitute "*mandatory*" for "desirable"? Or perhaps insert *conditionally* mandatory at least in the form of a *request for instructions* and the authority to decide without such instructions solely in cases of "specially urgent importance"?

Clause 4 could perhaps also be "amalgamate by agreement of the

---

2. Lenin, *CW,* vol. 42, pp. 421–23. Lenin's letter was not published in the Soviet Union until 1959. Major excerpts were cited by Leon Trotsky in his 1927 "Letter to the Bureau of Party History," which is included in Trotsky's book *The Stalin School of Falsification* (New York: Pathfinder, third edition, 1972); see pp. 65–66.

3. Lenin's views on relations between Soviet Russia and the Ukraine were set out in three 1919 articles. See Lenin, *CW,* vol. 30, pages 163–66, 270–71, and 295–97.

central executive committees"?

Perhaps add to clause 5: "with the establishment of joint (or general) conferences and congresses of a *purely consultative* nature (or perhaps of a *solely* consultative nature)?

Appropriate alterations in the first and second comments.

Stalin has agreed to delay submission of the resolution to the Political Bureau of the Central Committee until my return. I shall arrive on Monday, October 2. I should like to see you and Rykov for about two hours in the morning, say 12 noon to 2:00 P.M., and, if necessary, in the evening, say 5:00–7:00 or 6:00–8:00.

That is my tentative draft. I shall add or amend on the strength of talks with Mdivani and other comrades. I beg you to do the same and to reply to me.

Yours,

Lenin

P.S. Send copies to *all* members of the Political Bureau.

Letter to members of the Political Bureau
by Joseph Stalin

Copy

Strictly secret

To Comrades Lenin, Kamenev, and members of the Politburo: Comrades Zinoviev, Kalinin, Molotov, Rykov, Tomsky, Trotsky. (Answer to Comrade Lenin's letter to Comrade Kamenev.)[4]

1. As to paragraph 1 of the commission's resolution, in my opinion, it is possible to concur with Comrade Lenin's proposal by reformulating it as follows: "to consider expedient the formal unification of the Soviet socialist republics of the Ukraine, Belorussia, Georgia, Azerbaijan, and Armenia with the RSFSR in a union of Soviet socialist republics of Europe and Asia." (Bukhara, Khorezm, and the Far Eastern Republic, of which the first two are not socialist and the third has not yet been sovietized, are to remain for the time being outside the formal unification.)

2. As to paragraph 2, Comrade Lenin's amendment, proposing to create—side by side with the All-Russia Central Executive Committee of the RSFSR—another Federal All-Russia Central Executive Committee, should not be adopted in my opinion. The existence of two central executive committees in Moscow, one of which will obviously represent a "lower house" and the other an "upper house" will bring us nothing but conflicts and friction.

I propose the following amendment in place of Comrade Lenin's: "In accordance with this, the Central Executive Committee of the

RSFSR is to be reorganized into an All-Federal Central Executive Committee, the decisions of which are obligatory for the central institutions forming part of the union of republics."

I think that any other decision along the lines of Comrade Lenin's amendment must necessarily lead to the creation of a Russian Central Executive Committee with the exclusion from it of the eight autonomous republics (the Tatar Republic, the Turkmen Republic, and the others), which are members of the RSFSR, and to the proclamation of the latter as independent republics side by side with the Ukraine and other independent republics, to the creation of two houses in Moscow (a Russian chamber and a federal chamber), and in general to profound reorganizations that are not required at this time by any internal or external necessity, and that are inadvisable in my view under present conditions and, in any case, are premature.

3. As to paragraph 3, Comrade Lenin's unimportant amendments are of a purely editorial nature.

4. As to paragraph 4, in my opinion, Comrade Lenin himself has been "hasty," demanding the merging of the people's commissariats of finance, food supplies, labor, and national economy with the federal people's commissariats. There is hardly any doubt that this "hastiness" "provides material for the pro-independence forces," to the detriment of the national liberalism of Comrade Lenin.

5. As to paragraph 5, Comrade Lenin's amendment is, in my opinion, superfluous.

4. Translated from Jan M. Meijer, ed., *The Trotsky Papers* (The Hague: Mouton, 1971), vol. 2, pp. 752, 754. Major excerpts from this answer by Stalin to Lenin's September 27 letter were included in *Stalin School of Falsification;* see pp. 66–67.

Revised resolution on relations between the RSFSR and the independent republics

by Joseph Stalin and others

SUBMITTED TO CENTRAL COMMITTEE PLENUM, OCTOBER 5–6, 1922

1. It is considered necessary that a treaty be concluded between the Ukraine, Belorussia, the federation of Transcaucasian republics, and the RSFSR for their amalgamation in a union of socialist Soviet republics, each reserving the right to freely secede from membership of the union.[5]

2. The supreme body of the union shall be the union Central Executive Committee consisting of representatives of the central executive committees of the RSFSR, the Transcaucasian Federation,[6] the Ukraine, and Belorussia pro rata to the population they represent.

3. The executive organ of the union CEC shall be the union Council of People's Commissars appointed by the union CEC.

4. The people's commissariats of foreign affairs, foreign trade, military affairs, railways, and posts and telegraphs of the republics and federations comprising the union shall be merged with those of the union of Soviet socialist republics. The corresponding commissariats of the union of republics shall have in the republics and federations their agents and a small staff appointed by the people's commissars of the union by arrangement with the Central Executive Committees of the federations and republics.

NOTE: It is considered necessary for the republics concerned to be represented on the corresponding foreign agencies of the People's

Commissariat of Foreign Affairs and the People's Commissariat of Foreign Trade.

5. The people's commissariats of finance, food, national economy, labor, and inspection of the republics and federations comprising the union of republics and also their central agencies for fighting counterrevolution shall be subject to the directives of the corresponding people's commissariats and to the decisions of the Council of People's Commissars and the Council of Labor and Defense of the union of republics.

6. The remaining people's commissariats comprising the union of republics, namely, the commissariats of justice, education, internal affairs, agriculture, public health, and social security shall be considered independent.

5. Printed in the notes to Lenin, *CW,* vol. 42, pp. 604–5. This version of the commission's draft resolution, rewritten by Stalin, was submitted to the Central Committee after Lenin's letter of September 26 had been circulated. The CC approved the document, which bore the signatures of Stalin, Ordzhonikidze, V.M. Molotov, and A.F. Myasnikov.

6. The Transcaucasian Federation consisted of Armenia, Azerbaijan, and Georgia. These states, formed in 1918, were governed at first by petty-bourgeois and bourgeois parties hostile to Soviet rule, which was established in Azerbaijan and Armenia in 1920.

For three years Georgia, the most economically developed of these new states, was ruled by a bourgeois government led by the local wing of the Menshevik Party and headed by Noy Zhordania. Georgia was occupied by the German military in 1918 and then by British troops until July 1920. During the civil war it was a bastion of counterrevolutionary forces.

In February 1921, a pro-Soviet revolt took place in Georgia in an area close to the frontier. The Red Army crossed into Georgia to support the rebels. The Menshevik government surrendered after a month-long war. The new Soviet government was headed by the Communists who had led the party within Georgia. They sought to act with extreme care not to trample on the national aspirations of the Georgian masses, who were deeply suspicious of any government that seemed based in Russia.

The Communist Party, embracing Communists from all the republics, set out in 1921 to knit the region's peoples together through a series of steps leading to formation of the Transcaucasian Federation, which was established on March 12, 1922.

On combating dominant nation chauvinism
MEMO TO THE POLITICAL BUREAU

OCTOBER 6, 1922

I declare war to the death on dominant nation chauvinism.[7] I shall eat it with all my healthy teeth as soon as I get rid of this accursed bad tooth.[8] It must be *absolutely* insisted that the union Central Executive Committee should be *presided over* in turn by a Russian,
Ukrainian,
Georgian, etc.
Absolutely!
Yours,

Lenin

7. Lenin, *CW*, vol. 33, p. 372.
8. Lenin had been hit by a bad toothache, which, he wrote in another letter, "kept me from my work a . . . whole week."

On the foreign trade monopoly
LETTER TO JOSEPH STALIN FOR MEMBERS OF THE CENTRAL COMMITTEE

OCTOBER 13, 1922

To Comrade Stalin, secretary of the CC:[9]

The decision of the plenary meeting of the CC of October 6 (minutes no. 7, point 3) institutes what seems to be an unimportant, partial reform: "implement a number of separate decisions of the Council of Labor and Defense on temporary permission for the import and export of individual categories of goods or on granting the permission for specific frontiers."[10]

In actual fact, however, this wrecks the foreign trade monopoly. Small wonder that Comrade Sokolnikov has been trying to get this done and has succeeded. He has always been for it; he likes paradoxes and has always undertaken to prove that monopoly is not to our advantage. But it is surprising that people who in principle favor the monopoly have voted for this without asking for detailed information from any of the business executives.

What does the decision that has been adopted signify?

Purchasing offices are being opened for the import and export trade. The owner of such an office has the right to buy and sell only specially listed goods.

Where is the control over this? Where are the means of control?

In Russia flax costs 4 rubles 50 kopeks, in Britain it costs 14 rubles. All of us have read in *Capital* how capitalism changes internally and grows more daring when interest rates and profits rise quickly. All of us recall that capitalism is capable of taking deadly risks and that Marx recognized this long before the war and before capitalism began its "leaps."

What is the situation now? What force is capable of holding the peasants and the traders from extremely profitable deals? Cover Russia with a network of overseers? Catch the neighbor in a purchasing office and prove that his flax has been sold to be smuggled out of the country?

Comrade Sokolnikov's paradoxes are always clever, but one must distinguish between paradoxes and the grim truth.

No "legality" on such a question is at all possible in the Russian countryside. No comparison with smuggling in general ("All the same," they say, "smuggling is also flourishing in spite of the monopoly") is in any way correct; it is one thing to deal with the professional smuggler on the frontier and another with all the peasantry, who will *all* defend themselves and fight the authorities when they try to deprive them of the profit "belonging to them."

Before we have had an opportunity to test the monopoly system, which is only just beginning to bring us millions (and will give us tens of millions and more), we are introducing complete chaos. We are shaking loose the very supports that we have only just begun to strengthen.

We have begun to build up a system; the foreign trade monopoly

9. Lenin, *CW*, vol. 33, pp. 375–78.

10. Under the state monopoly on foreign trade, all exporting and importing activity was centralized in the hands of a state agency. There were continuing proposals to relax the monopoly from a number of party leaders, including Bukharin, Zinoviev, Kamenev, and Stalin. Lenin responded to these proposals with a letter on May 15, 1922, calling for "a *formal ban* on all talks and negotiations and commissions, etc., concerning the relaxation of the foreign trade monopoly." The Political Bureau adopted a motion to this effect, although Stalin expressed doubt that it would settle anything. "All the same, I think that mitigation [of the trade monopoly] is becoming indispensable," he jotted down on Lenin's memo.

In October 1922 the Central Committee adopted, at a session both Lenin and Trotsky were unable to attend, the proposal cited here by Lenin. Following a fight led by Lenin and backed by Trotsky, this decision was reversed by the Central Committee December 18.

and the cooperatives are both only in the process of being built up. Some results will be forthcoming in a year or two. The profit from foreign trade runs into hundreds percent, and we are *beginning* to receive millions and tens of millions. We have *begun* to build up mixed companies; we have begun to learn to receive *half* of their (monstrous) profits. We can already see signs of very substantial state profits. We are giving this up in the hope of duties which cannot yield any comparable profit; we are giving everything up and chasing a specter!

The question was brought up at the plenary meeting hastily. There was no serious discussion worth mentioning. We have no reason for haste. Our business executives are only just beginning to go into things. Is this anything like a correct approach to the matter— when major questions of trade policy are decided in a slapdash manner, without collecting the pertinent material, without weighing the *pros* and *cons* with documents and figures? Tired people vote in a few minutes and that's the end of it. We have weighed less complicated political questions over and over again, and frequently it took us several months to reach a decision.

I regret it very much that illness prevented me from attending the meeting on that day and that I am now compelled to seek an exception to the rule.

But I think that the question must be weighed and studied, that haste is harmful.

I propose that the decision on this question be deferred for two months, i.e., until the next plenary meeting; in the interim, information and verified *documents* on the experience of our trade policy should be collected.

V. Ulyanov (Lenin)

P.S. In the conversation I had with Comrade Stalin yesterday (I did not attend the plenary meeting and tried to get my information from the comrades who were there), we spoke, incidentally, of the proposal temporarily to open the Petrograd and Novorossiisk ports. It seems to me that both examples show the extreme danger of such experiments even for a most restricted list of goods. The opening of the Petrograd port would intensify the smuggling of flax across the Finnish frontier to prodigious proportions. Instead of combating professional smugglers we shall have to combat *all the peasantry* of the flax-growing region. In this fight we shall almost assuredly be beaten, and beaten irreparably. The opening of the Novorossiisk port would quickly drain us of surplus grain. Is this a cautious policy at a time when our reserves for war are small? When a series of systematic measures to increase them have not yet had time to show results?

Then the following should be given consideration. The foreign trade monopoly has started a stream of gold into Russia. It is only just becoming possible to calculate; the first trip of such-and-such a merchant to Russia for six months has given him, say, hundreds percent of profit; he increases his price for this right from 25 to 50 percent in favor of the Commissariat of Foreign Trade. Furthermore, it has become possible for us to learn and to *increase* this profit. Everything will at once collapse, the whole work will stop, because if here and there various ports are opened for a time, *not a single merchant will pay a penny for this kind of "monopoly."* That is obvious. Before taking such a risk things have to be thought over and weighed several times. Besides there is the political risk of letting through not foreign merchants by name, which we check, but the entire petty bourgeoisie in general.

With the start of foreign trade, we have begun to reckon on an influx of gold. I see no other settlement except for a liquor monopoly, but here there are very serious moral considerations and also some businesslike objections from Sokolnikov.

Lenin

P.P.S. I have just been informed (1:30 hours) that some business executives have applied for a postponement. I have not yet read this application, but I wholeheartedly support it. It is only a matter of two months.

Lenin

Letter to Central Committee members
by Joseph Stalin

OCTOBER 20, 1922

Comrade Lenin's letter did not dissuade me from the correctness of the October 6 Central Committee plenum's decision regarding foreign trade.[11] The Commissariat of Foreign Trade's "millions" (the figures must still be established and calculations made) lose their authority if you take into consideration the fact that they are surpassed many times over by the tens of millions in gold that the commissariat exports from Russia. Nevertheless, in view of Comrade Lenin's insistent proposal that implementation of the Central Committee's decision be postponed, I vote for postponement so that the question may be discussed with Lenin's participation at the next plenum.

11. The full text of Stalin's letter is unavailable; these excerpts are taken from L.A. Fotieva, *Iz vospominaniy o V.I. Lenine* (Pages from Lenin's life) (Moscow: Izdat. Politicheskoy Literatury, 1964), pp. 28–29.

Telegram to K.M. Tsintsadze
and S.I. Kavtaradze

OCTOBER 21, 1922

Code

Tsintsadze and Kavtaradze, Communist Party of Georgia CC, Tiflis[12]
Copy to Ordzhonikidze, CC member, and Orakhelashvili, secretary
of the Transcaucasian Regional Committee

I am surprised at the indecent tone of the direct wire message
signed by Tsintsadze and others, which was handed to me for some
reason by Bukharin instead of one of the CC secretaries. I was sure
that all the differences had been ironed out by the CC plenum resolutions with my indirect participation and with the direct participation of Mdivani. That is why I resolutely condemn the abuse against

12. Lenin, *CW*, vol. 45, p. 582.
In response to the stipulation in the revised draft resolution on relations
with the independent republics, that Georgia, Armenia, and Azerbaijan
were to be admitted to the new union not as full members but as the
components of the Transcaucasian Federation, the Central Committee in
Georgia reaffirmed that Georgia should enter as a separate entity. (See
Lenin's 1921 correspondence concerning Soviet Georgia and the prospects for a Transcaucasian Federation in appendix 1 to this volume.)
Ordzhonikidze, with the backing of the party's Organization Bureau in
Moscow, reacted by disciplining Communist leaders in Georgia, ordering
a number of them to leave Georgia and place themselves at the disposal
of the Central Committee of the party in Russia. The leaders in Georgia
sent a protest to Bukharin and Kamenev, hoping to circumvent the party
Secretariat, which was headed by Stalin and had consistently supported
Ordzhonikidze. Bukharin and Kamenev showed Lenin the message from

Ordzhonikidze and insist that your conflict should be referred in a decent and loyal tone for settlement by the RCP CC Secretariat, which has been handed your direct wire message.

Lenin

Georgia, prompting this brief note by him.

    On October 22, 1922, nine of the eleven members of the Central Committee in Georgia resigned from the body in protest against the measures of Ordzhonikidze and the party Secretariat; Ordzhonikidze replaced them with his supporters. The new Central Committee in Georgia changed the Georgian government's policy, lifting its objections to the proposed terms for constituting the new federation.

The Union of Soviet Socialist Republics was formed on December 30.

3

The NEP and the World Struggle for Socialism

Five years of the Russian revolution and the prospects of the world revolution

REPORT TO THE FOURTH CONGRESS OF THE COMMUNIST INTERNATIONAL

NOVEMBER 13, 1922

(*Lenin is met with stormy, prolonged applause and a general ovation.*[1] *All rise and join in singing "The Internationale."*) Comrades, I am down in the list as the main speaker, but you will understand that after my lengthy illness I am not able to make a long report. I can only make a few introductory remarks on the key questions. My subject will be a very limited one. The subject, "Five Years of the Russian Revolution and the Prospects of the World Revolution," is in general too broad and too large for one speaker to exhaust in a single speech. That is why I shall take only a small part of this subject, namely, the question of the New Economic Policy. I have deliberately taken only this small part in order to make you familiar with what is now the most important question—at all events, it is the most important to me, because I am now working on it.

And so I shall tell you how we launched the New Economic Policy, and what results we have achieved with the aid of this policy. If I confine myself to this question, I shall, perhaps, succeed in giving you a general survey and a general idea of it.

To begin with how we arrived at the New Economic Policy, I must quote from an article I wrote in 1918. At the beginning of 1918, in a brief polemic, I touched on the question of the attitude

Footnotes start on next page

97

we should adopt towards state capitalism. I then wrote:

"State capitalism would be a *step forward* as compared with the present state of affairs"—i.e., the state of affairs at that time—"in our Soviet republic. If in approximately six months' time state capitalism became established in our republic, this would be a great success and a sure guarantee that within a year socialism will have gained a permanently firm hold and will have become invincible in our country."[2]

Of course, this was said at a time when we were more foolish than we are now, but not so foolish as to be unable to deal with such matters.

Thus in 1918 I was of the opinion that with regard to the economic situation then obtaining in the Soviet republic, state capitalism would be a step forward. This sounds very strange, and perhaps even absurd, for already at that time our republic was a socialist republic and we were every day hastily—perhaps too hastily—adopting various new economic measures which could not be described as anything but socialist measures. Nevertheless, I then held the view that in relation to the economic situation then obtaining in the Soviet republic, state capitalism would be a step forward, and I explained my idea simply by enumerating the elements of the economic system of Russia. In my opinion these elements were the following: "(1) patriarchal, i.e., the most primitive form of agriculture; (2) small commodity production (this includes the majority of the peasants who trade in grain); (3) private capitalism; (4) state capitalism; and (5) socialism."[3]

All these economic elements were present in Russia at that time. I set myself the task of explaining the relationship of these elements to each other, and whether one of these nonsocialist elements, namely, state capitalism, should not be rated higher than socialism. I repeat: it seems very strange to everyone that a nonsocialist element should

1. Lenin, *CW*, vol. 33, pp. 418–32.
2. Lenin, "'Left-Wing' Childishness and the Petty-Bourgeois Mentality," in *CW*, vol. 27, pp. 334–35.
3. "'Left-Wing' Childishness," *CW*, vol. 27, pp. 335–36.

be rated higher than, regarded as superior to, socialism in a republic which declares itself a socialist republic. But the fact will become intelligible if you recall that we definitely did not regard the economic system of Russia as something homogeneous and highly developed; we were fully aware that in Russia we had patriarchal agriculture, i.e., the most primitive form of agriculture, alongside the socialist form. What role could state capitalism play in these circumstances?

I then asked myself which of these elements predominated? Clearly, in a petty-bourgeois environment the petty-bourgeois element predominates. I recognized then that the petty-bourgeois element predominated; it was impossible to take a different view. The question I then put to myself—this was in a specific controversy which had nothing to do with the present question—was: What is our attitude towards state capitalism? And I replied: Although it is not a socialist form, state capitalism would be for us, and for Russia, a more favorable form than the existing one. What does that show? It shows that we did not overrate either the rudiments or the principles of socialist economy, although we had already accomplished the social revolution. On the contrary, at that time we already realized to a certain extent that it would be better if we first arrived at state capitalism and only after that at socialism.

I must lay special emphasis on this, because I assume that it is the only point of departure we can take, first, to explain what the present economic policy is and, second, to draw very important practical conclusions for the Communist International. I do not want to suggest that we had then a ready-made plan of retreat. This was not the case. Those brief lines set forth in a polemic were not by any means a plan of retreat. For example, they made no mention whatever of that very important point, freedom to trade, which is of fundamental significance to state capitalism. Yet they did contain a general, even if indefinite, idea of retreat.

I think that we should take note of that not only from the viewpoint of a country whose economic system was, and is to this day, very backward, but also from the viewpoint of the Communist International and the advanced western European countries. For example, just now we are engaged in drawing up a program.[4] I personally think that it would be best to hold simply a general discussion on all the programs, to make the first reading, so to speak, and to get them printed, but not to take a final decision now, this year. Why? first of all, of course, because I do not think we have considered all of them in sufficient detail, and also because we have given scarcely any thought to possible retreat and to preparations for it. Yet that is a question which, in view of such fundamental changes in the world as the overthrow of capitalism and the building of socialism with all its enormous difficulties, absolutely requires our attention.

We must not only know how to act when we pass directly to the offensive and are victorious. In revolutionary times this is not so difficult, nor so very important; at least, it is not the most decisive thing. There are always times in a revolution when the opponent loses his head, and if we attack him at such a time we may win an easy victory. But that is nothing, because our enemy, if he has enough endurance, can rally his forces beforehand, and so forth. He can easily provoke us to attack him and then throw us back for many years. For this reason, I think, the idea that we must prepare for ourselves the possibility of retreat is very important, and not only from the theoretical point of view. From the practical point of view, too, all the parties which are preparing to take the direct offensive against capitalism in the near future must now give thought to the problem of preparing for a possible retreat. I think it will do us no harm to learn this lesson together with all the other lessons which the experience of our revolution offers. On the contrary, it may prove beneficial in many cases.

Now that I have emphasized the fact that as early as 1918 we regarded state capitalism as a possible line of retreat, I shall deal with the results of our New Economic Policy. I repeat: at that time it was

4. Draft programs were submitted to the International's fourth congress, held November 5–December 5, 1922, by Nikolai Bukharin of the Russian CP and by the Bulgarian, German, and Italian parties. None were adopted at the congress.

still a very vague idea, but in 1921, after we had passed through the most important stage of the civil war, and passed through it victoriously, we felt the impact of a grave—I think it was the gravest—internal political crisis in Soviet Russia. This internal crisis brought to light discontent not only among a considerable section of the peasantry but also among the workers.

This was the first and, I hope, the last time in the history of Soviet Russia that feeling ran against us among large masses of peasants, not consciously but instinctively. What gave rise to this peculiar and for us, of course, very unpleasant situation? The reason for it was that in our economic offensive we had run too far ahead, that we had not provided ourselves with adequate resources, that the masses sensed what we ourselves were not then able to formulate consciously but what we admitted soon after, a few weeks later, namely, that the direct transition to purely socialist forms, to purely socialist distribution, was beyond our available strength, and that if we were unable to effect a retreat so as to confine ourselves to easier tasks, we would face disaster.

The crisis began, I think, in February 1921. In the spring of that year we decided unanimously—I did not observe any considerable disagreement among us on this question—to adopt the New Economic Policy. Now, after eighteen months have elapsed, at the close of 1922, we are able to make certain comparisons. What has happened? How have we fared during this period of over eighteen months? What is the result? Has this retreat been of any benefit to us? Has it really saved us, or is the result still indefinite? This is the main question that I put to myself, and I think that this main question is also of first-rate importance to all the Communist parties, for if the reply is in the negative, we are all doomed. I think that all of us can, with a clear conscience, reply to this question in the affirmative, namely, that the past eighteen months provide positive and absolute proof that we have passed the test.

I shall now try to prove this. To do that, I must briefly enumerate all the constituent parts of our economy.

First of all I shall deal with our financial system and our famous

Russian ruble. I think we can say that Russian rubles are famous, if only for the reason that their number now in circulation exceeds a quadrillion. (*Laughter*) That is something! It is an astronomical figure. I am sure that not everyone here knows what this figure signifies. (*General laughter*) But we do not think that the figure is so very important even from the point of view of economic science, for the zeroes can always be crossed out. (*Laughter*) We have achieved a thing or two in this art, which is likewise of no importance from the economic point of view, and I am sure that in the further course of events we shall achieve much more. But what is really important is the problem of stabilizing the ruble. We are now grappling with this problem, our best forces are working on it, and we attach decisive importance to it.[5]

If we succeed in stabilizing the ruble for a long period, and then for all time, it will prove that we have won. In that case, all these astronomical figures, these trillions and quadrillions, will not have mattered in the least. We shall then be able to place our economy on a firm basis, and develop it further on a firm basis. On this question I think I can cite some fairly important and decisive data. In 1921 the rate of exchange of the paper ruble remained stable for a period of less than three months. This year, 1922, which has not yet drawn to a close, the rate remained stable for a period of over five months. I think that this proof is sufficient. Of course, if you demand scientific proof that we shall definitely solve this problem, then it is not sufficient; but in general, I do not think it is possible to prove this entirely and conclusively. The data I have cited show that between last year, when we started on the New Economic Policy, and the present day, we have already learned to make progress. Since we have learned to do this, I am sure

5. In 1922 a new currency issue was introduced in which one ruble was worth 10,000 rubles of previous issues. Late that year it was decided that one ruble of the 1923 issue would be worth 100 rubles of the 1922 issue. The decision to go over to a stable currency backed by gold was taken in July 1922, both to facilitate trade between town and country and to make possible a planned revival of industrial production. This change was accomplished through a gradual transition completed in early 1924.

we shall learn to achieve further successes along this road, provided we avoid doing anything very foolish.

The most important thing, however, is trade, namely, the circulation of commodities, which is essential for us. And since we have successfully coped with this problem for two years, in spite of having been in a state of war (for, as you know, Vladivostok was recaptured only a few weeks ago),[6] and in spite of the fact that only now we are able to proceed with our economic activities in a really systematic way—since we have succeeded in keeping the rate of the paper ruble stable for five months instead of only three months, I think I can say that we have grounds to be pleased.

After all, we stand alone. We have not received any loans and are not receiving any now. We have been given no assistance by any of the powerful capitalist countries, which organize their capitalist economy so "brilliantly" that they do not know to this day which way they are going. By the Treaty of Versailles, they have created a financial system that they themselves cannot make head or tail of.[7] If these great capitalist countries are managing things in this way, I think that we, backward and uneducated as we are, may be pleased with the fact that we have grasped the most important thing—the conditions for the stabilization of the ruble. This is proved not by theoretical analysis but by practical experience, which in my opinion is more important than all the theoretical discussions in the world. Practice shows that we have achieved decisive results in that field, namely, we are beginning to push our economy towards the stabilization of the ruble, which is of supreme importance for trade, for

6. Vladivostok, Russia's largest port on the Pacific Ocean, was occupied by troops of the Japanese government until late October 1922.

7. The Treaty of Versailles between Germany and the victorious Allied powers in World War I was signed June 28, 1919. Germany was declared responsible for the war, its armed forces were strictly limited, and its colonies were seized by the victorious powers. Onerous financial reparations were imposed, spurring massive currency production and runaway inflation in Germany, as well as currency destabilization throughout the capitalist world, in the early 1920s.

the free circulation of commodities, for the peasants, and for the vast masses of small producers.

Now I come to our social objectives. The most important factor, of course, is the peasantry. In 1921 discontent undoubtedly prevailed among a vast section of the peasantry. Then there was the famine. This was the severest trial for the peasants. Naturally, all our enemies abroad shouted: "There, that's the result of a socialist economy!" Quite naturally, of course, they said nothing about the famine actually being the terrible result of the civil war. All the landowners and capitalists who had begun their offensive against us in 1918 tried to make out that the famine was the result of socialist economy. The famine was indeed a great and grave disaster which threatened to nullify the results of all our organizational and revolutionary efforts.

And so I ask now, after this unprecedented and unexpected disaster, what is the position today, after we have introduced the New Economic Policy, after we have granted the peasants freedom to trade? The answer is clear and obvious to everyone; in one year the peasants have not only got over the famine but have paid so much tax in kind that we have already received hundreds of millions of poods of grain, and that almost without employing any measures of coercion. Peasant uprisings, which previously, before 1921, were, so to speak, a common occurrence in Russia, have almost completely ceased.

The peasants are satisfied with their present position. We can confidently assert that. We think that this evidence is more important than any amount of statistical proof. Nobody questions the fact that the peasants are a decisive factor in our country. And the position of the peasantry is now such that we have no reason to fear any movement against us from that quarter. We say that quite consciously, without exaggeration. This we have already achieved. The peasantry may be dissatisfied with one aspect or another of the work of our authorities. They may complain about this. That is possible, of course, and inevitable, because our machinery of state and our state-operated economy are still too inefficient to avert it; but any serious dissatisfaction with us on the part of the peasantry as a whole is quite out of the question. This has been achieved in the course of one year. I think that is already quite a lot.

Now I come to our light industry. In industry we have to make a distinction between heavy and light industry because the situation in them is different. As regards light industry, I can safely say that there is a general revival. I shall not go into details. I did not set out to quote a lot of statistics. But this general impression is based on facts, and I can assure you that it is not based on anything untrue or inaccurate. We can speak of a general revival in light industry, and, as a result, of a definite improvement in the conditions of the workers in Petrograd and Moscow. In other districts this is observed to a lesser degree, because heavy industry predominates in them. So this does not apply generally. Nevertheless, I repeat, light industry is undoubtedly on the upgrade and the conditions of the workers in Petrograd and Moscow have unquestionably improved. In the spring of 1921 there was discontent among the workers in both these cities. That is definitely not the case now. We, who watch the conditions and mood of the workers from day to day, make no mistake on that score.

The third question is that of heavy industry. I must say that the situation here is still grave. Some turn for the better occurred in 1921–22, so that we may hope that the situation will improve in the near future. We have already gathered some of the resources necessary for this. In a capitalist country a loan of hundreds of millions would be required to improve the situation in heavy industry. No improvement would be possible without it. The economic history of the capitalist countries shows that heavy industry in backward countries can only be developed with the aid of long-term loans of hundreds of millions of dollars or gold rubles. We did not get such loans, and so far have received nothing.

All that is now being written about concessions and so forth is not worth much more than the paper it is written on. We have written a great deal about this lately and in particular about the Urquhart concession.[8] Yet I think our concessions policy is a very good one. How-

8. The British capitalist Leslie Urquhart negotiated with the Soviet government during 1921–22 for a concession to operate some mining properties.

ever, we have not concluded a single profitable concession agreement so far. I ask you to bear that in mind. Thus, the situation in heavy industry is really a very grave problem for our backward country, because we cannot count on loans from the wealthy countries.

In spite of that, we see a tangible improvement, and we also see that our trading has brought us some capital. True, it is only a very modest sum as yet—a little over twenty million gold rubles. At any rate, a beginning has been made; our trade is providing us with funds which we can employ for improving the situation in heavy industry. At the present moment, however, our heavy industry is still in great difficulties. But I think that the decisive circumstance is that we are already in a position to save a little. And we shall go on saving. We must economize now though it is often at the expense of the population. We are trying to reduce the state budget, to reduce staffs in our government offices. Later on I shall have a few words to say about our state apparatus. At all events, we must reduce it. We must economize as much as possible. We are economizing in all things, even in schools. We must do this, because we know that unless we save heavy industry, unless we restore it, we shall not be able to build up an industry at all; and without an industry we shall go under as an independent country. We realize this very well.

The salvation of Russia lies not only in a good harvest on the peasant farms—that is not enough; and not only in the good condition of light industry, which provides the peasantry with consumer goods—this, too, is not enough; we also need *heavy* industry. And to put it in a good condition will require several years of work.

Heavy industry needs state subsidies. If we are not able to provide them, we shall be doomed as a civilized state, let alone as a socialist state. In this respect, we have taken a determined step. We have begun to accumulate the funds that we need to put heavy industry on its feet. True, the sum we have obtained so far barely exceeds twenty million gold rubles; but at any rate this sum is available, and it is earmarked exclusively for the purpose of reviving our heavy industry.

I think that, on the whole, I have, as I have promised, briefly outlined the principal elements of our economy, and feel that we may draw the conclusion from all this that the New Economic Policy has already yielded dividends. We already have proof that, as a state, we are able to trade, to maintain our strong positions in agriculture and industry, and to make progress. Practical activity has proved it. I think this is sufficient for us for the time being. We shall have to learn much, and we have realized that we still have much to learn. We have been in power for five years, and during these five years we have been in a state of war. Hence, we have been successful.

This is understandable, because the peasantry were on our side. Probably no one could have supported us more than they did. They were aware that the White Guards had the landowners behind them, and they hate the landowners more than anything in the world. That is why the peasantry supported us with all their enthusiasm and loyalty. It was not difficult to get the peasantry to defend us against the White Guards. The peasants, who had always hated war, did all they possibly could in the war against the White Guards, in the civil war against the landowners.

But this was not all, because in substance it was only a matter of whether power would remain in the hands of the landowners or of the peasants. This was not enough for us. The peasants know that we have seized power for the workers and that our aim is to use this power to establish the socialist system. Therefore, the most important thing for us was to lay the economic foundation for socialist economy. We could not do it directly. We had to do it in a roundabout way.

The state capitalism that we have introduced in our country is of a special kind. It does not correspond to the usual conception of state capitalism. We hold all the key positions. We hold the land—it belongs to the state. This is very important, although our opponents try to make out that it is of no importance at all. That is untrue. The fact that the land belongs to the state is extremely important, and economically it is also of great practical purport. This we have achieved, and I must say that all our future activities should develop only within that framework. We have already succeeded in making the peasantry content and in reviving both industry and trade. I have already said that our state capitalism differs from state capitalism in the literal sense of the term in that our proletarian state owns not only the land but also all the vital branches of industry. To begin with, we have leased out only a certain number of the small and medium plants, but all the rest remain in our hands.

As regards trade, I want to reemphasize that we are trying to found mixed companies, that we are already forming them, i.e., companies in which part of the capital belongs to private capitalists—and foreign capitalists at that—and the other part belongs to the state. First, in this way we are learning how to trade, and that is what we need. Second, we are always in a position to dissolve these companies if we deem it necessary, and do not, therefore, run any risks, so to speak. We are learning from the private capitalist and looking round to see how we can progress, and what mistakes we make. It seems to me that I need say no more.

I should still like to deal with several minor points. Undoubtedly, we have done, and will still do, a host of foolish things. No one can judge and see this better than I. (*Laughter*) Why do we do these foolish things? The reason is clear: first, because we are a backward country; second, because education in our country is at a low level; and third, because we are getting no outside assistance. Not a single civilized country is helping us. On the contrary, they are all working against us. Fourth, our machinery of state is to blame.

We took over the old machinery of state, and that was our misfortune. Very often this machinery operates against us. In 1917, after we seized power, the government officials sabotaged us. This frightened us very much and we pleaded: "Please come back." They all came back, but that was our misfortune. We now have a vast army of government employees but lack sufficiently educated forces to exercise real control over them.

In practice it often happens that here at the top, where we exercise political power, the machine functions somehow, but down below government employees have arbitrary control and they often exercise it in such a way as to counteract our measures. At the top, we have I don't know how many, but at all events, I think, no more than a few thousand, at the outside several tens of thousands of our own people. Down below, however, there are hundreds of thousands of old officials whom we got from the tsar and from bourgeois society and who, partly deliberately and partly unwittingly, work against us. It is clear that nothing can be done in that respect overnight. It will take many years of hard work to improve the machinery, to remodel it, and to enlist new forces. We are doing this fairly quickly, perhaps too quickly. Soviet schools and workers' faculties have been formed;[9] a few hundred thousand young people are studying; they are studying too fast perhaps, but at all events a start has been made, and I think this work will bear fruit. If we do not work too hurriedly we shall, in a few years' time, have a large body of young people capable of thoroughly overhauling our state apparatus.

I have said that we have done a host of foolish things, but I must also say a word or two in this respect about our enemies. If our enemies blame us and say that Lenin himself admits that the Bolsheviks have done a host of foolish things, I want to reply to this: yes, but you know, the foolish things we have done are nonetheless very different from yours. We have only just begun to learn but are learning so methodically that we are certain to achieve good results. But since our enemies, i.e., the capitalists and the heroes of the Second International, lay stress on the foolish things we have done, I take the liberty, for the sake of comparison, to cite the words of a celebrated Russian author, which I shall amend to read as follows: if the Bolsheviks do foolish things, the Bolshevik says, "Twice two are five," but when their enemies, i.e., the capitalists and the heroes of the Second International, do foolish things, they get, "Twice two make a tallow candle."[10]

9. The workers' faculties, first opened in 1919, offered a course of study averaging three to four years to prepare them to enter the university.

10. The allusion is to a passage in Ivan Turgenev's *Rudin*. One character says, "A man may, for example, say that twice two makes not four but five or three and a half, but a woman will say that twice two makes a tallow candle."

That is easily proved. Take, for example, the agreement concluded by the USA, Great Britain, France, and Japan with Kolchak.[11] I ask you, are there any more enlightened and more powerful countries in the world? But what has happened? They promised to help Kolchak without calculation, without reflection, and without circumspection. It ended in a fiasco, which, it seems to me, is difficult for the human intellect to grasp.

Or take another example, a closer and more important one: the Treaty of Versailles. I ask you, what have the "great" powers which have "covered themselves with glory" done? How will they find a way out of this chaos and confusion? I don't think it will be an exaggeration to repeat that the foolish things we have done are nothing compared with those done in concert by the capitalist countries—the capitalist world and the Second International. That is why I think that the outlook for the world revolution—a subject which I must touch on briefly—is favorable. And given a certain definite condition, I think it will be even better. I should like to say a few words about this.

At the Third Congress, in 1921, we adopted a resolution on the organizational structure of the Communist parties and on the methods and content of their activities.[12] The resolution is an excellent one, but it is almost entirely Russian, that is to say, everything in it is based on Russian conditions. This is its good point, but it is also its failing. It is its failing because I am sure that no foreigner can read it. I have read it again before saying this. In the first place, it is too long, containing fifty or more points. Foreigners are not usually able to

11. On July 12, 1919, Admiral Kolchak, the White Guard commander in Siberia, was officially recognized by the chief capitalist powers fighting to overthrow the Soviet government. By this time, however, Kolchak's armies were already in full retreat; by the end of 1919 they were disintegrating.

12. See Alan Adler, ed., *Theses, Resolutions and Manifestos of the First Four Congresses of the Third International* (London: Ink Links, 1980), pp. 234–61. For the complete record of these congresses, see the ongoing Pathfinder series The Communist International in Lenin's Time.

read such things. Second, even if they read it, they will not understand it because it is too Russian. Not because it is written in Russian—it has been excellently translated into all languages—but because it is thoroughly imbued with the Russian spirit. And third, if by way of exception some foreigner does understand it, he cannot carry it out. This is its third defect. I have talked with a few of the foreign delegates and hope to discuss matters in detail with a large number of delegates from different countries during the congress, although I shall not take part in its proceedings, for unfortunately it is impossible for me to do that. I have the impression that we made a big mistake with this resolution, namely, that we blocked our own road to further success.

As I have said already, the resolution is excellently drafted; I am prepared to subscribe to every one of its fifty or more points. But we have not learned how to present our Russian experience to foreigners. All that was said in the resolution has remained a dead letter. If we do not realize this, we shall be unable to move ahead. I think that after five years of the Russian revolution the most important thing for all of us, Russian and foreign comrades alike, is to sit down and study. We have only now obtained the opportunity to do so. I do not know how long this opportunity will last. I do not know for how long the capitalist powers will give us the opportunity to study in peace. But we must take advantage of every moment of respite from fighting, from war, to study, and to study from scratch.

The whole party and all strata of the population of Russia prove this by their thirst for knowledge. This striving to learn shows that our most important task today is to study and to study hard. Our foreign comrades, too, must study. I do not mean that they have to learn to read and write and to understand what they read, as we still have to do. There is a dispute as to whether this concerns proletarian or bourgeois culture.[13] I shall leave that question open. But one

13. Some writers and artists in Russia held that the culture developed under the old ruling classes had to be rejected and replaced by a new "proletarian culture."

thing is certain: we have to begin by learning to read and write and to understand what we read. Foreigners do not need that. They need something more advanced: first of all, among other things they must learn to understand what we have written about the organizational structure of the Communist parties and what the foreign comrades have signed without reading and understanding. This must be their first task.

That resolution must be carried out. It cannot be carried out overnight—that is absolutely impossible. The resolution is too Russian, it reflects Russian experience. That is why it is quite unintelligible to foreigners, and they cannot be content with hanging it in a corner like an icon and praying to it. Nothing will be achieved that way. They must assimilate part of the Russian experience. Just how that will be done, I do not know. The fascists in Italy may, for example, render us a great service by showing the Italians that they are not yet sufficiently enlightened and that their country is not yet ensured against the Black Hundreds.[14] Perhaps this will be very useful. We Russians must also find ways and means of explaining the principles of this resolution to the foreigners. Unless we do that, it will be absolutely impossible for them to carry it out.

I am sure that in this connection we must tell not only the Russians, but the foreign comrades as well, that the most important thing in the period we are now entering is to study. We are studying in the general sense. They, however, must study in the special sense, in order that they may really understand the organization, structure, method, and content of revolutionary work. If they do that, I am sure the prospects of the world revolution will be not only good, but excellent. (*Stormy, prolonged applause. Shouts of "Long live our Comrade Lenin!" evoke a fresh stormy ovation.*)

---

14. The Italian fascists staged a coup October 31, two weeks before Lenin's speech to the Fourth Congress. The Black Hundreds were police-inspired monarchist gangs in tsarist Russia notorious for the murder of revolutionaries and instigation of pogroms against Jews.

Motion on the reduction of the army

NOVEMBER 13, 1922

Comrade Stalin,

Please obtain today a *viva voce* [oral] vote of the Politburo members on this motion of mine:[15]

That Comrade Trotsky's plan for submitting to the government a proposal for reducing the army by 200,000 men in the course of January be endorsed;

That Comrade Trotsky be asked to state when he considers it possible for such a question to be introduced to the Council of People's Commissars in the form of a completed draft.

Lenin

15. Lenin, *CW*, vol. 42, p. 425.

At several international conferences in 1922, the Soviet government called on the capitalist powers to join it in reduction of armaments. In December, the Soviet government acted unilaterally. The Tenth All-Russia Congress of Soviets implemented a 25 percent reduction in the Red Army—a proposal Lenin had made the previous May. The Soviet government and Communist Party also demanded that the imperialist powers revise the Treaty of Versailles, grant self-determination to all peoples including colonial subjects, and cancel all war debts and reparations.

To the Russian community in North America

NOVEMBER 14, 1922

Comrade Reichel, a representative of the American Society for Technical Aid for Soviet Russia, told me about the incorrect view on the New Economic Policy prevalent among some members of the Russian community in North America.[16]

This incorrect view could, I believe, be the result of deliberate misinterpretation of this policy by the capitalist press and the ridiculous tales spread by the embittered White Guards, who have been driven out of Soviet Russia, as well as by the Mensheviks and Socialist Revolutionaries.

In Europe these tales about us and especially about our New Economic Policy are falling into disuse. The New Economic Policy has changed nothing radically in the social system of Soviet Russia, nor can it change anything so long as the power is in the hands of the workers—and that Soviet power has come to stay, no one now, I think, can have any doubt. The malevolence of the capitalist press and the influx of Russian White Guards in America merely prove our strength.

The state capitalism which is one of the principal aspects of the New Economic Policy is, under Soviet power, a form of capitalism that is deliberately permitted and restricted by the working class. Our state capitalism differs essentially from the state capitalism in countries that have bourgeois governments in that the state with us

114

is represented not by the bourgeoisie but by the proletariat, which has succeeded in winning the full confidence of the peasantry.

Unfortunately, the introduction of state capitalism with us is not proceeding as quickly as we would like it. For example, so far we have not had a single important concession, and without foreign capital to help develop our economy, the latter's quick rehabilitation is inconceivable.

Those to whom the question of our New Economic Policy—the only correct policy—is not quite clear, I would refer to the speeches of Comrade Trotsky and me at the Fourth Congress of the Communist International devoted to this question.[17]

Comrade Reichel has told me about the preparatory work which the Society for Technical Aid is doing to organize American agricultural and other producers' communes who wish to come out to work in Russia and intend to bring with them new instruments of production, tractors, seeds of improved cultures, and so on.

I have already expressed my gratitude to the American comrades in my letters to the Society for Technical Aid and the Society of Friends for Soviet Russia in connection with the very successful work of their agricultural communes and units in Russia in the summer of 1922.[18]

---

16. Lenin, *CW*, vol. 42, pp. 425–27. Lenin's letter was first published in *Russky golos* (Russian voice) of New York, January 10, 1923.

17. Trotsky's report, along with the theses on the NEP he drafted for the congress, can be found in Leon Trotsky, *The First Five Years of the Communist International* (New York: Pathfinder, 1972), vol. 2, pp. 220–74.

18. See Lenin, "To the Society of Friends of Soviet Russia (in the United States)," in *CW*, vol. 33, p. 380; and "To the Society for Technical Aid for Soviet Russia," p. 381 of the same volume.

One of the most successful units from the United States was a group of ten farmers led by Harold Ware that came in 1922. Bringing with them twenty tractors, implements, and tools for a machine shop, they demonstrated U.S. farmers' techniques by plowing thousands of acres on a large state farm near Perm. At that time there were fewer than 400 working tractors in the Soviet republic. Lenin wrote to the Perm soviet executive committee October 20, calling for "maximum support" for Ware's group, whose aid was "most desirable and timely."

I take this opportunity to thank you once more on behalf of the Soviet government and to stress the fact that of all the forms of aid, the aid to our agriculture is the most important and valuable for us.

V. Ulyanov (Lenin)
Chairman, Council of People's Commissars

Speech at a plenary session of
the Moscow soviet

NOVEMBER 20, 1922

(*Stormy applause. "The Internationale" is sung.*)[19] Comrades, I regret very much and apologize that I have been unable to come to your session earlier. As far as I know you intended a few weeks ago to give me an opportunity of attending the Moscow soviet. I could not come because after my illness—from December onwards—I was incapacitated (to use the professional term) for quite a long time, and because of this reduced ability to work had to postpone my present address from week to week. A very considerable portion of my work which, as you will remember, I had first piled on Comrade Tsyurupa, and then on Comrade Rykov, I also had to pile additionally on Comrade Kamenev. And I must say that, to employ a simile I have already used, he was suddenly burdened with two loads. Though, to continue the simile, it should be said that the horse has proved to be an exceptionally capable and zealous one. (*Applause*) All the same, however, nobody is supposed to drag two loads, and I am now waiting impatiently for Comrades Tsyurupa and Rykov to return, and we shall divide up the work at least a little more fairly. As for myself, in view of my reduced ability to work it takes me much more time to look into matters than I should like.

In December 1921, when I had to stop working altogether, it was the year's end. We were effecting the transition to the New Economic Policy, and it turned out already then that, although we had embarked upon this transition in the beginning of 1921, it was quite a difficult, I would say a very difficult, transition. We have now been effecting this transition for more than eighteen months, and one would think that it was time the majority took up new places and disposed themselves according to the new conditions, particularly those of the New Economic Policy.

As to foreign policy, we had the fewest changes in that field. We pursued the line that we had adopted earlier, and I think I can say with a clear conscience that we pursued it quite consistently and with enormous success. There is no need, I think, to deal with that in detail; the capture of Vladivostok, the ensuing dem-onstration, and the declaration of federation which you read in the press the other day have proved and shown with the utmost clarity that no changes are necessary in this respect.[20] The road we are on is absolutely clearly and well defined and has ensured us success in face of all the countries of the world, although some of them are still prepared to declare that they refuse to sit at one table with us. Nevertheless, economic relations, followed by dip-lomatic relations, are improving, must improve, and certainly will improve.

Every country which resists this risks being late, and, perhaps in some quite substantial things, it risks being at a disadvantage. All of us see this now, and not only from the press, from the newspapers. I think that in their trips abroad comrades are also finding the changes very great. In that respect, to use an old simile, we have not changed to other trains or to other conveyances.

But as regards our home policy, the change we made in the spring of 1921, which was necessitated by such extremely powerful and convincing circumstances that no debates or disagreements arose

19. Lenin, CW, vol. 33, pp. 435–43.
20. Taking advantage of the Japanese government's withdrawal from Vladivostok, the People's Assembly of the Far Eastern Republic, compris-ing a large stretch of territory between Lake Baikal and the Pacific, voted on November 14, 1922, to join the Russian Soviet Federated Socialist Republic.

among us about it—that change continues to cause us some difficulties, great difficulties, I would say. Not because we have any doubts about the need for the turn—no doubts exist in that respect—not because we have any doubts as to whether the test of our New Economic Policy has yielded the successes we expected. No doubts exist on that score—I can say this quite definitely—either in the ranks of our party or in the ranks of the huge mass of nonparty workers and peasants.

In this sense the problem presents no difficulties. The difficulties we have stem from our being faced with a task whose solution very often requires the services of new people, extraordinary measures, and extraordinary methods. Doubts still exist among us as to whether this or that is correct. There are changes in one direction or another. And it should be said that both will continue for quite a long time.

"The New Economic Policy!" A strange title. It was called a New Economic Policy because it turned things back. We are now retreating, going back, as it were; but we are doing so in order, after first retreating, to take a running start and make a bigger leap forward. It was on this condition alone that we retreated in pursuing our New Economic Policy. Where and how we must now regroup, adapt, and reorganize in order to start a most stubborn offensive after our retreat, we do not yet know. To carry out all these operations properly we need, as the proverb says, to look not ten but a hundred times before we leap. We must do so in order to cope with the incredible difficulties we encounter in dealing with all our tasks and problems.

You know perfectly well what sacrifices have been made to achieve what has been achieved, you know how long the civil war has dragged on and what effort it has cost. Well now, the capture of Vladivostok has shown all of us (though Vladivostok is a long way off, it is after all one of our own towns) (*prolonged applause*) everybody's desire to join us, to join in our achievements. The Russian Soviet Federated Socialist Republic now stretches from here to there. This desire has rid us both of our civil enemies and of the foreign enemies who attacked us. I am referring to Japan.

We have won quite a definite diplomatic position, recognized by the whole world. All of you see it. You see its results, but how much time we needed to get it! We have now won the recognition of our rights by our enemies both in economic and in commercial policy. This is proved by the conclusion of trade agreements.

We can see why we, who eighteen months ago took the path of the so-called New Economic Policy, are finding it so incredibly difficult to advance along that path. We live in a country devastated so severely by war, knocked out of anything like the normal course of life, in a country that has suffered and endured so much, that willy-nilly we are beginning all our calculations with a very, very small percentage—the percentage of the prewar level. We apply this yardstick to the conditions of our life, we sometimes do so very impatiently, heatedly, and always end up with the conviction that the difficulties are vast. The task we have set ourselves in this field seems all the more vast because we are comparing it with the state of affairs in any ordinary bourgeois country. We have set ourselves this task because we understood that it was no use expecting the wealthy powers to give us the assistance usually forthcoming under such circumstances.[21] After the civil war, we have been subjected to very nearly a boycott, that is, we have been told that the economic ties that are customary and normal in the capitalist world will not be maintained in our case.

Over eighteen months have passed since we undertook the New Economic Policy and even a longer period has passed since we con-

---

21. The stenographic transcript of Lenin's report includes the following passage, not published in *Pravda* at the time: "and that even if we took into consideration the extremely high, say such-and-such a rate of interest, that is imposed in these circumstances on a country that, to use the accepted term, is rendered aid. Properly speaking, these rates of interest are very far from being aid. To put it bluntly, they would deserve a far less polite term than the word aid. But even these usual conditions would have been onerous for us."

cluded our first international treaty.[22] Nonetheless, this boycott of us by all the bourgeoisie and all governments continues to be felt. We could not count on anything else when we entered the new economic conditions, yet we had no doubt that we had to make the change and achieve success single-handedly. The further we go, the clearer it becomes that any aid that may be rendered to us, that will be rendered to us by the capitalist powers, will, far from eliminating this condition, in all likelihood and in the overwhelming majority of cases intensify it, accentuate it still further.

"Single-handed," we told ourselves. "Single-handed," we are told by almost every capitalist country with which we have concluded any deals, with which we have undertaken any engagements, with which we have begun any negotiations. And that is where the special difficulty lies. We must realize this difficulty. We have built up our own political system in more than three years of work, incredibly hard work that was incredibly full of heroism. In the position in which we were till now we had no time to see whether we would smash something needlessly, no time to see whether there would be many sacrifices, because there were sacrifices enough, because the struggle which we then began (you know this perfectly well and there is no need to dwell on it) was a life-and-death struggle against the old social system, against which we fought to forge for ourselves a right to existence, to peaceful development. And we have won it.

It is not we who say this, it is not the testimony of witnesses who may be accused of being partial to us. It is the testimony of witnesses who are in the camp of our enemies and who are naturally partial— not in our favor, however, but against us. These witnesses were in Denikin's camp. They directed the occupation. And we know that their partiality cost us very dear, cost us colossal destruction. We suffered all sorts of losses on their account and lost values of all

22. Some of the initial treaties signed with capitalist states were the peace treaty of Brest-Litovsk with Germany and its allies, signed March 3, 1918; the treaty with Estonia of February 2, 1920; the treaty with Afghanistan of February 28, 1921; the peace treaty with Poland of March 18, 1921; and the Treaty of Rapallo with Germany of April 16, 1922.

kinds, including the greatest of all values—human lives—on an incredibly large scale.

Now we must scrutinize our tasks most carefully and understand that the main task will be not to give up our previous gains. We shall not give up a single one of our old gains. (*Applause*) Yet we are also faced with an entirely new task; the old may prove a downright obstacle. To understand this task is most difficult. Yet it must be understood so that we may learn how to work when, so to speak, it is necessary to turn ourselves inside out. I think, comrades, that these words and slogans are understandable, because for nearly a year, during my enforced absence, you have had in practice, handling the jobs on hand, to speak and think of this in various ways and on hundreds of occasions, and I am confident that your reflections on that score can only lead to one conclusion, namely, that today we must display still more of the flexibility which we employed till now in the civil war.

We must not abandon the old. The series of concessions that adapt us to the capitalist powers is a series of concessions that enables them to make contact with us, ensures them a profit which is sometimes bigger, perhaps, than it should be. At the same time, we are conceding but a little part of the means of production, which are held almost entirely by our state.

The other day the papers discussed the concession proposed by the Englishman Urquhart, who has hitherto been against us almost throughout the civil war. He used to say: "We shall achieve our aim in the civil war against Russia, against the Russia that has dared to deprive us of this and of that." And after all that, we had to enter into negotiations with him. We did not refuse them, we undertook them with the greatest joy, but we said: "Beg your pardon, but we shall not give up what we have won. Our Russia is so big, our economic potentialities are so numerous, and we feel justified in not rejecting your kind proposal, but we shall discuss it soberly, like businessmen."

True, nothing came of our first talk, because we could not agree to his proposal for political reasons. We had to reject it. So long as the British did not entertain the possibility of our participating in the negotiations on the Straits, the Dardanelles, we had to reject it, but right after doing so we had to start examining the matter in substance.[23] We discussed whether or not it was of advantage to us, whether we would profit from concluding this concession agreement, and if so, under what circumstances it would be profitable. We had to talk about the price. That, comrades, is what shows you clearly how much our present approach to problems should differ from our former approach.

Formerly the Communist said: "I give my life," and it seemed very simple to him, although it was not always so simple. Now, however, we Communists face quite another task. We must now take all things into account and each of you must learn to be prudent. We must calculate how, in the capitalist environment, we can ensure our existence, how we can profit by our enemies, who, of course, will bargain, who have never forgotten how to bargain and will bargain at our expense. We are not forgetting that either, and do not in the least imagine commercial people anywhere turning into lambs and, having turned into lambs, offering us blessings of all sorts for nothing. That does not happen and we do not expect it, but count on the fact that we, who are accustomed to putting up a fight, will find a way out and prove capable of trading and profiting and emerging safely from difficult economic situations. That is a very difficult task. That is the task we are working on now.

23. Before the October revolution, Urquhart had owned vast mining properties in Russia. Lenin opposed a preliminary agreement with Urquhart in September 1922 for a concession to operate some of these mines, on the grounds that the terms would permit him to draw profits without any immediate investment of capital.

The Soviet government subsequently announced that Urquhart would not be granted the concession, citing London's exclusion of Soviet Russia from a conference on the Middle East that was to take up naval passage through the Bosporus and Dardanelles Straits into the Black Sea. Lenin and other Soviet leaders considered amendments to Urquhart's proposal that would make it acceptable. No agreement was ever concluded, however.

I should like us to realize clearly how great is the abyss between
the old and the new tasks. However great the abyss may be, we
learned to maneuver during the war, and we must understand that
the maneuver we now have to perform, in the midst of which we
now are, is the most difficult one. But then it seems to be our last
maneuver. We must test our strength in this field and prove that we
have learned more than just the lessons of yesterday and do not just
keep repeating the fundamentals. Nothing of the kind. We have begun to relearn and shall relearn in such a way that we shall achieve
definite and obvious success. And it is for the sake of this relearning,
I think, that we must again firmly promise one another that under
the name of the New Economic Policy we have turned back, but
turned back in such a way as to surrender nothing of the new and
yet to give the capitalists such advantages as will compel any state,
however hostile to us, to establish contacts and to deal with us.

Comrade Krasin, who has had many talks with Urquhart, the
head and backbone of the whole intervention, said that Urquhart,
after all his attempts to foist the old system on us at all costs,
throughout Russia, seated himself at the same table with him, with
Krasin, and began asking: "What's the price? How much? For how
many years?" (*Applause*) This is still quite far from our concluding
concession deals and thus entering into treaty relations that are perfectly precise and binding—from the viewpoint of bourgeois society—but we can already see that we are coming to it, have nearly
come to it, but have not quite arrived. We must admit that, comrades, and not have swelled heads. We are still far from having fully
achieved the things that will make us strong, self-reliant, and calmly
confident that no capitalist deals can frighten us; calmly confident
that however difficult a deal may be we shall conclude it, we shall
get to the bottom of it and settle it. That is why the work—both political and party—that we have begun in this sphere must be continued, and that is why we must change from the old methods to entirely new ones.

We still have the old machinery, and our task now is to remold it
along new lines. We cannot do so at once, but we must see to it that

the Communists we have are properly placed. What we need is that they, the Communists, should control the machinery they are assigned to and not, as so often happens with us, that the machinery should control them. We should make no secret of it, and speak of it frankly. Such are the tasks and the difficulties that confront us—and that at a moment when we have set out on our practical path, when we must not approach socialism as if it were an icon painted in festive colors. We need to take the right direction, we need to see that everything is checked, that the masses, the entire population, check the path we follow and say: "Yes, this is better than the old system." That is the task we have set ourselves.

Our party, a little group of people in comparison with the country's total population, has tackled this job. This tiny nucleus has set itself the task of remaking everything, and it will do so. We have proved that this is no utopia but a cause which people live by. We have all seen this. This has already been done. We must remake things in such a way that the great majority of the masses, the peasants and workers, will say: "It is not you who praise yourselves, but we. We say that you have achieved splendid results, after which no intelligent person will ever dream of returning to the old." We have not reached that point yet. *That is why NEP remains the main, current, and all-embracing slogan of today.*

We shall not forget a single one of the slogans we learned yesterday. We can say that quite calmly, without the slightest hesitation, say it to anybody, and every step we take demonstrates it. But we still have to adapt ourselves to the New Economic Policy. We must know how to overcome, to reduce to a definite minimum all its negative features, which there is no need to enumerate and which you know perfectly well. We must know how to arrange everything shrewdly. Our legislation gives us every opportunity to do so.

Shall we be able to get things going properly? That is still far from being settled. We are making a study of things. Every issue of our party newspaper offers you a dozen articles which tell you that at such-and-such a factory, owned by so-and-so, the rental terms are such-and-such, whereas at another, where our Communist comrade is the manager, the terms are such-and-such. Does it yield a profit or not, does it pay its way or not? We have approached the very core of the everyday problems, and that is a tremendous achievement. Socialism is no longer a matter of the distant future, or an abstract picture, or an icon. Our opinion of icons is the same as before—a very negative one. We have brought socialism into everyday life and must here see how matters stand. That is the task of our day, the task of our epoch.

Permit me to conclude by expressing confidence that difficult as this task may be, new as it may be compared with our previous task, and numerous as the difficulties may be that it entails, we shall all—not in a day, but in a few years—all of us together fulfill it whatever the cost, so that NEP Russia will become socialist Russia. (*Stormy, prolonged applause.*)

Draft resolution on the question of the program of the Communist International

PROPOSALS ADOPTED AT A MEETING OF THE CC FIVE
(LENIN, TROTSKY, ZINOVIEV, RADEK, BUKHARIN)

NOVEMBER 20, 1922

1. All the programs are to be handed to the executive of the Comintern or to a committee appointed by it for detailed working up and study.[24]

The executive of the Comintern is obliged within the shortest possible time to publish all the draft programs forwarded to it.

2. The congress confirms that all the national parties which do not yet have their own national programs must immediately start drafting them so that they may be submitted to the executive not later than three months prior to the next congress, which shall endorse them.

3. The necessity of fighting for transitional demands subject to appropriate reservations making these demands dependent on concrete conditions of place and time should be stated explicitly and categorically in the national programs.[25]

4. The theoretical basis for all such transitional or limited demands should be definitely stated in the general program, the Fourth Congress declaring that the Comintern emphatically condemns both the attempts to represent the inclusion of limited demands in the program as opportunism and all and any attempts to use limited demands to obscure and sidetrack the basic revolutionary task.

5. The general program should clearly state the basic historical

types of transitional demands of the national parties that flow from cardinal differences of economic structure, as for example, Britain and India, and suchlike.

24. Lenin, *CW*, vol. 42, pp. 427–28. This resolution was drafted by the Russian delegation's Bureau, which was made up of the five Central Committee members centrally involved in the Communist International's work, and was adopted by the Comintern's Fourth Congress.

25. In 1921 the Communist International's Third Congress had called for putting forward "a system of demands which in their totality disintegrate the power of the bourgeoisie, organize the proletariat, represent stages in the struggle for the proletarian dictatorship, and each of which expresses in itself the need of the broadest masses." Such demands arising from the objective needs of the working class became known as "transitional demands." At the Fourth Congress, some delegates criticized raising such demands as a concession to opportunism. See Jane DeGras, ed., *The Communist International 1919–1943: Documents* (London: Frank Cass & Co., 1971), vol. 1, p. 249.

To the congress of the Soviet Employees Union

NOVEMBER 22, 1922

Dear comrades,

The primary, immediate task of the present day, and of the next few years, is systematically to reduce the size and the cost of the Soviet machinery of state by cutting down staffs, improving organization, eliminating red tape and bureaucracy, and by reducing unproductive expenditure.[26] In this field your union has a great deal of work before it.

Wishing the Fifth All-Russia Congress of the Soviet Employees Union success and fruitful work, I hope that it will give particular attention to the question of the Soviet machinery of state.

V. Ulyanov (Lenin)
Chairman of the Council of
People's Commissars

26. Lenin, CW, vol. 33, p. 444.

Memorandum to Political Bureau members and draft letter to Herbert Hoover

Top Secret

Haskell reported to me the tentative proposal he made to Comrade Kamenev.[27] I expressed full agreement and showered him with compliments. At Haskell's request I want to give him the following letter. I ask members of the Politburo and Comrade Chicherin to address the question of whether you consider it expedient to put such a letter in Haskell's hands, or whether you think it more prudent, since the political situation in America is not clear to us, that I plead illness and avoid giving Haskell any letter at all.

A decision must be reached no later than tomorrow morning.

To Mr. Hoover

Dear Mr. Hoover,

Colonel Haskell told Comrade Kamenev, with whom he is in constant contact regarding the American Relief Administration—and then conveyed to me at a special meeting—that under certain conditions you would agree to come to Russia and devote yourself to work for its economic reconstruction. I welcome this offer with great interest and I thank you in advance. I repeat what I told Mr. Haskell—namely that assistance from an eminent organizer and "captain of industry" of a country whose economic system has principles contrary to ours would be exceptionally significant and especially desirable and gratifying to us.

In accordance with Mr. Haskell's wish, this entire matter will remain strictly confidential until your decision is made.[28]

Sincerely yours,

Lenin

27. First published in English in the present work. Translated from the fifth Russian edition of Lenin's works. Lenin, *Polnoye sobraniye sochineniy* (Collected works) (Moscow: 1967–70), vol. 54, pp. 311–12.

Hoover, then U.S. secretary of commerce, was also head of the American Relief Administration, which during the 1921 famine in Russia was a major source of material aid. William Haskell represented Hoover's organization in Russia.

28. Hoover never visited Soviet Russia.

To Leon Trotsky

Comrade Trotsky, copies to Zinoviev, Bukharin, Radek, Stalin, and Kamenev[29]

1. About Bordiga, I very strongly advise the adoption of your proposal that we send a letter from our CC to the Italian delegates and insistently recommend that they adopt the tactics you have outlined, otherwise the actions of the latter will be highly harmful for the Italian Communists in everything they subsequently do.[30]

2. I have read your theses concerning NEP and on the whole find them very good, and some formulations extremely felicitous, but a small part of the points seemed to me to be dubious. I would advise that they be published in the newspapers for the time being and then reissued in a pamphlet without fail.[31] With some comments, they will be especially appropriate for informing the foreign public about our New Economic Policy.   Lenin

29. Lenin, *CW*, vol. 45, p. 593.

30. After expelling its reformist minority in October 1922, the Italian Socialist Party applied to join the Communist International. Doing so entailed fusing with the Italian Communist Party, then led by Amadeo Bordiga, which initially rejected such a fusion. The fourth Comintern congress won agreement from the two parties to set up a joint committee to lead a fusion process. There were hesitations on both sides, however, and the fusion remained unconsummated when the blows of fascist repression disrupted the functioning of the two parties' leaderships in the course of 1923. See also Lenin, *CW*, vol. 45, p. 600.

31. Trotsky's theses were published in *Pravda* December 6, 1922, and in pamphlet form early the following year.

On reducing the repair and construction program of naval vessels

NOVEMBER 25, 1922

To Comrade Stalin:

(For now let this be a private discussion, with the request for consultation with other Central Committee members.)[32]

I am sending you a summary list on the question of the ship repair program. We need to reach a decision with dispatch, possibly even today. Yesterday, discussing this in detail with Sklyansky, I was somewhat hesitant, but the expenditure of ten million is so outrageously high that I must all the same propose the following:

To approve completion of the cruiser *Nakhimov*, then to reduce by one-third the number of the remaining large vessels (destroyers, battleships, and so on), and to instruct the department to reduce all remaining expenditures accordingly. I believe that we may on the whole go down to seven million. It will be much more correct to use the remaining funds to raise expenditures on schools. Enclosed is a strictly confidential summary list, as well as results of work done by Pyatakov's commission,[33] which, according to Comrade Sklyansky, has already reduced expenditures by nearly sixteen million.

I think that the navy at its present size is an excessive luxury for

32. Published here in English for the first time. Translated from the fifth Russian-language edition of Lenin's works, vol. 45, pp. 311–13.

33. The reference is to a commission of the Communist Party Central Committee charged with reviewing the annual plan for shipbuilding and defense projects.

us—even though it is really a small navy, as Sklyansky correctly remarks. The *Nakhimov* must be finished, since we will sell it for a
profit, but as for the rest I am convinced that our naval specialists
are all getting far too carried away. We do not need a navy, while
we desperately need an increase in expenditures for schools.

Lenin

To Leon Trotsky, Gregory Zinoviev, Nikolai Bukharin, and Karl Radek

NOVEMBER 26, 1922

Comrades Trotsky, Zinoviev, Bukharin, and Radek:[34]

I have read the document which you have sent me, namely, the draft in German entitled "Outline of Agrarian Action Program," compiled mainly by Varga and approved by the commission, and I very much hesitate to support it.[35] I feel that the draft gives virtually nothing new in comparison with the resolution of the Second Congress of the Comintern on the agrarian question. I very much fear that some formulations, diverging, perhaps even accidentally, from the Second Congress resolution, may cause misunderstanding and breed artificial talk about a discrepancy between this draft and the Second Congress resolution. There also seems to be a distinct element which weakens what was said there about supporting the peasant movement and which is capable of producing some dissent between the needy peasantry and the rural proletariat.

I am unable to go into this question in greater detail and make a sentence-by-sentence comparison between Varga's draft resolution which you have sent in and the Second Congress resolution. I consider it necessary to warn that we should not let ourselves accumulate numerous resolutions on one and the same question which are capable of producing misunderstanding and confusion.

As a minimum, I would propose:

1. To compare the new resolution with the Second Congress

resolution sentence by sentence.

2. To give the new resolution the character of something like a partial commentary.

I personally feel that the new resolution is of very doubtful value.[36]

Lenin

34. Lenin, *CW*, vol. 45, pp. 593–94.

35. The Communist International's Fourth Congress had appointed a commission on the agrarian question to draw up a resolution for submission to plenary debate.

36. Copies of Lenin's letter in four languages were distributed to delegates and the Comintern congress. The agrarian commission made several changes in Varga's draft resolution to clarify its relationship to that of the Second Congress, including addition of the subtitle, "Directives on the Application of the Agrarian Theses of the Second Congress." The resolution was then adopted.

The final text of the theses is printed in *Theses, Resolutions and Manifestos of the First Four Congresses of the Third International*, pp. 331–36. The theses of the Second Congress (and Lenin's draft, which differs substantially) can be found in John Riddell, ed., *Workers of the World and Oppressed Peoples, Unite! Proceedings and Documents of the Second Congress, 1920* (New York: Pathfinder, 1991), pp. 660–70, 960–71.

On reducing the repair and construction program of naval vessels (continuation)

NOVEMBER 29, 1922

To Comrade Stalin,

As for the charge that I am using a "rough guess" as a basis for cutting back the ship repair program,[37] I must explain the following:

The ship repair program, in all its aspects, must be brought into line (and only specialists, of course, are in a position to do this) with the size of the navy that we for political and economic reasons decide to maintain. I have been fully convinced that the cruiser *Nakhimov* must form part of our navy, since as a last resort we would have the option of selling it for a profit. In addition, our ship repair program includes a number of destroyers, some battleships, and some submarines, and so on. The total number of these vessels seems to me to be excessive, not justified by the state of our naval forces in general, and far beyond our budget as well. I cannot say just how much this part of the navy can be cut back. Nor do I believe that the Pyatakov/Sokolnikov commission was able to determine this on the basis of rational, economic, and—especially—political considerations.

For me one thing is clear: the total expense of ten million is beyond our strength. Therefore, I propose to limit this total to seven million, leaving it to the military specialists to calculate, on the basis of this estimate, the overall number of destroyers, battleships, submarines, and so on, that the navy will receive, adding in the additional figures corresponding to the quantity of our vessels in the navy. In my opinion, there is no other way to carry out a reduction in our navy successfully, for the naval specialists, naturally, get carried away by their work and will inflate every figure. Meanwhile, given the enormous expense that we allocate to aviation, we ought to be five, ten times more cautious regarding our naval budget—all the more since there will probably be very large expenses called for by the reoccupation of Vladivostok.

As for Kamenev's views on giving the promised orders to the metal factories and to the Chief Electricity Committee,[38] it must be stated that we must give such orders to meet the needs of the peasantry and by no means for any such thing as the navy. Due to economic and political considerations, it is impossible to maintain a navy of any significant size. Therefore, I propose that after cutting the general expenses by three million, we calculate how the remaining sum should be apportioned for this or that goal within the framework of the ship repair program. We should then figure out how to start right now converting the above-mentioned proportion of our shipyards to metal goods needed by the peasantry.[39]

Lenin

37. The criticism Lenin is replying to had been made by Trotsky.

38. Kamenev had argued for maintaining planned shipyard expenditures, since the orders had already gone out to the factories.

39. On November 30 the Communist Party Political Bureau voted to reduce naval expenditure for ship repair to eight million rubles and to transfer the resources saved to the People's Commissariat of Education.

To Comrade Münzenberg

DECEMBER 2, 1922

Supplementing your report at the Fourth Congress of the Comintern, I should like in a few words to point out the significance of the organization of aid.[40]

The assistance given to the starving by the international working class helped Soviet Russia in considerable measure to endure the painful days of last year's famine and to overcome it. At the present time we have to heal the wounds inflicted by the famine, provide in the first place for many thousands of orphaned children, and restore our agriculture and industry, which have suffered heavily as a result of the famine.

In this sphere, too, the fraternal aid of the international working class has already begun to operate. The American tractor column near Perm, the agricultural groups of the American Technical Aid, the agricultural and industrial undertakings of the International Workers' Aid, the allocation of and subscriptions to the first proletarian loan, through the Workers' Aid to Soviet Russia—all these are very promising beginnings in the cause of workers' fraternal aid to promote the economic restoration of Soviet Russia.

The work of economic assistance, so happily begun by the International Workers' Aid to Soviet Russia, should be supported in every possible way by the workers and toilers of the whole world. Side by side with the continuing strong political pressure on the governments of the bourgeois countries over the demand for recognition of the Soviet government, widespread economic aid by the world proletariat is at present the best and most practical support of Soviet Russia in her difficult economic war against the imperialist concerns and the best support for her work of building a socialist economy.

V.I. Ulyanov (Lenin)
Moscow

40. Lenin, CW, vol. 35, pp. 559–60.

To I.I. Khodorovsky

DECEMBER 4, 1922

Comrade Khodorovsky,

Comrade Molotov informs me that you have had experience in Novo-Nikolayevsk [Novosibirsk] in arranging help from city cells to rural cells and vice versa.[41] Will you collect material about this—written or printed—or, if you have no time to do this before the Congress of Soviets, will you write a couple of words, or perhaps we shall find time to talk it over.

Lenin

---

41. Lenin, *CW*, vol. 45, pp. 595–96.

Lenin was referring to the practice of "sponsorship," by which a party cell based among urban workers would adopt another in a rural area, in order to learn of its work and provide it with assistance. Lenin returns to this topic in "Pages from a Diary" in chapter 6.

On the tasks of our delegation at The Hague

DECEMBER 4, 1922

On the question of combating the danger of war, in connection with the conference at The Hague, I think that the greatest difficulty lies in overcoming the prejudice that this is a simple, clear, and comparatively easy question.[42]

"We shall meet the outbreak of war by a strike or a revolution"— that is what all the prominent reformist leaders usually say to the working class. And very often the seeming radicalness of the measures proposed satisfies and appeases the workers, cooperators, and peasants.[43]

Perhaps the most correct method would be to start with the sharpest refutation of this opinion; to declare that particularly now, after the recent war, only the most foolish or utterly dishonest people can assert that such an answer to the question of combating war is of any use; to declare that it is impossible to "respond" to war by a strike, just as it is impossible to "respond" to war by revolution in the simple and literal sense of these terms.

We must explain the real situation to the people, show them that war is hatched in the greatest secrecy and that the ordinary workers organizations, even if they call themselves revolutionary organizations, are utterly helpless in face of a really impending war.

We must explain to the people again and again in the most concrete manner possible how matters stood in the last war and why they could not have been otherwise.

We must take special pains to explain that the question of "defense of the fatherland" will inevitably arise and that the overwhelming majority of the working people will inevitably decide it in favor of their bourgeoisie.

Therefore, first, it is necessary to explain what "defense of the fatherland" means. Second, in connection with this, it is necessary to explain what "defeatism" means. Lastly, we must explain that the only possible method of combating war is to preserve existing and to form new, illegal organizations in which all revolutionaries taking part in a war carry on *prolonged* antiwar activities—all this must be brought into the forefront.[44]

42. Lenin, *CW*, vol. 33, pp. 447–51.

The Hague International Peace Congress, held December 10–15, 1922, was called by the reformist-led International Federation of Trade Unions. Unions from Soviet Russia secured an invitation, and their delegates called on the conference to adopt plans for united international working-class action against war. The struggle against war, they argued, could be effectively conducted only on the basis of a class struggle against the bourgeoisie. The reformist leaders, who dominated the conference, rejected united action with Communists and charged them with splitting the labor movement, repressing their opponents in Russia, and violating the independence of Georgia.

43. Before World War I, a widely held view in the Second International was that in case of war, the Social Democratic parties of belligerent countries would respond by calling a general strike. This threat, it was hoped, would deter capitalist governments from war. A resolution adopted by the International's 1907 Stuttgart congress called on all parties to combat the threat of war with all possible means. Revolutionary forces, led by Lenin and Rosa Luxemburg, won inclusion of a passage calling on the working class, if war was declared, to utilize the resulting crisis to "hasten the downfall of capitalist class rule." See Riddell, ed., *Lenin's Struggle for a Revolutionary International*, pp. 20–47.

This revolutionary perspective was reaffirmed at the International's 1912 congress in Basel. When World War I broke out in 1914, however, a large majority of the International's leaders, including prominent advocates of a general strike against war, rallied to support the war effort of their respective ruling classes.

44. Lenin explained the Bolshevik viewpoint on these questions in his 1915 pamphlet, "Socialism and War," in *CW*, vol. 21, pp. 295–338, and

Boycott war—that is a silly catchphrase. Communists must take part in every war, even the most reactionary.

Examples from, say, prewar German literature, and in particular, the example of the Basel congress of 1912, should be used as especially concrete proof that the theoretical admission that war is criminal, that socialists cannot condone war, etc., turn out to be empty phrases, because there is nothing concrete in them. The masses are not given a really vivid idea of how war may and will creep up on them. On the contrary, every day the dominant press, in an infinite number of copies, obscures this question and weaves such lies around it that the feeble Socialist press is absolutely impotent against it, the more so that even in time of peace it propounds fundamentally erroneous views on this point. In all probability, the Communist press in most countries will also disgrace itself.

I think that our delegates at the international congress of cooperators and trade unionists should distribute their functions among themselves and expose all the sophistries that are being advanced at the present time in justification of war.

These sophistries are, perhaps, the principal means by which the bourgeois press rallies the masses in support of war. The main reason why we are so impotent in face of war is either that we do not expose these sophistries beforehand or still more that we, in the spirit of the Basel Manifesto of 1912, waive them aside with the cheap, boastful, and utterly empty phrase that we shall not allow war to break out, that we fully understand that war is a crime, etc.

I think that if we have several people at The Hague conference who are capable of delivering speeches against war in various languages, the most important thing would be to refute the opinion that the delegates at the conference are opponents of war, that they understand how war may and will come upon them at the most unexpected moment, that they to any extent understand what methods should be adopted to combat war, that they are to any extent in a

in other articles printed in *Lenin's Struggle*, pp. 135–38, 162–70, 178–79, 193–210.

position to adopt reasonable and effective measures to combat war.

Using the experience of the recent war to illustrate the point, we must explain what a host of both theoretical and practical questions will arise on the morrow of the declaration of war and that the vast majority of the men called up for military service will have no opportunity to examine these questions with anything like clear heads or in a conscientious and unprejudiced manner.

I think that this question must be explained in extraordinary detail, and in two ways:

First, by relating and analyzing what happened during the last war and telling all those present that they are ignorant of this, or pretend that they know about it while actually shutting their eyes to what is the very pivot of the question which must be understood if any real efforts are to be made to combat war. On this point I think it is necessary to examine all the opinions and shades of opinion that arose among Russian socialists concerning the last war. We must show that those shades of opinion did not emerge accidentally but arose out of the very nature of modern wars in general. We must prove that without an analysis of these opinions, without ascertaining why they inevitably arise and why they are of decisive significance in the matter of combating war—without such an analysis it is utterly impossible to make any preparations for war or even to take an intelligent stand on it.

Second, we must take the present conflicts, even the most insignificant, to illustrate the fact that war may break out any day as a consequence of a dispute between Great Britain and France over some point of their treaty with Turkey, or between the USA and Japan over some trivial disagreement on any Pacific question, or between any of the big powers over colonies, tariffs, or general commercial policy, etc., etc. It seems to me that if there is the slightest doubt about being able at The Hague to say all we want to say against war with the utmost freedom, we should consider various stratagems that will enable us to say at least what is most important and to publish in pamphlet form what could not be said. We must take the risk of our speaker being stopped by the chair.

I think that for the same purpose the delegation should consist not only of speakers who are able, and whose duty it shall be, to make speeches against war as a whole, i.e., to enlarge on all the main arguments and all the conditions for combating war, but also of people who know all the three principal foreign languages, whose business it shall be to enter into conversation with the delegates and to ascertain how far they understand the main arguments, what need there is to advance certain arguments, and to quote certain examples.

Perhaps on a number of questions the mere quoting of facts of the last war will be sufficient to produce serious effect. Perhaps on a number of other questions serious effect can be produced only by explaining the conflicts that exist today between the various countries and how likely they are to develop into armed collisions.

Apropos of a question of combating war, I remember that a number of declarations have been made by our Communist deputies, in parliament and outside parliament, which contain monstrously incorrect and monstrously thoughtless statements on this subject. I think these declarations, particularly if they have been made since the war, must be subjected to determined and ruthless criticism and the name of each person who made them should be mentioned. Opinion concerning these speakers may be expressed in the mildest terms, particularly if circumstances require it, but not a single case of this kind should be passed over in silence, for thoughtlessness on this question is an evil that outweighs all others and cannot be treated lightly.

A number of decisions have been adopted by workers congresses which are unpardonably foolish and thoughtless.[45]

---

45. For example, on February 3, 1922, the reformist-led International Union of Metal Workers, meeting in Hanover, Germany, adopted a resolution in favor of calling a general strike if war broke out. On hearing of this, Lenin proposed that the Soviet press and the Communist International call to mind the failure of the 1912 Basel Manifesto. They should point out, he stated in a letter to Political Bureau members, that "only a ready and experienced revolutionary party, with a good illegal machin-

All material should be immediately collected and all the separate parts and particles of the subject and the whole "strategy" to be pursued should be thoroughly discussed at a congress.

On such a question, not only a mistake, but even lack of thoroughness on our part will be unpardonable.

---

ery, can successfully wage a struggle against war, and that the means of struggle is not a strike against war, but the formation of revolutionary groups in the warring armies and their preparation for the carrying out of a revolution." (Lenin, "On the Question of Struggle against War," in *CW*, vol. 36, p. 559.)

Re draft proposal on the report of the State Supplies Commission

DECEMBER 6–7, 1922

All schools, including teachers and pupils, to have their requirements in bread fully provided for over and above the given calculations, and Comrades Kamenev, Tsyurupa, and Yakovleva to figure out exactly what amount of bread should be earmarked for this purpose, with the addition of a minimum, specially verified, quantity for office employees.[46]

Another one million gold rubles to be added for school expenses.

Lenin

46. Lenin, *CW*, vol. 42, p. 429. The Council of People's Commissars subsequently decided to allocate for education two million gold rubles saved by cutbacks in the ship repair program.

Proposals concerning the work routine of the deputy chairmen and chairman of the Council of People's Commissars

DECEMBER 9, 1922

Work routine of the deputy chairmen and the chairman of the CPC:[47]

1. Working hours: 11-2, 6-9; together with the CPC chairman on *Monday and Tuesday, Thursday and Friday.*

2. Special meetings of all the deputies and the chairman of the CLD [Council of Labor and Defense] (minus the Politburo, CPC, and CLD) on these days and at these hours whenever there is need, but *generally not less than* twice a week for one hour. This hour is to be fixed the evening before not later than 9 P.M.

3. All the work of the deputies is divided into:

a) Close supervision over the work of the Narrow CPC.[48]

b) Similar supervision over the work of the business meetings of the CLD.

(It is necessary to resume the business meetings of the CLD in order to disengage the deputies for other more important work. The business meetings are *not* chaired by the deputies but *their* signatures *alone* endorse the decisions of these meetings.)

c) Chairmanship at those parts of the CPC and CLD meetings where the chairman of the CPC does not preside.

d) Participation in the Financial Committee (plus Sokolnikov and his deputy and the chairman of the Narrow CPC; the latter need not attend all meetings of the Financial Committee).

(Perhaps arrange a meeting of the Financial Committee once a week for one hour chaired by the CPC chairman? Think this over.)

e) Determining the agenda of all bodies, including the Narrow CPC, and the order of priority, the most important questions being chosen by all four under the chairmanship of the CPC chairman.

f) Close supervision of the various people's commissariats and their apparatus both by means of instructions to the people's commissars and their deputies personally and by means of studying their apparatus top and bottom.

g) The commissariats, for this purpose (point f), are allocated among the deputies, such allocation to be endorsed by the chairman of the CPC.

4. All the above-mentioned work is distributed among the deputies in such a way that each of the three (and if need be their assistants from among the business managers) handles a definite job *for two months* and afterwards *changes it* for another.

(This is necessary in order that all the deputies may acquaint themselves with the *entire* apparatus and in order to achieve real unity of management.)

5. The draft of such a distribution among the three deputies is to be drawn up by them immediately and approved by all four.

6. The work of improving and correcting the whole apparatus is far more important than the work of chairmanship and the chatting with deputy people's commissars and people's commissars, which

47. Lenin, *CW*, vol. 42, pp. 430–432.

This letter and that of December 13 (see chapter 4) address a task discussed by Lenin in the final section of his report to the eleventh Communist Party congress (see chapter 1). Lenin dealt with these matters in greater detail in his "Decree on the Functions of the Deputy Chairmen of the Council of People's Commissars and of the Council of Labor and Defense," April 11, 1922, and "Reply to Remarks Concerning the Functions of the Deputy Chairmen of the Council of People's Commissars and of the Council of Labor and Defense," May 5, 1922. See Lenin, *CW*, vol. 33, pp. 335–43, 353–55.

48. The "Narrow" or "Little" Council of People's Commissars was an executive body within the CPC that met several times a week.

has up till now fully occupied all the deputies' time. It is therefore necessary to arrange and strictly carry out a practice under which each deputy, *for not less than two hours* a week, "goes down to the bottom," makes a personal study of all the various parts of the apparatus, top and bottom, and the most unexpected ones at that. The official record of such a study, made, confirmed, and communicated (in certain cases) to *all* government departments, should lead to a *reduction* in staff and tighten up discipline throughout our state machinery.

Lenin

To the All-Ukraine Congress of Soviets

DECEMBER 10, 1922

I welcome the opening of the All-Ukraine Congress of Soviets.[49]

One of the most important problems which the congress has to solve is that of uniting the republics. The proper solution of this problem will determine the future organization of our machinery of state, the glaring defects of which were so vividly and strikingly revealed by the recent census of Soviet employees in Moscow, Petrograd, and Kharkov.[50]

The second problem to which the congress must devote special attention is that of our heavy industry. To raise the output of the Donbas and of the oil and iron and steel industries to prewar levels is the fundamental problem of our entire economy, and we must concentrate all our efforts on solving this problem.

I am firmly convinced that the congress will find the correct solutions for these problems and with all my heart I wish you success in your work.

Lenin

49. Lenin, CW, vol. 33, p. 454.

50. Despite an energetic effort to cut down the inflated staffs in government offices, an October 1922 census of public employees revealed a total of 243,000 in Moscow—12,000 more than four years earlier. See Lenin, "Speech at the Fourth Session of the All-Russia CEC, October 31, 1922," in CW, vol. 33, pp. 394–95.

4

Defending the State Monopoly of Foreign Trade

To Leon Trotsky

DECEMBER 12, 1922

Comrade Trotsky,

I am sending you Krestinsky's letter.[1] Write me as soon as possible whether you agree; at the plenum, I am going to fight for the monopoly.

What about you?

Yours,

Lenin

P.S. It would be best returned *soon.*

---

1. Lenin, *CW*, vol. 45, p. 601.

N.N. Krestinsky, RSFSR plenipotentiary representative in Germany, had written on prospects for improving trade with Germany and the need to maintain the state monopoly of foreign trade. The letters to Trotsky in this chapter were first made available by Trotsky in his "Letter to the Bureau of Party History" of 1927. See Trotsky, *Stalin School of Falsification,* pp. 59–63. They first appeared in the Soviet Union in the fifth Russian edition of Lenin's works.

Letter to Lenin
by Leon Trotsky

DECEMBER 12, 1922

To Comrade Lenin

V.I.,

Maintaining and *strengthening* the monopoly of foreign trade is a matter of absolute necessity.[2] But right now, in practice, opponents of foreign trade are not waging any frontal attacks on this but are using complex flanking tactics. On the other hand, modification and improvement of the methods of foreign trade is absolutely essential.

The danger is that under the guise of improving the implementation of the monopoly, measures that essentially undermine the monopoly may be slipped in.

Comrade Avanesov visited me today and told me of the basic conclusions of his commission. As far as I understood him, he wants the monopoly of foreign trade to be implemented not directly by the People's Commissariat of Foreign Trade but by large management units (syndicates, concerns) under the control of the commissariat. Krestinsky proposes, apparently in agreement with Stomonyakov, that the most important economic units (that is, once again, obviously the syndicates and concerns and in part the departments) have permanent representation at appropriate points and that these representatives constitute sections within the trade delegations. This plan has something in common with that of Avanesov. There is a

Footnotes start on next page

very basic difference, however; Krestinsky bases his plan on the trade delegations being the direct trading (selling and buying) organ of the republic. Individual economic units carry out their operations through the sections of the trade delegations, while these sections are organized in agreement with the corresponding economic units. But Avanesov right off suggests that these syndicate representatives serve as the basic vehicle for trade, reserving for the trade delegations a supervisory role.

Perhaps the evolution of both plans would lead to the same thing, but at the moment it would be safer to accept the trade delegations as the basis. Perhaps, however, I have not fully grasped the plan of Avanesov's commission. He has promised to send the proposals in writing tomorrow.

The most important question, nevertheless, has been and remains the regulation of our export trade out of Russia in connection with our economic work as a whole. Someone must be in charge of what may or may not be imported, what must be exported and what we should keep for ourselves. Here decisions are needed not on the level of legislative regulations, of fixed categories; they should be practical, flexible, and always adjusted to the needs of the economy as a whole. Clearly this should be the job of the State Planning Commission, which comes under the rubric of industrial development of the state. But that is another subject on which I have written more than once. Avanesov's commission has confirmed only that no *such* accounting of our exports and imports has been made yet.

Trotsky

2. Translated from Meijer, *Trotsky Papers*, vol. 2, pp. 778, 780.

To M.I. Frumkin
and B.S. Stomonyakov

DECEMBER 12, 1922

To Comrades Frumkin and Stomonyakov, copy to Trotsky.

In view of my increasing sickness, I cannot be present at the plenum.[3] I am fully aware how awkwardly, and even worse than awkwardly, I am behaving in relation to you, but all the same, I cannot possibly speak.

Today I received the enclosed letter from Comrade Trotsky, with which I agree in all essentials, with the exception perhaps of the last lines about the State Planning Commission. I will write Trotsky of my agreement with him and ask him to take upon himself, in view of my sickness, the defense of my position at the plenum.

I think that this defense ought to be divided into three parts.

First, defense of the fundamental principle of the monopoly of foreign trade, giving it full and final confirmation.

Second, delegating to a special commission the detailed consideration of those practical plans for realizing this monopoly advanced by Avanesov. At least half of this commission ought to consist of representatives from the Commissariat of Foreign Trade.

Third, separate consideration of the work of the State Planning Commission. By the way, I think that there will probably be no disagreement between Trotsky and me, if he confines himself to the demand that the work of the State Planning Commission, carried on under the heading of the development of state industry, should have repercussions on all aspects of the activity of the People's Commissariat of Foreign Trade.

I hope to write again today or tomorrow and send you my declaration to the Central Committee plenum on the essence of this problem. At any rate, I think this question is of such fundamental importance that in case I do not get the agreement of the plenum, I must take it into the party congress, and before that, announce the existence of this disagreement in the fraction of our party at the coming Congress of Soviets.

Lenin

DICTATED TO L.F. [LYDIA FOTIEVA]

3. Translated from Meijer, *Trotsky Papers,* vol. 2, pp. 774–76. Included by Trotsky in his "Letter to the Bureau of Party History" and first published in 1928 in Trotsky, *The Real Situation in Russia.* The letter is not found in the *Collected Works.*

Letter on the distribution of work between the deputy chairmen

DECEMBER 13, 1922

Comrades Kamenev, Rykov, and Tsyurupa:

Owing to a recurrence of my illness I must wind up all political work and take a holiday again.[4] Therefore our disagreements with you lose their practical significance. I must say, however, that I utterly disagree with Rykov's practical addendum, and I move the exact opposite against it—namely, that reception should be quite free, unlimited, and even extended.[5] I am leaving the details to a meeting in person.

To a considerable extent I disagree also with the distribution of the commissariats. I think this distribution should be more closely adjusted to the ability of each deputy for purely administrative work. In my opinion, the chief fault of your yesterday's distribution consists in the lack of such adjustment. The functions of chairmanship and supervision of the proper legal wording of both legislative acts and decisions of the Financial Committee and so forth should be far more strictly separated from the functions of checking and improving the administrative apparatus. Comrade Kamenev is more suitable for the former functions (i.e., chairmanship, supervision of proper wording, etc.) whereas the purely administrative functions are more in Tsyurupa's and Rykov's line.

For the general reason mentioned above I must defer this question until my return from leave. But please bear in mind that I give my consent to your proposed distribution not for three months (as you suggest) but pending my return to work, should this take place earlier than within three months.

I see that your distribution has overlooked such an important organ as *Ekonomicheskaya zhizn* [Economic life], which needs someone to keep a special eye on it. I think this could best be done by Rykov.[6]

4. Lenin, *CW*, vol. 42, pp. 432–33.

5. Rykov had suggested that Lenin should receive visitors only after preliminary selection by the deputy chairmen of the Council of People's Commissars or the secretary of the Communist Party Central Committee.

6. Lenin's views on the need to make this publication into "a real *business management* paper, into a real organ of socialist construction" can be found in "Decree on the Functions of the Deputy Chairmen of the Council of People's Commissars and of the Council of Labor and Defense" and "Letter to the Editors of *Ekonomicheskaya zhizn*," Lenin, *CW*, vol. 33, pp. 339 and 36–38 respectively.

To Leon Trotsky

DECEMBER 13, 1922

Copy to Frumkin and Stomonyakov

Comrade Trotsky,

I have received your comments on Krestinsky's letter and Avanesov's plans.[7] I think that you and I are in maximum agreement, and I believe that the State Planning Commission question, as presented in this case, rules out (or postpones) any discussion on whether the State Planning Commission needs to have any administrative rights.

At any rate, I would urge that at the forthcoming plenum you should undertake the defense of our common standpoint on the unconditional need to maintain and consolidate the foreign trade monopoly. The preceding plenum passed a decision in this respect which runs entirely counter to the foreign trade monopoly, and there can be no concessions on this matter. I believe, therefore, as I say in my letter to Frumkin and Stomonyakov, that in the event of our defeat on this question we must refer the question to a party congress. This will require a brief exposition of our differences before the party group of the forthcoming Congress of Soviets. If I have time, I shall write this, and I would be very glad if you did the same. Hesitation on this question is doing us unprecedented harm, and the negative arguments boil down entirely to accusations of shortcomings in the apparatus. But our apparatus is everywhere imperfect, and to abandon the monopoly because of an imperfect apparatus would be throwing out the baby with the bathwater.

Lenin

7. Lenin, CW, vol. 45, pp. 601–2.

Re the monopoly of foreign trade

DECEMBER 13, 1922

To Comrade Stalin for the plenary meeting of the Central Committee.

I think it is most important to discuss Comrade Bukharin's letter.[8] His first point says that "neither Lenin nor Krasin says a word about the incalculable losses that are borne by the economy of the country as a consequence of the inefficiency of the People's Commissariat of Foreign Trade due to the 'principles' on which it is organized; they do not say a word about the losses incurred because we ourselves are unable (and will not be able for a long time for quite understandable reasons) to mobilize the peasants' stocks of goods and use them for international trade."

This statement is positively untrue, for in his paragraph two Krasin clearly discusses the formation of mixed companies as a means first, of mobilizing the peasants' stocks of goods, and second, of obtaining for our exchequer no less than half the profits accruing from this mobilization. Thus it is Bukharin who is trying to evade the issue, for he refuses to see that the profits accruing from the "mobilization of the peasants' stocks of goods" will go wholly and entirely into the pockets of the Nepmen.[9] The question is: Will our People's Commissariat of Foreign Trade operate for the benefit of the Nepmen or of our proletarian state? This is a fundamental question over which a fight can and should be put up at a party congress.

Compared with this primary, fundamental question of principle, the question of the inefficiency of the People's Commissariat of Foreign Trade is only a minor one, for this inefficiency is only part and parcel of the inefficiency of all our people's commissariats and is due to their general social structure; to remedy this we shall require many years of persistent effort to improve education and to raise the general standard.

The second point in Bukharin's theses says that "points like paragraph five of Krasin's theses, for example, are fully applicable to concessions in general." This, too, is glaringly untrue, for Krasin's fifth thesis states that "the most pernicious exploiter, the merchant, profiteer, the agent of foreign capital, operating with dollars, pounds, and Swedish crowns, will be artificially introduced into the rural districts." Nothing of the kind will happen in the case of concessions, which not only stipulate territory but also envisage special permission to trade in specified articles; and what is most important, we control the trade in the articles specified in the concession. Without saying a single word in opposition to Krasin's argument that we shall be unable to keep free trade within the limits laid down by the decision of the plenary meeting of October 6, that trade will be torn out of our hands by pressure brought to bear not only by smugglers but also by the entire peasantry—without saying a word in answer to this fundamental economic and class argument, Bukharin hurls accusations against Krasin that are amazingly groundless.

In the third point of his letter Bukharin writes "Paragraph three of Krasin's theses." (By mistake he mentions paragraph three instead of paragraph four.) "We are maintaining our frontiers," and he asks: "What does this mean? In reality, this means that we are doing nothing. It is exactly like a shop with a splendid window, but with

8. Lenin, *CW*, vol. 33, pp. 455–59. Bukharin had argued against the monopoly of foreign trade in a letter to the Central Committee, October 15, 1922. Krasin, the people's commissar of foreign trade, was a leading ally of Lenin in defense of the trade monopoly.

9. "Nepmen" was a disparaging term for petty traders, merchants, and swindlers who took advantage of profit-making opportunities under the NEP.

nothing on its shelves (the 'shut-the-shops system')." Krasin very definitely says that we are maintaining our frontiers not so much by tariffs or frontier guards as by means of our monopoly of foreign trade. Bukharin does not say a word to refute this obvious, positive, and indisputable fact, nor can he do so. His sneering reference to the "shut-the-shops system" belongs to the category of expressions to which Marx, in his day, retorted with the expression "free-trader *vulgaris*," for it is nothing more than a vulgar free-trader catch-phrase.

Further, in his fourth point, Bukharin accuses Krasin of failing to realize that we must improve our tariff system, and at the same time he says that I am wrong in talking about having inspectors all over the country, because export and import bases are the only point under discussion. Here, too, Bukharin's objections are amazingly thoughtless and quite beside the point, for Krasin not only realizes that we must improve our tariff system and not only fully admits it, but says so with a definiteness that leaves no room for the slightest doubt. This improvement consists first, in our adopting the monopoly of foreign trade, and second, in the formation of mixed companies.

Bukharin does not see—this is his most amazing mistake, and a purely theoretical one at that—that no tariff system can be effective in the epoch of imperialism when there are monstrous contrasts between pauper countries and immensely rich countries. Several times Bukharin mentions tariff barriers, failing to realize that under the circumstances indicated any of the wealthy industrial countries can completely break down such tariff barriers. To do this it will be sufficient for it to introduce an export bounty to encourage the export to Russia of goods upon which we have imposed high import duties. All of the industrial countries have more than enough money for this purpose, and by means of such a measure any of them could easily ruin our home industry.

Consequently, all Bukharin's arguments about the tariff system would in practice only leave Russian industry entirely unprotected and lead to the adoption of free trading under a very flimsy veil. We must oppose this with all our might and carry our opposition right to a party congress, for in the present epoch of imperialism the only system of protection worthy of consideration is the monopoly of foreign trade.

Bukharin's accusation (in his fifth point) that Krasin fails to appreciate the importance of increasing circulation is utterly refuted by what Krasin says about mixed companies, for these mixed companies have no other purpose than to increase circulation and to provide real protection for our Russian industry and not the fictitious protection of tariff barriers.

Further, in point six, in answer to me, Bukharin writes as if he attaches no importance to the fact that the peasants will enter into profitable transactions and as if the struggle will proceed between the Soviet government and the exporters and not between the peasants and the Soviet government. Here, too, he is absolutely wrong, for with the difference in prices that I have indicated (for example, in Russia the price of flax is 4 rubles 50 kopeks, while in Britain it is 14 rubles), the exporter will be able to mobilize all the peasants around himself in the swiftest and most certain manner.

In practice, Bukharin is acting as an advocate of the profiteer, of the petty bourgeois, and of the upper stratum of the peasantry in opposition to the industrial proletariat, which will be totally unable to reconstruct its own industry and make Russia an industrial country unless it has the protection, not of tariffs, but of the monopoly of foreign trade. In view of the conditions at present prevailing in Russia, any other form of protection would be absolutely fictitious; it would be merely paper protection, from which the proletariat would derive no benefit whatever. Hence, from the viewpoint of the proletariat and of its industry, the present fight rages around fundamental principles. The mixed company system is the only system that can be really effective in improving the defective machinery of the People's Commissariat of Foreign Trade, for under this system foreign and Russian merchants will be operating side by side. If we fail to learn the business thoroughly even under such circumstances, it will prove that ours is a nation of hopeless fools.

By talking about "tariff barriers," we shall only be concealing from ourselves the dangers which Krasin points out quite clearly, and which Bukharin has failed to refute in the slightest degree.

I will add that the partial opening of the frontiers would be fraught with grave currency dangers, for in practice we should be reduced to the position of Germany; there would be the grave danger that the petty bourgeoisie and all sorts of agents of émigré Russia would penetrate into Russia without our having the slightest possibility of exercising control over them.

The utilization of mixed companies as a means to long and serious self-instruction is the only road to the restoration of our industry.

Lenin

To V.A. Avanesov

DECEMBER 14, 1922

Comrade Avanesov,

I am sending you my letter.[10] Return by 7:00.

Think out thoroughly what should be added or eliminated. *How should the struggle be arranged?*

Yours,

Lenin

10. Lenin, *CW*, vol. 45, p. 602. Lenin refers to his letter of December 13 to the Central Committee plenum.

Letter to Joseph Stalin for Central Committee members

DECEMBER 15, 1922

I have now finished winding up my affairs and can leave with my mind at peace.[11] I have also come to an agreement with Trotsky on the defense of my views on the monopoly of foreign trade. Only one circumstance still worries me very much; it is that it will be impossible for me to speak at the Congress of Soviets. My doctors are coming on Tuesday and we shall see if there is even a small chance of my speaking. I would consider it a great inconvenience to miss the opportunity of speaking, to say the least. I finished preparing the summary a few days ago.[12] I therefore propose that the writing of a report which somebody will deliver should go ahead, and that the possibility be left open until Wednesday that I will perhaps personally make a speech, a much shorter one than usual, for example, one that will take three-quarters of an hour. Such a speech would in no way hinder the speech of my deputy (whoever you may appoint for this purpose), but would be useful politically and from the personal angle, as it would eliminate cause for great anxiety. Please have this in mind, and if the opening of the congress is delayed, inform me in good time through my secretary.[13]

Lenin

DECEMBER 15, 1922

I am emphatically against any procrastination of the question of the monopoly of foreign trade. If any circumstance (including the circumstance that my participation is desirable in the debate over this question) gives rise to the idea to postpone it to the next plenary meeting, I would most emphatically be against it because, first, I am sure Trotsky will uphold my views as well as I; second, the statements that you, Zinoviev, and, according to rumors, Kamenev have made prove that some members of the CC have already changed their minds; third, and most important, any further vacillation over this extremely important question is absolutely impermissible and will wreck all our work.

Lenin

11. Lenin, *CW,* vol. 33, pp. 460–61.

12. For the outline of this speech, see Lenin, *CW,* vol. 36, pp. 588–89.

13. On December 16 Lenin sent word that he would not be able to speak to the congress, which opened December 23.

To Leon Trotsky

DECEMBER 15, 1922

Comrade Trotsky:

I consider that we have quite reached agreement.[14] I ask you to declare our solidarity at the plenum. I hope that our decision will be passed because some of those who had voted against it in October have now partially or all together switched to our side.

If for some reason our decision should not be passed, we shall turn to our fraction at the Congress of Soviets and declare that we are referring the question to the party congress.

In that case, inform me and I shall send in my statement.

Yours,

Lenin

P.S. If this question should be removed from the present plenum (which I do not expect and against which you should, of course, protest as strongly as you can on our common behalf), I think that we should apply to our fraction at the Congress of Soviets anyway and demand that the question be referred to the party congress, because any further hesitation is absolutely intolerable.

You can keep all the material I have sent you until after the plenum.

14. Lenin, *CW*, vol. 45, p. 604.

Letter to Lenin
by M.I. Frumkin

DECEMBER 15, 1922

Dear Vladimir Ilyich,

I began to worry yesterday that the question of the monopoly of foreign trade might be removed from the plenum agenda on the grounds that in view of your interest in this question, the discussion should be postponed until the next plenum so that you can participate.[15] Rumors reached me today that there is a proposal to this effect.

I consider it absolutely essential to resolve this question. Any further uncertainty over the situation would be counterproductive in every way. Is there any possibility that you could discuss this question with Stalin and Kamenev?

With communist greetings.

Yours,

Frumkin

15. Translated from Meijer, *Trotsky Papers,* vol. 2, p. 786.

To Leon Trotsky

DECEMBER 15, 1922

Comrade Trotsky,

I am sending on to you Frumkin's letter which I have received to-day.[16] I also think that it is absolutely necessary to have done with this question once and for all. If there are any fears that I am being worried by this question and that it could even have an effect on my health, I think that this is absolutely wrong, because I am infinitely more worried by the delay which makes our policy on one of the most basic questions quite unstable. That is why I call your attention to the enclosed letter and ask you to support an immediate discussion of this question. I am sure that if we are threatened with the danger of failure, it would be much better to fail before the party congress, and at once to apply to our fraction at the congress than to fail after the congress. Perhaps an acceptable compromise is that we pass a decision just now confirming the monopoly, and still bring up the question at the party congress, making an arrangement about this right away. I do not believe that we could accept any other compromise either in our own interests or the interests of the cause.

Lenin

16. Translated from Meijer, *Trotsky Papers*, vol. 2, p. 786, 788.

To Leon Trotsky

DECEMBER 21, 1922

It looks as though it has been possible to take the position without a single shot, by a simple maneuver.[17] I suggest that we should not stop and should continue the offensive and for that purpose put through a motion to raise at the party congress the question of consolidating our foreign trade and of measures to improve its implementation. This to be announced in our fraction at the Congress of Soviets. I hope that you will not object to this, and will not refuse to give a report in the group.

N. Lenin

P.S. Vladimir Ilyich also asks that you telephone your reply. N.K. Ulyanova [Krupskaya].[18]

17. Lenin, *CW*, vol. 45, p. 606.
18. This postscript is not found in the English-language edition of Lenin's works and is translated from the fifth Russian-language edition of Lenin's works, vol. 54, p. 672. It was included with Lenin's letter as published by Trotsky in his "Letter to the Bureau of Party History."

Letter to L.B. Kamenev
on Stalin's conduct

by N.K. Krupskaya

DECEMBER 23, 1922

Lev Borisovich:

Yesterday Stalin subjected me to a storm of coarse abuse concerning a brief little note that Lenin had dictated to me with the doctors' consent.[19] I did not join the party just yesterday. In all of thirty years I have never heard a single rude word from any comrade, and the interests of the party and of Ilyich are no less dear to me than to Stalin. Right now I need all the self-control I can muster. I know better than any doctor, and in any case better than Stalin, what one may and may not discuss with Ilyich, what does and does not upset him.

19. An incomplete version of this letter is found in the fifth Russian-language edition of Lenin's works, vol. 54, pp. 786, 788. That edition omits the first half of paragraph two (the wording "I am turning to you and to Gregory [Zinoviev] as much closer comrades of V.I. and"). The full text is contained in Robert H. McNeal, *Bride of the Revolution: Krupskaya and Lenin* (London: Victor Gollancz Ltd., 1973), p. 221.

On December 16 Lenin had again fallen ill. This was followed on December 22–23 by another serious attack, after which paralysis returned to his right arm and leg.

Lenin's doctors ordered him on December 24 to discontinue dictating notes and letters. Lenin insisted that he be permitted to dictate at least a few minutes each day. The doctors immediately met with Stalin, Kamenev, and Bukharin. Their written order to Lenin's secretaries and family members, dated December 24, stated, "(1) Vladimir Ilyich is permitted to dictate five to ten minutes a day, but this must not take the form of corre-

I am turning to you and to Gregory [Zinoviev] as much closer comrades of V.I. and I beg you to protect me from rude interference in my personal life and from vile invective and threats.

There is no doubt in my mind regarding some unanimous decision of the Control Commission, which Stalin presumes to threaten me with, but I have neither the strength nor the time to waste on this stupid squabble. I too am human, and my nerves are strained to the limit.

N. Krupskaya

---

spondence, and he should not expect any replies. Visitors are forbidden. (2) To avoid giving Vladimir Ilyich cause for reflection or anxiety, his family and friends must not give him political news."

Stalin had been appointed by the Central Committee to oversee Lenin's medical treatment. On learning that Krupskaya, Lenin's wife, had taken dictation from Lenin December 21—the note to Trotsky proposing to take their position on the foreign trade monopoly to the upcoming twelfth party congress—Stalin telephoned Krupskaya and reproached her in an abusive manner. It appears that Lenin did not learn of this incident until two months later. His response to Stalin is printed in chapter 9.

5

Lenin's Letter to the Party Congress

Letter to the Congress

(1) DECEMBER 23, 1922

I would urge strongly that at this congress a number of changes be made in our political structure.[1]

I want to tell you of the considerations to which I attach most importance.

At the head of the list I set an increase in the number of Central Committee members to a few dozen or even a hundred.[2] It is my opinion that without this reform our Central Committee would be in great danger unless the course of events were entirely favorable to us (and that is something we cannot count on).

Then, I intend to propose that the congress should on certain conditions invest the decisions of the State Planning Commission with legislative force, meeting, in this respect, the wishes of Comrade Trotsky—to a certain extent and on certain conditions.

As for the first point, i.e., increasing the number of CC members, I think it must be done in order to raise the prestige of the Central Committee, to do a thorough job of improving our administrative machinery and to prevent conflicts between small sections of the CC from acquiring excessive importance for the future of the party.

It seems to me that our party has every right to demand from the working class 50 to 100 CC members, and that it should get them

Footnotes start on next page

from it without unduly taxing the resources of that class.

Such a reform would considerably increase the stability of our party and ease its struggle in the encirclement of hostile states, which, in my opinion, is likely to and must become much more acute in the next few years. I think that the stability of our party would gain a thousandfold by such a measure.

Lenin

TAKEN DOWN BY M.V. [MARIA VOLODICHEVA]

(2)   DECEMBER 24, 1922

CONTINUATION OF THE NOTES

By stability of the Central Committee, of which I spoke above, I mean measures against a split, as far as such measures can at all be taken.[3] For, of course, the White Guard in *Russkaya mysl* [Russian

1. Lenin, *CW*, vol. 36, pp. 593–97.

During the week following his stroke of December 22–23, Lenin dictated these notes on key questions before the twelfth congress of the Russian Communist Party, then planned for March 1923. His notes began with the title, "Letter to the Congress"; additional titles marked off notes devoted to the State Planning Commission and on internationalism and relations with the nationalities oppressed under tsarism.

On December 23 Lenin sent the first of these notes to Stalin; there is no record that Stalin passed it on to the Political Bureau. Lenin kept the rest confidential. According to Lenin's secretary M.A. Volodicheva, he asked that a copy of each note be placed in a sealed envelope to be opened in the event of his death.

2. The April 1922 party congress had elected 46 full and alternate members to the Central Committee. The average age of the 27 full members of the committee was 39 and they had been party members for an average of twenty years. Only one had been a member for fewer than fifteen years.

3. As indicated in a December 29, 1922, letter from Lenin's secretary Fotieva to L.B. Kamenev, this section of Lenin's letter to the congress, evaluating the party's central leaders, had already that month been sum-

thought] (it seems to have been S.S. Oldenburg) was right when, first, in the White Guards' game against Soviet Russia he banked on a split in our party and when, second, he banked on grave differences in our party to cause that split.

Our party relies on two classes and therefore its instability would be possible and its downfall inevitable if there could be no agreement between those two classes. In that event this or that measure and generally all talk about the stability of our CC would be futile. No measures of any kind could prevent a split in such a case. But I hope that this is too remote a future and too improbable an event to talk about.

I have in mind stability as a guarantee against a split in the immediate future, and I intend to deal here with a few ideas concerning personal qualities.

I think that from this standpoint the prime factors in the question of stability are such members of the CC as Stalin and Trotsky. I think relations between them make up the greater part of the danger of a

---

marized by Fotieva to Stalin and some other Political Bureau members. See Roy A. Medvedev, *Let History Judge: The Origins and Consequences of Stalinism* (New York: Columbia University Press, 1989), pp. 84–85.

This section was kept secret until May 1924, when, on Krupskaya's initiative, it was read to groups of delegates to a party congress. The delegates were instructed not to take notes or to mention the document in the congress sessions. At the party congress in 1927, however, the leadership then dominated by Stalin felt compelled to distribute it to the delegates, who voted to publish the letter.

The decision was not carried out. During the frame-up purges of the 1930s, the letter was proclaimed a forgery, and many Communists were sentenced to long prison terms for "possession of a counterrevolutionary document, the so-called Testament of Lenin."

The same section, including the January 4, 1923, postscript, was published by Max Eastman in 1926 in the *New York Times* and, two years later, as an appendix to a collection of Trotsky's articles, *The Real Situation in Russia*. Trotsky's 1932 article on Lenin's document, "On Lenin's Testament," out of print for several years, is due to be published as an appendix to Pathfinder's reprinting of *The Stalin School of Falsification*. Lenin's letter as a whole, including the notes on the State Planning Commission and the nationalities question, was not published until 1956, when layers of the dominant caste headed by Soviet premier Nikita Khrushchev sought to distance themselves from the policies of Stalin.

split, which could be avoided, and this purpose, in my opinion, would be served, among other things, by increasing the number of CC members to 50 or 100.

Comrade Stalin, having become general secretary, has concentrated unlimited authority in his hands, and I am not sure whether he will always be capable of using that authority with sufficient caution. Comrade Trotsky, on the other hand, as his struggle against the CC on the question of the People's Commissariat of Communications has already proved, is distinguished not only by outstanding ability. He is personally perhaps the most capable man in the present CC, but he has displayed excessive self-assurance and shown excessive preoccupation with the purely administrative side of the work.[4]

These two qualities of the two outstanding leaders of the present CC can inadvertently lead to a split, and if our party does not take steps to avert this, the split may come unexpectedly.

I shall not give any further appraisals of the personal qualities of other members of the CC. I shall just recall that the October episode with Zinoviev and Kamenev was, of course, no accident, but neither can the blame for it be laid upon them personally, any more than

---

4. In March 1920 Trotsky was appointed people's commissar of communications to lead the effort to prevent the collapse of Soviet railroads and organize their recovery. Trotsky instituted the application of military discipline to railroad workers, removed the railroad union leaders, and replaced the unions with a new structure under government control.

Under emergency conditions (the war with Poland was then at its height), the Communist Party Central Committee endorsed these actions as "temporary" measures, urging that normal union structures and functions be restored "as soon as possible." As the war drew to a close late in 1920 and railway transport revived, union leaders pressed to restore the railway unions. Trotsky proposed instead that measures similar to those used to "shake up" the railway unions be applied to other unions, in order to accelerate the revival of production.

Trotsky's views were rejected by the Central Committee and by the tenth party congress in March 1921. Lenin's position on the trade unions' role in the Soviet state was developed in several speeches and articles in 1920–21. See especially Lenin, CW, vol. 32, pp. 19–107.

non-Bolshevism can upon Trotsky.[5]

Speaking of the young CC members, I wish to say a few words about Bukharin and Pyatakov. They are, in my opinion, the most outstanding figures (among the youngest ones), and the following must be borne in mind about them: Bukharin is not only a most valuable and major theorist of the party; he is also rightly considered the favorite of the whole party, but his theoretical views can be classified as fully Marxist only with great reserve, for there is something scholastic about him (he has never made a study of dialectics, and, I think, never fully understood it).

DECEMBER 25, 1922

As for Pyatakov, he is unquestionably a man of outstanding will and outstanding ability, but shows too much zeal for administrating and the administrative side of the work to be relied upon in a serious political matter.

Both of these remarks, of course, are made only for the present, on the assumption that both these outstanding and devoted party workers fail to find an occasion to enhance their knowledge and amend their one-sidedness.

Lenin

TAKEN DOWN BY M.V.[6]

5. In October 1917, Kamenev and Zinoviev had publicly opposed the preparation and launching at that time of an armed insurrection under Bolshevik leadership to establish a revolutionary government based on the soviets. Trotsky had stood outside the Bolshevik Party before 1917, opposing its policies on several important questions. He and his co-thinkers fused with the Bolsheviks in August 1917.

6. A postscript written January 4, 1923, appears at this point in many editions of Lenin's "Letter to the Congress." In the present work, Lenin's postscript is found at the end of this chapter.

(3)   DECEMBER 26, 1922

CONTINUATION OF THE NOTES

The increase in the number of CC members to 50 or even 100 must, in my opinion, serve a double or even a treble purpose: the more members there are in the CC the more people will be trained in CC work and the less danger there will be of a split due to some indiscretion.

The enlistment of many workers to the CC will help the workers to improve our administrative machinery, which is pretty bad. We inherited it, in effect, from the old regime, for it was absolutely impossible to reorganize it in such a short time, especially in conditions of war, famine, etc. That is why those "critics" who point to the defects of our administrative machinery out of mockery or malice may be calmly answered that they do not in the least understand the conditions of the revolution today.

It is altogether impossible in five years to reorganize the machinery adequately, especially in the conditions in which our revolution took place. It is enough that in five years we have created a new type of state in which the workers are leading the peasants against the bourgeoisie, and in a hostile international environment this in itself is a gigantic achievement.

But knowledge of this must on no account blind us to the fact that, in effect, we took over the old machinery of state from the tsar and the bourgeoisie and that now, with the onset of peace and the satisfaction of the minimum requirements against famine, all our work must be directed towards improving the administrative machinery.

I think that a few dozen workers, added to the CC, can deal better than anybody else with checking, improving, and remodeling our state apparatus. The Workers and Peasants Inspection on whom this function devolved at the beginning proved unable to cope with it and can be used only as an "appendage" or, on certain conditions, as an assistant to these members of the CC. In my opinion, the workers admitted to the Central Committee should come preferably not from among those who have had long service in Soviet bodies (in this part of my letter the term workers everywhere includes peasants), because those workers have already acquired the very traditions and the very prejudices which it is desirable to combat.

The working-class members of the CC must be mainly workers of a lower stratum than those promoted in the last five years to work in Soviet bodies; they must be people closer to being rank-and-file workers and peasants who, however, do not fall into the category of direct or indirect exploiters. I think that by attending all sittings of the CC and all sittings of the Political Bureau, and by reading all the documents of the CC, such workers can form a staff of devoted supporters of the Soviet system, able first, to give stability to the CC itself, and second, to work effectively on the renewal and improvement of the state apparatus.

Lenin

TAKEN DOWN BY L.F.

Plan for future work

DECEMBER 27 OR 28, 1922

Memorandum:

In the letter on increasing the number of members of the Central Committee a point has been omitted on the relations between the enlarged Central Committee and the Workers and Peasants Inspection.[7]

Subjects to consider:

1. The Union of Consumer Cooperatives and its importance from the point of view of the NEP.

2. The relationship between the Central Vocational Education Board and general educational work among the people.

3. The national question and internationalism (with respect to the recent conflict in the Georgian party).

4. The new book of statistics on national education published in 1922.

---

7. Translated from the fifth Russian-language edition of Lenin's works, vol. 45, p. 592.

Letter to the Congress (continuation)

(4)   DECEMBER 27, 1922

Granting legislative functions to the State Planning Commission

CONTINUATION OF THE NOTES

This idea was suggested by Comrade Trotsky, it seems, quite a long time ago.[8] I was against it at the time, because I thought that there would then be a fundamental lack of coordination in the system of our legislative institutions. But after closer consideration of the matter I find that in substance there is a sound idea in it, namely: the State Planning Commission stands somewhat apart from our legislative institutions, although, as a body of experienced people, experts, representatives of science and technology, it is actually in a better position to form a correct judgment of affairs.

However, we have so far proceeded from the principle that the State Planning Commission must provide the state with critically analyzed material, and the state institutions must decide state matters. I think that in the present situation, when affairs of state have become unusually complicated, when it is necessary time and again to settle questions of which some require the expert opinion of the members of the State Planning Commission and some do not, and, what is more, to settle matters which need the expert opinion of the State Planning Commission on some points but not on others—I think that we must now take a step towards extending the competence of the State Planning Commission.

I imagine that step to be such that the decisions of the State Planning Commission could not be rejected by ordinary procedure in Soviet bodies, but would need a special procedure to be reconsidered. For example, the question should be submitted to a session of the All-Russia Central Executive Committee, prepared for reconsideration according to a special instruction, involving the drawing up, under special rules, of memoranda to examine whether the State Planning Commission decision is subject to reversal. Lastly, special time limits should be set for the reconsideration of State Planning Commission decisions, etc.

In this respect I think we can and must accede to the wishes of Comrade Trotsky, but not in the sense that specifically any one of our political leaders or the chairman of the Supreme Economic Council, etc., should be chairman of the State Planning Commission.[9] I think that personal matters are at present too closely interwoven with the question of principle. I think that the attacks which are now made against the chairman of the State Planning Commission, Comrade Krzhizhanovsky, and Comrade Pyatakov, his deputy, and which proceed along two lines, so that, on the one hand, we hear charges of extreme leniency, lack of independent judgment,

8. Lenin, CW, vol. 36, pp. 598–611.
In February 1921 the Soviet government established the State Planning Commission with the goal of beginning to work toward a single comprehensive plan for industry. In May of that year, Trotsky wrote to Lenin proposing strengthening the powers of the State Planning Commission. Trotsky wrote letters to the Political Bureau along these lines on April 21, 1922, and January 15, 1923. (See Meijer, Trotsky Papers, vol. 2, pp. 730–37 and 816–23.) Lenin explained the reasons for his disagreement with Trotsky's proposals in his May 5, 1922, "Reply to Remarks Concerning the Functions of the Deputy Chairmen of the Council of People's Commissars" (Lenin, CW, vol. 33, pp. 353–55).
9. In his April 21, 1922, memorandum, Trotsky had proposed that one of the deputy chairmen of the Council of People's Commissars should be head of the State Planning Commission. The Supreme Economic Council was formed in 1917 as overall organizer of economic activity.

and lack of backbone and, on the other, charges of excessive coarseness, drill sergeant methods, lack of solid scientific background, etc.—I think these attacks express two sides of the question, exaggerating them to the extreme, and that in actual fact we need a skillful combination in the State Planning Commission of two types of character, of which one may be exemplified by Comrade Pyatakov and the other by Comrade Krzhizhanovsky.

I think that the State Planning Commission must be headed by someone who, on the one hand, has scientific education, namely, either technical or agronomic, with decades of experience in practical work in the field of technology or of agronomy. I think this person must possess not so much the qualities of an administrator as broad experience and the ability to enlist the services of others.

Lenin

TAKEN DOWN BY M.V.

(5)   DECEMBER 28, 1922

Continuation of the letter on the legislative nature of State Planning Commission decisions

I have noticed that some of our comrades who are able to exercise a decisive influence on the direction of state affairs exaggerate the administrative side, which, of course, is necessary in its time and place, but which should not be confused with the scientific side, with a grasp of the broad facts, the ability to recruit people, etc.

In every state institution, especially in the State Planning Commission, the combination of these two qualities is essential. When Comrade Krzhizhanovsky told me that he had enlisted the services of Comrade Pyatakov for the commission and had come to terms with him about the work, I, in consenting to this, on the one hand entertained certain doubts and on the other sometimes hoped that we would thus get the combination of the two types of statesmen. To see whether those hopes are justified, we must now wait and consider the matter on the strength of somewhat longer experience, but in principle, I think, there can be no doubt that such a combination of temperaments and types (of people and qualities) is absolutely necessary for the correct functioning of state institutions. I think that here it is just as harmful to exaggerate "administrating" as it is to exaggerate anything at all. The head of a state institution must possess to a high degree the ability to enlist people's services and sufficiently solid scientific and technical knowledge to be able to check people's work. That much is basic. Without it the work cannot be done properly. On the other hand, it is very important that he should be capable of administering and should have a worthy assistant, or assistants, in the matter. The combination of these two qualities in one person will hardly be found, and it is hardly necessary.

Lenin

TAKEN DOWN BY L.F.

(6)   DECEMBER 29, 1922

Continuation of the notes on the State Planning Commission

The State Planning Commission is apparently developing in all respects into a commission of experts. Such an institution cannot be headed by anybody except someone with great experience and an all-round scientific education in technology. The administrative element must in essence be subsidiary. A certain independence and autonomy of the State Planning Commission is essential for the prestige of this scientific institution and depends on one thing, namely, the conscientiousness of its workers and their conscientious desire to turn our plan of economic and social development into reality.

This last quality may, of course, be found now only as an exception, for the overwhelming majority of scientists, who naturally make up the commission, are inevitably infected with bourgeois ideas and bourgeois prejudices. The check on them from this standpoint must be the job of several persons who can form the presidium of the commission. These must be Communists, to keep a day-to-day check on the extent of the bourgeois scientists' devotion to our cause displayed in the whole course of the work and see that they abandon bourgeois prejudices and gradually adopt the socialist standpoint. This work along the twin lines of scientific checking and pure administration should be the ideal of those who run the State Planning Commission in our republic.

Lenin

TAKEN DOWN BY M.V.

DECEMBER 29, 1922

Is it rational to divide the work of the State Planning Commission into separate jobs? Should we not, on the contrary, try to build up a group of permanent specialists who would be systematically checked by the presidium of the commission and could solve the whole range of problems within its ambit? I think that the latter would be the more reasonable and that we must try to cut down the number of temporary and urgent tasks.

Lenin

TAKEN DOWN BY M.V.

(7)   DECEMBER 29, 1922

(Addition to the section on increasing the number of CC members)

CONTINUATION OF THE NOTES

In increasing the number of its members, the CC, I think, must also and perhaps mainly devote attention to checking and improving our administrative machinery, which is no good at all. For this we must enlist the services of highly qualified specialists, and the task of supplying those specialists must devolve upon the Workers and Peasants Inspection.

How are we to combine these checking specialists, people with adequate knowledge, and the new members of the CC? This problem must be resolved in practice.

It seems to me that the Workers and Peasants Inspection (as a result of its development and of our perplexity about its development) has led all in all to what we now observe, namely, to an intermediate position between a special people's commissariat and a special function of the members of the CC; between an institution that inspects anything and everything and an aggregate of not very numerous but first-class inspectors, who must be well paid (this is especially indispensable in our age when everything must be paid for and inspectors are directly employed by the institutions that pay them better).

If the number of CC members is increased in the appropriate way and they go through a course of state management year after year with the help of highly qualified specialists and of members of the Workers and Peasants Inspection who are highly authoritative in every branch—then, I think, we shall successfully solve this problem which we have not managed to do for such a long time.

To sum up, 100 members of the CC at the most and not more than 400-500 assistants, members of the Workers and Peasants Inspection, engaged in inspecting under their direction.

TAKEN DOWN BY M.V.   Lenin

The question of nationalities or 'autonomization'

DECEMBER 30, 1922

CONTINUATION OF THE NOTES

I suppose I have been very remiss with respect to the workers of Russia for not having intervened energetically and decisively enough in the notorious question of autonomization, which, it appears, is officially called the question of the union of Soviet socialist republics.

When this question arose last summer, I was ill; and then in the autumn I placed too much hope on my recovery and on the October and December plenary meetings giving me an opportunity of intervening in this question. However, I did not manage to attend the October plenary meeting (when this question came up) or the one in December, and so the question passed me by almost completely.

I have only had time for a talk with Comrade Dzerzhinsky, who came from the Caucasus and told me how this matter stood in Georgia. I have also managed to exchange a few words with Comrade Zinoviev and express my apprehensions on this matter. From what I was told by Comrade Dzerzhinsky, who was at the head of the commission sent by the CC to "investigate" the Georgian incident, I could only draw the greatest apprehensions. If matters had come to such a pass that Ordzhonikidze could go to the extreme of applying physical violence, as Comrade Dzerzhinsky informed me, we can imagine what a mess we have got ourselves into.[10] Obviously the whole business of "autonomiza-

10. At a private gathering in Ordzhonikidze's Tiflis apartment in November 1922 attended by Rykov of the Political Bureau, Ordzhonikidze flew into a rage and struck one of the dissenting Georgian Communists, A. Kobakhidze, who had accused Ordzhonikidze of corruption with regard to a white horse Ordzhonikidze had received as a gift during an official visit to the Caucasian Mountaineer Republic. This fact first came to light during the investigation by a Political Bureau–appointed commission of inquiry, headed by Dzerzhinsky. The commission's report, which Dzerzhinsky summarized to Lenin on December 12, sustained Ordzhonikidze and Stalin.

The commission's report had yet to be discussed by the Political Bureau on December 30, when Lenin began dictating these notes.

tion" was radically wrong and badly timed.

It is said that a united apparatus was needed. Where did that assurance come from? Did it not come from that same Russian apparatus which, as I pointed out in one of the preceding sections of my diary, we took over from tsarism and slightly anointed with Soviet oil?

There is no doubt that that measure should have been delayed somewhat until we could say that we vouched for our apparatus as our own. But now we must, in all conscience, admit the contrary; the apparatus we call ours is, in fact, still quite alien to us. It is a bourgeois and tsarist hodgepodge. There has been no possibility of getting rid of it in the course of the past five years, given the lack of help of other countries and given that we have been "busy" most of the time with military engagements and the fight against famine.

It is quite natural that in such circumstances the "freedom to secede from the union" by which we justify ourselves will be a mere scrap of paper, unable to defend the non-Russians from the onslaught of that really Russian man, the Great Russian chauvinist, in substance a rascal and a tyrant, such as the typical Russian bureaucrat is. There is no doubt that the infinitesimal percentage of Soviet and sovietized workers will drown in that tide of chauvinistic Great Russian riffraff like a fly in milk.

It is said in defense of this measure that the people's commissariats directly concerned with national psychology and national education were set up as separate bodies. But there the question arises: Can these people's commissariats be made quite independent? And secondly: Were we careful enough to take measures to provide the non-Russians with a real safeguard against the truly Russian bully? I do not think we took such measures, although we could and should have done so.

I think that Stalin's haste and his infatuation with pure administration, together with his spite against the notorious "nationalist socialism," played a fatal role here. In politics spite generally plays the basest of roles.

I also fear that Comrade Dzerzhinsky, who went to the Caucasus to investigate the "crime" of those "nationalist-socialists," distinguished himself there by his truly Russian frame of mind (it is common knowledge that people of other nationalities who have become Russified overdo this Russian frame of mind)[11] and that the impartiality of his whole commission was typified well enough by Ordzhonikidze's "manhandling." I think that no provocation or even insult can justify such Russian manhandling and that Comrade Dzerzhinsky was inexcusably guilty in adopting a lighthearted attitude towards it.

For all the citizens in the Caucasus Ordzhonikidze was the authority. Ordzhonikidze had no right to display that irritability to which he and Dzerzhinsky referred. On the contrary, Ordzhonikidze should have behaved with a restraint which cannot be demanded of any ordinary citizen, still less of someone accused of a "political" crime. And, to tell the truth, those nationalist socialists were citizens who were accused of a political crime, and the terms of the accusation were such that it could not be described otherwise.

Here we have an important question of principle: How is internationalism to be understood?

Lenin

TAKEN DOWN BY M.V.

DECEMBER 31, 1922

Continuation of the notes on the question of nationalities or 'autonomization'

In my writings on the national question I have already said that an abstract presentation of the question of nationalism in general is of no use at all. A distinction must necessarily be made between the nationalism of an oppressor nation and that of an oppressed nation, the nationalism of a big nation and that of a small nation.

---

11. Dzerzhinsky was Polish, and the other two commission members were also of non-Russian nationality.

In respect of the second kind of nationalism we, nationals of a big nation, have nearly always been guilty, in historic practice, of an infinite number of cases of violence; furthermore, we commit violence and insult an infinite number of times without noticing it. It is sufficient to recall my Volga reminiscences of how non-Russians are treated; how the Poles are not called by any other name than Polyachishka, how the Tatar is nicknamed Prince, how the Ukrainians are always Khokhols and the Georgians and other Caucasian nationals always Kapkasians.

That is why internationalism on the part of oppressors or "great" nations, as they are called (though they are great only in their violence, only great as bullies), must consist not only in the observance of the formal equality of nations but even in an inequality, through which the oppressor nation, the great nation, would compensate for the inequality which obtains in real life. Anybody who does not understand this has not grasped the real proletarian attitude to the national question; he is still essentially petty bourgeois in his point of view and is, therefore, sure to descend to the bourgeois point of view.

What is important for the proletarian? For the proletarian it is not only important, it is absolutely essential that he should be assured that the non-Russians place the greatest possible trust in the proletarian class struggle. What is needed to ensure this? Not merely formal equality. In one way or another, by one's attitude or by concessions, it is necessary to compensate the non-Russians for the lack of trust, for the suspicion and the insults to which the government of the "dominant" nation subjected them in the past.

I think it is unnecessary to explain this to Bolsheviks, to Communists, in greater detail. And I think that in the present instance, as far as the Georgian nation is concerned, we have a typical case in which a genuinely proletarian attitude makes profound caution, thoughtfulness, and a readiness to compromise a matter of necessity for us. The Georgian who is disdainful of this aspect of the question, or who carelessly flings about accusations of "nationalist socialism" (whereas he himself is a real and true "nationalist socialist" and even a vulgar Great Russian bully), violates, in substance, the interests of proletarian class solidarity, for nothing holds up the development and strengthening of proletarian class solidarity so much as national injustice. "Offended" nationals are not sensitive to anything so much as to the feeling of equality and the violation of this equality, if only through negligence or jest to the violation of that equality by their proletarian comrades. That is why in this case it is better to overdo rather than underdo the concessions and leniency towards the national minorities. That is why, in this case, the fundamental interest of proletarian solidarity and consequently of the proletarian class struggle requires that we never adopt a formal attitude to the national question, but always take into account the specific attitude of the proletarian of the oppressed (or small) nation towards the oppressor (or great) nation.

Lenin

TAKEN DOWN BY M.V.

DECEMBER 31, 1922

CONTINUATION OF THE NOTES

What practical measures must be taken in the present situation?

First, we must maintain and strengthen the union of socialist republics. Of this there can be no doubt. This measure is necessary for us and it is necessary for the world communist proletariat in its struggle against the world bourgeoisie and its defense against bourgeois intrigues.

Second, the union of socialist republics must be retained for its diplomatic apparatus. By the way, this apparatus is an exceptional component of our state apparatus. We have not allowed a single influential person from the old tsarist apparatus into it. All sections with any authority are composed of Communists. That is why it has already won for itself (this may be said boldly) the name of a reliable communist apparatus purged to an incomparably greater extent of the old tsarist, bourgeois, and petty-bourgeois elements than that which we have had to make do with in other people's commissariats.

Third, exemplary punishment must be inflicted on Comrade Ordzhonikidze (I say this all the more regretfully as I am one of his personal friends and have worked with him abroad), and the investigation of all the material which Dzerzhinsky's commission has collected must be supplemented or started over again to correct the enormous mass of wrongs and biased judgments which it doubtlessly contains. The political responsibility for all this truly Great Russian nationalist campaign must, of course, be laid on Stalin and Dzerzhinsky.

Fourth, the strictest rules must be introduced on the use of the national language in the non-Russian republics of our union, and these rules must be checked with special care. There is no doubt that our apparatus being what it is, there is bound to be, on the pretext of unity in the railway service, unity in the fiscal service and so on, a mass of truly Russian abuses. Special ingenuity is necessary for the struggle against these abuses, not to mention special sincerity on the part of those who undertake this struggle. A detailed code will be required and only the nationals living in the republic in question can draw it up at all successfully. Moreover we must not in any way reject in advance that as a result of all this work we may well take a step backward at our next Congress of Soviets, namely, retaining the union of Soviet socialist republics only for military and diplomatic affairs and in all other respects restoring full independence to the individual people's commissariats.

It must be borne in mind that the decentralization of the people's commissariats and the lack of coordination in their work as far as Moscow and other centers are concerned can be compensated sufficiently by party authority if it is exercised with sufficient prudence and impartiality. The harm that can result to our state from a lack of unification between the national apparatuses and the Russian apparatus is infinitely less than that which will be done not only to us but to the whole International and to the hundreds of millions of the peoples of Asia, which are destined to follow us onto the stage of history in the near future.

It would be unpardonable opportunism if, on the eve of the debut of the East, just as it is awakening, we undermined our prestige with its peoples, even if only by the slightest crudity or injustice towards our own non-Russian nationalities. The need to rally against the imperialists of the West, who are defending the capitalist world, is one thing. There can be no doubt about that and it would be superfluous for me to speak about my unconditional approval of it. It is another thing when we ourselves lapse, even if only in trifles, into imperialist attitudes towards oppressed nationalities, thus undermining all our principled sincerity, all our principled defense of the struggle against imperialism. But the morrow of world history will be a day when the awakening peoples oppressed by imperialism are finally aroused and the decisive long and hard struggle for their liberation begins.

Lenin

TAKEN DOWN BY M.V.

Addition to the letter of December 24, 1922

JANUARY 4, 1923

Stalin is too rude and this defect, although quite tolerable in our midst and in dealings among us Communists, becomes intolerable in a general secretary.[12] That is why I suggest that the comrades think about a way of removing Stalin from that post and appointing another man in his stead who in all other respects differs from Comrade Stalin in having only one advantage, namely, that of being more tolerant, more loyal, more polite, and more considerate to the comrades, less capricious, etc. This circumstance may appear to be a

12. Lenin, CW, vol. 36, p. 596. This addition was written as a postscript to the notes dictated by Lenin on December 24, 1922.

negligible detail. But I think that from the standpoint of safeguards against a split and from the standpoint of what I wrote above about the relationship between Stalin and Trotsky it is not a detail, or it is a detail which can assume decisive importance.

Lenin

TAKEN DOWN BY L.F.

6

Strengthening the Alliance
with the Peasantry

Pages from a diary

JANUARY 2, 1923

The recent publication of the report on literacy among the population of Russia, based on the census of 1920 ("Literacy in Russia," issued by the Central Statistical Board, Public Education Section, Moscow, 1922) is a very important event.[1]

Below I quote a table from this report on the state of literacy among the population of Russia in 1897 and 1920:

	LITERATES PER					
	THOUSAND MALES		THOUSAND FEMALES		THOUSAND POPULATION	
	1897	1920	1897	1920	1897	1920
1. European Russia	326	422	136	255	229	330
2. North Caucasus	241	357	56	215	150	281
3. Siberia (western)	170	307	46	134	108	218
Overall average	318	409	131	244	223	319

At a time when we hold forth on proletarian culture and the relation in which it stands to bourgeois culture, facts and figures reveal that we are in a very bad way even as far as bourgeois culture is concerned. As might have been expected, it appears that we are still

Footnotes start on next page

203

a very long way from attaining universal literacy and that even compared with tsarist times (1897) our progress has been far too slow.[2] This should serve as a stern warning and reproach to those who have been soaring in the empyreal heights of "proletarian culture."[3] It shows what a vast amount of urgent spadework we still have to do to reach the standard of an ordinary western European civilized country.

It also shows what a vast amount of work we have to do today to achieve, on the basis of our proletarian gains, anything like a real cultural standard.

We must not confine ourselves to this incontrovertible but too theoretical proposition. The very next time we revise our quarterly budget we must take this matter up in a practical way as well. In the first place, of course, we shall have to cut down the expenditure of government departments other than the People's Commissariat of Education, and the sums thus released should be assigned for the latter's needs. In a year like the present, when we are relatively well supplied, we must not be chary in increasing the bread ration for schoolteachers.

Generally speaking, it cannot be said that the work now being done in public education is too narrow. Quite a lot is being done to get the old teachers out of their rut, to attract them to the new problems, to rouse their interest in new methods of education and in such problems as religion.

1. Lenin, *CW*, vol. 33, pp. 462–66.

2. Despite the difficult conditions of the civil war, the school system expanded following the Russian revolution. The number of students receiving primary education in early 1921 was more than 20 percent higher than in 1914–15. During the first eighteen months of the NEP, however, education suffered. In line with overall austerity measures, expenditure on education was cut back sharply. Local soviets, lacking the funds to pay teachers on their own, began to close down schools. By December 1922 more than twenty thousand schools had been shut, about 30 percent of the total.

3. See Lenin's reference to "proletarian culture" in his report to the Fourth Congress of the Communist International, in chapter 3.

But we are not doing the main thing. We are not doing anything—or doing far from enough—to raise the schoolteacher to the level that is absolutely essential if we want any culture at all, proletarian or even bourgeois. We must bear in mind the semi-Asiatic ignorance from which we have not yet extricated ourselves and from which we cannot extricate ourselves without strenuous effort—although we have every opportunity to do so, because nowhere are the masses of the people so interested in real culture as they are in our country. Nowhere are the problems of this culture tackled so thoroughly and consistently as they are in our country. In no other country is state power in the hands of the working class which, in its mass, is fully aware of the deficiencies, I shall not say of its culture, but of its literacy. Nowhere is the working class so ready to make, and nowhere is it actually making, such sacrifices to improve its position in this respect as in our country.

Too little, far too little, is still being done by us to adjust our state budget to satisfy, as a first measure, the requirements of elementary public education. Even in our People's Commissariat of Education we all too often find disgracefully inflated staffs in some state publishing establishment, which is contrary to the concept that the state's first concern should not be publishing houses but that there should be people to read, that the number of people able to read is greater, so that book publishing should have a wider political field in future Russia. Owing to the old (and bad) habit, we are still devoting much more time and effort to technical questions, such as the question of book publishing, than to the general political question of literacy among the people.

If we take the Central Vocational Education Board, we are sure that there too we shall find far too much that is superfluous and inflated by departmental interests, much that is ill-adjusted to the requirements of broad public education. Far from everything that we find in the Central Vocational Education Board can be justified by the legitimate desire first of all to improve and give a practical slant to the education of our young factory workers. If we examine the staff of the Central Vocational Education Board carefully, we shall find very much that is inflated and is in that respect fictitious and should be done away with. There is still very much in the proletarian and peasant state that can and must be economized for the purpose of promoting literacy among the people. This can be done by closing institutions which are playthings of a semiaristocratic type, or institutions we can still do without and will be able to do without, and shall have to do without for a long time to come, considering the state of literacy among the people as revealed by the statistics.

Our schoolteacher should be raised to a standard he has never achieved and cannot achieve in bourgeois society. This is a truism and requires no proof. We must strive for this state of affairs by working steadily, methodically, and persistently to raise the teacher to a higher cultural level, to train him thoroughly for his really high calling and—mainly, mainly, and mainly—to improve his position materially.

We must systematically step up our efforts to organize the schoolteachers so as to transform them from the bulwark of the bourgeois system that they still are in all capitalist countries without exception into the bulwark of the Soviet system, in order, through their agency, to divert the peasantry from alliance with the bourgeoisie and to bring them into alliance with the proletariat.

I want briefly to emphasize the special importance in this respect of regular visits to the villages; such visits, it is true, are already being practiced and should be regularly promoted. We should not stint money—which we all too often waste on the machinery of state that is almost entirely a product of the past historical epoch—on measures like these visits to the villages.

For the speech I was to have delivered at the Congress of Soviets in December 1922 I collected data on the sponsorship undertaken by urban workers of villagers. Part of this data was obtained for me by Comrade Khodorovsky, and since I have been unable to deal with this problem and give it publicity through the congress, I submit the matter to the comrades for discussion now.[4]

4. See Lenin's letter to Khodorovsky in chapter 3.

Here we have a fundamental political question—the relations between town and country—which is of decisive importance for the whole of our revolution. While the bourgeois state methodically concentrates all its efforts on doping the urban workers, adapting all the literature published at state expense and at the expense of the tsarist and bourgeois parties for this purpose, we can and must utilize our political power to make the urban worker an effective vehicle of communist ideas among the rural proletariat.

I said "communist," but I hasten to make a reservation for fear of causing a misunderstanding, or of being taken too literally. Under no circumstances must this be understood to mean that we should immediately propagate purely and strictly communist ideas in the countryside. As long as our countryside lacks the material basis for communism, it will be, I should say, harmful, in fact, I should say, fatal, for communism to do so.

That is a fact. We must start by establishing contacts between town and country without the preconceived aim of implanting communism in the rural districts. It is an aim which cannot be achieved at the present time. It is inopportune, and to set an aim like that at the present time would be harmful instead of useful to the cause.

But it is our duty to establish contacts between the urban workers and the rural working people, to establish between them a form of comradeship which can easily be created. This is one of the fundamental tasks of the working class which holds power. To achieve this we must form a number of associations (party, trade union, and private) of factory workers, which would devote themselves regularly to assisting the villages in their cultural development. Is it possible to "attach" all the urban groups to all the village groups, so that every working-class group may take advantage regularly of every opportunity, of every occasion to serve the cultural needs of the village group it is "attached" to? Or will it be possible to find other forms of contact? I here confine myself solely to formulating the question in order to draw the comrades' attention to it, to point out the available experience of western Siberia (to which Comrade

Khodorovsky drew my attention) and to present this gigantic, historic cultural task in all its magnitude.

We are doing almost nothing for the rural districts outside our official budget or outside official channels. True, in our country the nature of the cultural relations between town and village is automatically and inevitably changing. Under capitalism the town introduced political, economic, moral, physical, etc., corruption into the countryside. In our case, towns are automatically beginning to introduce the very opposite of this into the countryside. But, I repeat, all this is going on automatically, spontaneously, and can be improved (and later increased a hundredfold) by doing it consciously, methodically, and systematically.

We shall begin to advance (and shall then surely advance a hundred times more quickly) only after we have studied the question, after we have formed all sorts of workers organizations—doing everything to prevent them from becoming bureaucratic—to take up the matter, discuss it, and get things done.

On cooperation

(1)   JANUARY 4, 1923

It seems to me that not enough attention is being paid to the co-operative movement in our country.[5] Not everyone understands that now, since the time of the October revolution and quite apart from NEP (on the contrary, in this connection we must say—because of NEP), our cooperative movement has become one of great significance. There is a lot of fantasy in the dreams of the old cooperators. Often they are ridiculously fantastic. But why are they fantastic? Because people do not understand the fundamental, the rock-bottom significance of the working-class political struggle for the overthrow of the rule of the exploiters. We have overthrown the rule of the exploiters, and much that was fantastic, even romantic, even banal in the dreams of the old cooperators is now becoming unvarnished reality.

Indeed, since political power is in the hands of the working class, since this political power owns all the means of production, the only task, indeed, that remains for us is to organize the population in cooperative societies. With most of the population organized in cooperatives, the socialism which in the past was legitimately treated with ridicule, scorn, and contempt by those who were rightly convinced that it was necessary to wage the class struggle, the struggle for political power, etc., will achieve its aim automatically. But not all comrades realize how vastly, how infinitely important it is now to organize the population of Russia in cooperative societies. By adopting NEP we made a concession to the peasant as a trader, to the principle of private trade; it is precisely for this reason (contrary to what some people think) that the cooperative movement is of such immense importance.

All we actually need under NEP is to organize the population of Russia in cooperative societies on a sufficiently large scale, for we have now found that degree of combination of private interest, of private commercial interest, with state supervision and control of this interest, that degree of its subordination to the common interests which was formerly the stumbling block for very many socialists. Indeed, the power of the state over all large-scale means of production, political power in the hands of the proletariat, the alliance of this proletariat with the many millions of small and very small peasants, the assured proletarian leadership of the peasantry, etc.— is this not all that is necessary to build a complete socialist society out of cooperatives, out of cooperatives alone, which we formerly ridiculed as huckstering and which from a certain aspect we have the right to treat as such now, under NEP? Is this not all that is necessary to build a complete socialist society? It is still not the building of socialist society, but it is all that is necessary and sufficient for it.

It is this very circumstance that is underestimated by many of our practical workers. They look down upon our cooperative societies, failing to appreciate their exceptional importance, first, from the standpoint of principle (the means of production are owned by the state), and second, from the standpoint of transition to the new system by means that are the *simplest, easiest, and most acceptable to the peasant.*

But this again is of fundamental importance. It is one thing to draw up fantastic plans for building socialism through all sorts of workers associations, and quite another to learn to build socialism in practice in such a way that every *small* peasant could take part in it. That is the very stage we have now reached. And there is no

5. Lenin, *CW*, vol. 33, pp. 467–75.

doubt that, having reached it, we are taking too little advantage of it.

We went too far when we introduced NEP, but not because we attached too much importance to the principle of free enterprise and trade—we went too far because we lost sight of the cooperatives, because we now underrate the cooperatives, because we are already beginning to forget the vast importance of the cooperatives from the above two points of view.

I now propose to discuss with the reader what can and must at once be done practically on the basis of this "cooperative" principle. By what means can we and must we start at once to develop this "cooperative" principle so that its socialist meaning may be clear to all?

Cooperation must be politically so organized that it will not only generally and always enjoy certain privileges, but that these privileges should be of a purely material nature (a favorable bank rate, etc.). The cooperatives must be granted state loans that are greater, if only by a little, than the loans we grant to private enterprises, even to heavy industry, etc.

A social system emerges only if it has the financial backing of a definite class. There is no need to mention the hundreds of millions of rubles that the birth of "free" capitalism cost. At present we have to realize that the cooperative system is the social system to which we must now give more than ordinary assistance—and we must actually give that assistance. But it must be assistance in the real sense of the word, i.e., it will not be enough to interpret it to mean assistance for any kind of cooperative trade; by assistance we must mean aid to cooperative trade in which *really large masses of the population actually take part*. It is certainly a correct form of assistance to give a bonus to peasants who take part in cooperative trade, but the whole point is to verify the nature of this participation, to verify the awareness behind it, and to verify its quality. Strictly speaking, when a cooperator goes to a village and opens a cooperative store, the people take no part in this whatever, but at the same time guided by their own interests they will hasten to try to take part in it.

There is another aspect to this question. From the point of view of the "enlightened" (primarily, literate) European there is not much left for us to do to induce absolutely everyone to take not a passive but an active part in cooperative operations. Strictly speaking, there is *"only"* one thing we have left to do and that is to make our people so "enlightened" that they understand all the advantages of everybody participating in the work of the cooperatives and organize this participation. *"Only"* that. There are now no other devices needed to advance to socialism.

But to achieve this "only," there must be a veritable revolution— the entire people must go through a period of cultural development. Therefore, our rule must be: as little philosophizing and as few acrobatics as possible. In this respect NEP is an advance, because it is adjustable to the level of the most ordinary peasant and does not demand anything higher of him. But it will take a whole historical epoch to get the entire population into the work of the cooperatives through NEP. At best we can achieve this in one or two decades. Nevertheless, it will be a distinct historical epoch. And without this historical epoch, without universal literacy, without a proper degree of efficiency, without training the population sufficiently to acquire the habit of book reading, and without the material basis for this, without a certain sufficiency to safeguard against, say, bad harvests, famine, etc.—without this we shall not achieve our object.

The thing now is to learn to combine the wide revolutionary range of action, the revolutionary enthusiasm which we have displayed, and displayed abundantly, and crowned with complete success—to learn to combine this with (I am almost inclined to say) the ability to be an efficient and capable trader, which is quite enough to be a good cooperator. By ability to be a trader I mean the ability to be a cultured trader. Let those Russians, or peasants, who imagine that since they trade they are good traders, get that well into their heads. This does not follow at all. They do trade, but that is far from being cultured traders. They now trade in an Asiatic manner, but to be a good trader one must trade in the European manner. They are a whole epoch behind in that.

In conclusion: a number of economic, financial, and banking privileges must be granted to the cooperatives—this is the way our socialist state must promote the new principle on which the population must be organized. But this is only the general outline of the task. It does not define and depict in detail the entire content of the practical task, i.e., we must find what form of "bonus" to give for joining the cooperatives (and the terms on which we should give it), the form of bonus by which we shall assist the cooperatives sufficiently, the form of bonus that will produce the civilized cooperator. And given social ownership of the means of production, given the class victory of the proletariat over the bourgeoisie, the system of civilized cooperators is the system of socialism.

(2)   JANUARY 6, 1923

Whenever I wrote about the New Economic Policy I always quoted the article on state capitalism which I wrote in 1918.[6] This has more than once aroused doubts in the minds of certain young comrades. But their doubts were mainly on abstract political points.

It seemed to them that the term "state capitalism" could not be applied to a system under which the means of production were owned by the working class, a working class that held political power. They did not notice, however, that I used the term "state capitalism," *first,* to connect historically our present position with the position adopted in my controversy with the so-called Left Communists; also, I argued at the time that state capitalism would be superior to our existing economy. It was important for me to show the continuity between ordinary state capitalism and the unusual, even very unusual, state capitalism to which I referred in in-

6. See Lenin, "'Left-Wing' Childishness and the Petty-Bourgeois Mentality," in *CW*, vol. 27, pp. 323–54.

troducing the reader to the New Economic Policy. *Second,* the practical purpose was always important to me. And the practical purpose of our New Economic Policy was to lease out concessions. In the prevailing circumstances, concessions in our country would unquestionably have been a pure type of state capitalism. That is how I argued about state capitalism.

But there is another aspect of the matter for which we may need state capitalism, or at least a comparison with it. It is the question of cooperatives.

In the capitalist state, cooperatives are no doubt collective capitalist institutions. Nor is there any doubt that under our present economic conditions, when we combine private capitalist enterprises—but in no other way than on nationalized land and in no other way than under the control of the working-class state—with enterprises of a consistently socialist type (the means of production, the land on which the enterprises are situated, and the enterprises as a whole belonging to the state), the question arises about a third type of enterprise, the cooperatives, which were not formerly regarded as an independent type differing fundamentally from the others. Under private capitalism, cooperative enterprises differ from capitalist enterprises as collective enterprises differ from private enterprises. Under state capitalism, cooperative enterprises differ from state capitalist enterprises first, because they are private enterprises and second, because they are collective enterprises. Under our present system, cooperative enterprises differ from private capitalist enterprises because they are collective enterprises but do not differ from socialist enterprises if the land on which they are situated and the means of production belong to the state, i.e., the working class.

This circumstance is not considered sufficiently when cooperatives are discussed. It is forgotten that owing to the special features of our political system, our cooperatives acquire an altogether exceptional significance. If we exclude concessions, which, incidentally, have not developed on any considerable scale, cooperation under our conditions nearly always coincides fully with socialism.

Let me explain what I mean. Why were the plans of the old cooperators, from Robert Owen onwards, fantastic? Because they dreamed of peacefully remodeling contemporary society into socialism without taking account of such fundamental questions as the class struggle, the capture of political power by the working class, the overthrow of the rule of the exploiting class. That is why we are right in regarding as entirely fantastic this "cooperative" socialism, and as romantic, and even banal, the dream of transforming class enemies into class collaborators and class war into class peace (so-called class truce) by merely organizing the population in cooperative societies.

Undoubtedly we were right from the point of view of the fundamental task of the present day, for socialism cannot be established without a class struggle for political power in the state.

But see how things have changed now that political power is in the hands of the working class, now that the political power of the exploiters is overthrown and all the means of production (except those which the workers state voluntarily abandons on specified terms and for a certain time to the exploiters in the form of concessions) are owned by the working class.

Now we are entitled to say that for us the mere growth of cooperation (with the "slight" exception mentioned above) is identical with the growth of socialism, and at the same time we have to admit that there has been a radical modification in our whole outlook on socialism. The radical modification is this: formerly we placed, and had to place, the main emphasis on the political struggle, on revolution, on winning political power, etc. Now the emphasis is changing and shifting to peaceful, organizational, "cultural" work. I should say that emphasis is shifting to educational work were it not for our international relations, were it not for our obligation to fight for our position on a world scale. If we leave that aside, however, and confine ourselves to internal economic relations, the emphasis in our work is certainly shifting to education.

Two main tasks confront us, which constitute the epoch: to reorganize our machinery of state, which is utterly useless, and which we took over in its entirety from the preceding epoch. During the past five years of struggle we did not, and could not, drastically reorganize it. Our second task is educational work among the peasants. And the economic object of this educational work among the peasants is to organize the latter in cooperative societies. If the whole of the peasantry had been organized in cooperatives, we would by now have been standing with both feet on the soil of socialism. But the organization of the entire peasantry in cooperative societies presupposes a standard of culture among the peasants (precisely among the peasants as the overwhelming mass) that cannot, in fact, be achieved without a cultural revolution.

Our opponents told us repeatedly that we were rash in undertaking to implant socialism in an insufficiently cultured country. But they were misled by our having started from the opposite end to that prescribed by theory (the theory of pedants of all kinds), because in our country the political and social revolution preceded the cultural revolution, that very cultural revolution which nevertheless now confronts us.

This cultural revolution would now suffice to make our country a completely socialist country; but it presents immense difficulties of a purely cultural (for we are illiterate) and material character (for to be cultured we must achieve a certain development of the material means of production, must have a certain material base).

7

Socialist Revolution, Russia, and the East

Our Revolution

(APROPOS OF N. SUKHANOV'S NOTES)

(1)   JANUARY 16–17, 1923

I have lately been glancing through Sukhanov's *Notes on the Revolution.*[1] What strikes one most is the pedantry of all our petty-bourgeois democrats and of all the heroes of the Second International. Apart from the fact that they are all extremely fainthearted, that when it comes to the minutest deviation from the German model[2] even the best of them fortify themselves with reservations— apart from this characteristic, which is common to all petty-bourgeois democrats and has been abundantly manifested by them throughout the revolution, what strikes one is their slavish imitation of the past.

They all call themselves Marxists, but their conception of Marxism is impossibly pedantic. They have completely failed to understand what is decisive in Marxism, namely, its revolutionary dialectics. They have even absolutely failed to understand Marx's plain statements that in times of revolution the utmost flexibility is demanded, and have even failed to notice, for instance, the statements Marx made in his letters—I think it was in 1856—expressing the hope of combining a peasant war in Germany, which might create a revolutionary situation, with the working-class movement[3]—they avoid even this plain statement and walk round and about it like a

Footnotes begin on next page

cat around a bowl of hot porridge.

Their conduct betrays them as cowardly reformists who are afraid to deviate from the bourgeoisie, let alone break with it, and at the same time they disguise their cowardice with the wildest rhetoric and braggartry. But what strikes one in all of them even from the purely theoretical point of view is their utter inability to grasp the following Marxist considerations: up to now they have seen capitalism and bourgeois democracy in western Europe follow a definite path of development, and cannot conceive that this path can be taken as a model only *mutatis mutandis,* only with certain amendments (quite insignificant from the standpoint of the general development of world history).

First, the revolution connected with the first imperialist world war. Such a revolution was bound to reveal new features, or variations, resulting from the war itself, for the world has never seen such a war in such a situation. We find that since the war, the bourgeoisie of the wealthiest countries have to this day been unable to restore "normal" bourgeois relations. Yet our reformists—petty bourgeois who make a show of being revolutionaries—believed, and still be-

1. Lenin, *CW,* vol. 33, pp. 476–80. Sukhanov's work, published in Russia and Germany in the early 1920s, was the most comprehensive record of the 1917 revolution written from a Menshevik viewpoint.

2. Before 1914 the German working-class movement was the largest in the Socialist International. The Social Democratic Party and German trade unions were widely regarded as a model for workers in other countries. Likewise, the industrial capitalism of western Europe, as well as the parliamentary structures and forms of bourgeois democracy characteristic of much of capitalist Europe, were seen by most leaders of the International, including the Menshevik Party leadership, as a stage through which not only Russia but all nations still saddled with precapitalist economic and social relations would have to pass. This model of development was inevitable, they said, in order to develop the forces of production and cultural level needed to make socialism possible.

3. Marx wrote in an April 16, 1856, letter to Engels, "The whole thing in Germany will depend on the possibility of backing the proletarian revolution by some second edition of the Peasant War. Then the affair will be splendid." Marx and Engels, *Selected Correspondence* (Moscow: Progress Publishers, 1955), p. 111.

lieve, that normal bourgeois relations are the limit (thus far shalt thou go and no farther). And even their conception of "normal" is extremely stereotyped and narrow.

Second, they are complete strangers to the idea that while the development of world history as a whole follows general laws, it is by no means precluded but, on the contrary, presumed, that certain periods of development may display peculiarities in either the form or the sequence of this development. For instance, it does not even occur to them that because Russia stands on the borderline between the civilized countries and the countries which this war has for the first time definitely brought into the orbit of civilization—all the Oriental, non-European countries—she could and was, indeed, bound to reveal certain distinguishing features. Although these, of course, are in keeping with the general line of world development, they distinguish her revolution from those which took place in the western European countries and introduce certain partial innovations as the revolution moves on to the countries of the East.

Infinitely stereotyped, for instance, is the argument they learned by rote during the development of western European Social Democracy, namely, that we are not yet ripe for socialism, that, as certain "learned" gentlemen among them put it, the objective economic premises for socialism do not exist in our country. It does not occur to any of them to ask: But what about a people that found itself in a revolutionary situation such as that created during the first imperialist war? Might it not, influenced by the hopelessness of its situation, fling itself into a struggle that would offer it at least some chance of securing conditions for the further development of civilization that were somewhat unusual?

"The development of the productive forces of Russia has not attained the level that makes socialism possible." All the heroes of the Second International, including, of course, Sukhanov, beat the drums about this proposition. They keep harping on this incontrovertible proposition in a thousand different keys and think that it is the decisive criterion of our revolution.

But what if the situation, which drew Russia into the imperialist world war that involved every more or less influential western European country and made her a witness of the eve of the revolutions maturing or partly already begun in the East, gave rise to circumstances that put Russia and her development in a position which enabled us to achieve precisely that combination of a "peasant war" with the working-class movement suggested in 1856 by no less a Marxist than Marx himself as a possible prospect for Prussia?

What if the complete hopelessness of the situation, by stimulating the efforts of the workers and peasants tenfold, offered us the opportunity to create the fundamental requisites of civilization in a different way from that of the western European countries? Has that altered the general line of development of world history? Has that altered the basic relations between the basic classes of all the countries that are being, or have been, drawn into the general course of world history?

If a definite level of culture is required for the building of socialism (although nobody can say just what that definite "level of culture" is, for it differs in every western European country), why cannot we begin by first achieving the prerequisites for that definite level of culture in a revolutionary way and then, with the aid of the workers and peasants government and the Soviet system, proceed to overtake the other nations?

(2)   JANUARY 17, 1923

You say that civilization is necessary for the building of socialism. Very good. But why could we not first create such prerequisites of civilization in our country as the expulsion of the landowners and the Russian capitalists, and then start moving towards socialism? Where, in what books, have you read that such variations of the customary historical sequence of events are impermissible or impossible?

Napoleon, I think, wrote: *"On s'engage et puis . . . on voit."* Rendered freely this means: "First engage in a serious battle and then see what happens." Well, we did first engage in a serious battle in October 1917 and then saw such details of development (from the standpoint of world history they were certainly details) as the Brest peace, the New Economic Policy, and so forth. And now there can be no doubt that in the main we have been victorious.

Our Sukhanovs, not to mention Social Democrats still farther to the right, never even dream that revolutions cannot be made otherwise. Our European philistines never even dream that the subsequent revolutions in Oriental countries, which possess much vaster populations and a much vaster diversity of social conditions, will undoubtedly display even greater distinctions than the Russian revolution.

It need hardly be said that a textbook written on Kautskyan lines was a very useful thing in its day.[4] But it is time, for all that, to abandon the idea that it foresaw all the forms of development of subsequent world history. It would be timely to say that those who think so are simply fools.

4. Karl Kautsky (1854–1938) was a collaborator of Frederick Engels and longtime leader of the German Social Democratic Party. His well-known works included *The Economic Doctrines of Karl Marx* (1887) and *The Class Struggle* (1892). Increasingly aligning himself with the reformist majority of the Social Democratic Party that capitulated to the German bourgeoisie at the opening of World War I, Kautsky in 1918 wrote *The Dictatorship of the Proletariat,* directed against the Russian revolution of October 1917. Lenin responded in *The Proletarian Revolution and the Renegade Kautsky.*

8

The Workers and Peasants Inspection

How we should reorganize the Workers and Peasants Inspection

RECOMMENDATION TO THE TWELFTH PARTY CONGRESS

JANUARY 23, 1923

It is beyond question that the Workers and Peasants Inspection is an enormous difficulty for us and that so far this difficulty has not been overcome.[1] I think that the comrades who try to overcome the difficulty by denying that the Workers and Peasants Inspection is useful and necessary are wrong.[2] But I do not deny that the problem presented by our state apparatus and the task of improving it is very difficult, that it is far from being solved, and is an extremely urgent one.

With the exception of the People's Commissariat of Foreign Affairs, our state apparatus is to a considerable extent a survival of the past and has undergone hardly any serious change. It has only been slightly touched up on the surface, but in all other respects it is a most typical relic of our old state machine. And so, to find a method of really renovating it, I think we ought to turn for experience to our civil war.

How did we act in the more critical moments of the civil war?

We concentrated our best party forces in the Red Army, we mobilized the best of our workers, we looked for new forces at the deepest roots of our dictatorship.

I am convinced that we must go to the same source to find the

Footnotes start on next page

227

means of reorganizing the Workers and Peasants Inspection. I recommend that our twelfth party congress adopt the following plan of reorganization, based on some enlargement of our Central Control Commission.[3]

The plenary meetings of the Central Committee of our party are already revealing a tendency to develop into a kind of supreme party conference. They take place on the average not more than once in two months, while the routine work is conducted, as we know, on behalf of the Central Committee by our Political Bureau, our Organization Bureau, our Secretariat, and so forth. I think we ought to follow the road we have thus taken to the end and definitely transform the ple-

1. Lenin, CW, vol. 33, pp. 481–86. Lenin's notes for this article and a first draft dictated to his secretaries can be found in appendix 2 to this volume and in Lenin, CW, vol. 42, pp. 433–34.

The Workers and Peasants Inspection was established by the Executive Committee of the All-Russia Congress of Soviets in early 1920 through a reorganization of the previous State Control Commissariat. Stalin chaired the WPI from its origins through 1922. Lenin's view on the importance of such a body in drawing both party and nonparty workers and peasants into greater inspection and control of the state and party apparatus were outlined in notes to Stalin dated March 8, 1919, and January 24, 1920, as well as a January 23, 1920, motion by Lenin adopted by the Political Bureau. These three items are also reprinted here in appendix 2.

During 1920–21 more than one hundred thousand volunteers participated in the work of the Workers and Peasants Inspection. But by 1922 the number of volunteer participants in the WPI's work dropped to twenty-five thousand. Some of Lenin's initial views on reorganizing the WPI from the year or so prior to the January 1923 article can be found in Lenin, CW, vol. 42, pp. 306–7; vol. 45, pp. 480, 493–94; vol. 36, p. 580; and vol. 33, pp. 42–48, 353–54.

2. In a May 5, 1922, letter to the Political Bureau, Lenin explained his view on why Trotsky's proposal to "dispense with the Workers and Peasants Inspection" was "fundamentally wrong." See Lenin, CW, vol. 33, pp. 353–54. Lenin was referring to a 1920 report by Trotsky to the Eighth Congress of Soviets, cited by Isaac Deutscher in The Prophet Unarmed: Trotsky 1921–29, pp. 47–48.

3. The Central Control Commission had seven members when Lenin wrote proposing its enlargement and amalgamation with the Workers and Peasants Inspection.

The Control Commission had been formed by the party's September 1920

nary meetings of the Central Committee into supreme party conferences convened once in two months jointly with the Central Control
Commission. The Central Control Commission should be amalgamated with the main body of the reorganized Workers and Peasants
Inspection on the following lines.

I propose that the congress should elect 75 to 100 new members
to the Central Control Commission. They should be workers and
peasants and should go through the same party screening as ordinary members of the Central Committee, because they are to enjoy
the same rights as the members of the Central Committee.

On the other hand, the staff of the Workers and Peasants Inspection should be reduced to three or four hundred persons, specially
screened for conscientiousness and knowledge of our state apparatus.[4] They must also undergo a special test as regards their knowledge of the principles of scientific organization of labor in general,
and of administrative work, office work, and so forth, in particular.

In my opinion, such an amalgamation of the Workers and Peas-

---

all-Russia conference. The conference resolution said that it would be "composed of the comrades with the greatest background in party affairs, the most
experienced, the most impartial, and those best able to implement strict party
control." The body was mandated "to receive all manner of complaints and
reach conclusions on them," making recommendations to the Central Committee. The Control Commission and Central Committee were authorized to
meet jointly when necessary or to refer questions to a party congress.

The Control Commission's purpose was defined by the tenth party congress
in March 1921 as including "combating the bureaucratism and careerism that
have crept into the party, combating misuse of party and soviet positions by
party members, violations of comradely relations within the party, dissemination of unfounded and unsubstantiated rumors and insinuations," and combating dissemination of other information that "violates the unity and authority of the party."

The tenth congress resolution stipulated that commission members
were not to be members of other leading committees of the party or the
government administration.

Control commissions were formed not only on the central leadership
level but also in the regional and provincial party organizations.

4. The reference here is to the commissariat's central apparatus, which
included 1,200 staff members at that time.

ants Inspection with the Central Control Commission will be beneficial to both these institutions. On the one hand, the Workers and Peasants Inspection will thus obtain such high authority that it will certainly not be inferior to the People's Commissariat of Foreign Affairs. On the other hand, our Central Committee, together with the Central Control Commission, will definitely take the road of becoming a supreme party conference, which in fact it has already taken, and along which it should proceed to the end so as to be able to fulfill its functions properly in two respects: in respect to *its own* methodical, expedient, and systematic organization and work and in respect to maintaining contacts with the broad masses through the medium of the best of our workers and peasants.

I foresee an objection that, directly or indirectly, may come from those spheres which make our state apparatus antiquated, i.e., from those who urge that its present utterly impossible, indecently prerevolutionary form be preserved (incidentally, we now have an opportunity which rarely occurs in history of ascertaining the period necessary for bringing about radical social changes; we now see clearly what can be done in five years, and what requires much more time).

The objection I foresee is that the change I propose will lead to nothing but chaos. The members of the Central Control Commission will wander around all the institutions, not knowing where, why, or to whom to apply, causing disorganization everywhere and distracting employees from their routine work, etc., etc.

I think that the malicious source of this objection is so obvious that it does not warrant a reply. It goes without saying that the Presidium of the Central Control Commission, the people's commissar of the Workers and Peasants Inspection and his collegium (and also, in the proper cases, the Secretariat of our Central Committee) will have to put in years of persistent effort to get the commissariat properly organized, and to get it to function smoothly in conjunction with the Central Control Commission.

In my opinion, the people's commissar of the Workers and Peasants Inspection, as well as the whole collegium, can (and should) remain and guide the work of the entire Workers and Peasants Inspection, including the work of all the members of the Central Control Commission who will be "placed under his command." The three or four hundred employees of the Workers and Peasants Inspection that are to remain, according to my plan, should, on the one hand, perform purely secretarial functions for the other members of the Workers and Peasants Inspection and for the supplementary members of the Central Control Commission and, on the other hand, they should be highly skilled, specially screened, particularly reliable, and highly paid, so that they may be relieved of their present truly unhappy (to say the least) position of Workers and Peasants Inspection officials.

I am sure that the reduction of the staff to the number I have indicated will greatly enhance the efficiency of the Workers and Peasants Inspection personnel and the quality of all its work, enabling the people's commissar and the members of the collegium to concentrate their efforts entirely on organizing the work and on systematically and steadily improving its efficiency, which is so absolutely essential for our workers and peasants government and for our Soviet system.

On the other hand, I also think that the people's commissar of the Workers and Peasants Inspection should work on partly amalgamating and partly coordinating those higher institutions for the organization of labor (the Central Institute of Labor, the Institute for the Scientific Organization of Labor, etc.) of which there are now no fewer than twelve in our republic. Excessive uniformity and a consequent desire to amalgamate will be harmful. On the contrary, what is needed here is a reasonable and expedient mean between amalgamating all these institutions and properly delimiting them, allowing for a certain independence for each of them.

Our own Central Committee will undoubtedly gain no less from this reorganization than the Workers and Peasants Inspection. It will gain because its contacts with the masses will be greater and because the regularity and effectiveness of its work will improve. It will then be possible (and necessary) to institute a stricter and more responsible procedure of preparing for the meetings of the Political Bureau, which should be attended by a definite number of members of the Central Control Commission determined either for a definite period or by some organizational plan.

In distributing work to the members of the Central Control Commission, the people's commissar of the Workers and Peasants Inspection, in conjunction with the Presidium of the Central Control Commission, should impose on them the duty either of attending the meetings of the Political Bureau for the purpose of examining all the documents appertaining to matters that come before it in one way or another; or of devoting their working time to theoretical study, to the study of scientific methods of organizing labor; or of taking a practical part in the work of supervising and improving our machinery of state, from the higher state institutions to the lower local bodies, etc.

I also think that in addition to the political advantages accruing from the fact that the members of the Central Committee and the Central Control Commission will, as a consequence of this reform, be much better informed and better prepared for the meetings of the Political Bureau, (all the documents relevant to the business to be discussed at these meetings should be sent to all the members of the Central Committee and the Central Control Commission not later than the day before the meeting of the Political Bureau, except in absolutely urgent cases, for which special methods of informing the members of the Central Committee and the Central Control Commission and of settling these matters must be devised) there will also be the advantage that the influence of purely personal and incidental factors in our Central Committee will diminish, and this will reduce the danger of a split.

Our Central Committee has grown into a strictly centralized and highly authoritative group, but the conditions under which this group is working are not commensurate with its authority. The reform I recommend should help to remove this defect. The members of the Central Control Commission, whose duty it will be to attend all meetings of the Political Bureau in a definite number, will have to form a compact group which should not allow anybody's authority without exception, neither that of the general secretary nor of any other member of the Central Committee, to prevent them from putting questions, verifying documents, and, in general, from keeping themselves fully informed of all things and from exercising the strictest control over the proper conduct of affairs.

Of course, in our Soviet republic, the social order is based on the collaboration of two classes: the workers and peasants, in which the "Nepmen," i.e., the bourgeoisie, are now permitted to participate on certain terms. If serious class disagreements arise between these classes, a split will be inevitable. But the grounds for such a split are not inevitable in our social system, and it is the principal task of our Central Committee and Central Control Commission, as well as of our party as a whole, to watch very closely over such circumstances as may cause a split and to forestall them. For in the final analysis the fate of our republic will depend on whether the peasant masses will stand by the working class, loyal to their alliance, or whether they will permit the "Nepmen," i.e., the new bourgeoisie, to drive a wedge between them and the working class, to split them off from the working class. The more clearly we see this alternative, the more clearly all our workers and peasants understand it, the greater are the chances that we shall avoid a split, which would be fatal for the Soviet republic.

9

Preparing the Twelfth
Party Congress

Better fewer, but better

MARCH 2, 1923

In the matter of improving our state apparatus, the Workers and Peasants Inspection should not, in my opinion, either strive after quantity or hurry.[1] We have so far been able to devote so little thought and attention to the efficiency of our state apparatus that it would now be quite legitimate if we took special care to secure its thorough organization, and concentrated in the Workers and Peasants Inspection a staff of workers really abreast of the times, i.e., not inferior to the best western European standards.

For a socialist republic this condition is, of course, too modest. But our experience of the first five years has fairly crammed our heads with mistrust and skepticism. These qualities assert themselves involuntarily when, for example, we hear people dilating at too great length and too flippantly on "proletarian" culture. For a start, we should be satisfied with real bourgeois culture; for a start, we should be glad to dispense with the cruder types of prebourgeois culture, i.e., bureaucratic culture or serf culture, etc. In matters of culture, haste and sweeping measures are most harmful. Many of our young writers and Communists should get this well into their heads.

Thus, in the matter of our state apparatus we should now draw

Footnotes start on next page

237

the conclusion from our past experience that it would be better to proceed more slowly.

Our state apparatus is so deplorable, not to say wretched, that we must first think very carefully how to combat its defects, bearing in mind that these defects are rooted in the past, which, although it has been overthrown, has not yet been overcome, has not yet reached the stage of a culture that has receded into the distant past.

I say culture deliberately, because in these matters we can only regard as achieved what has become part and parcel of our culture, of our social life, our habits. We might say that the good in our social system has not been properly studied, understood, and taken to heart; it has been hastily grasped at; it has not been verified or tested, corroborated by experience, and not made durable, etc. Of course, it could not be otherwise in a revolutionary epoch, when development proceeded at such breakneck speed that in a matter of five years we passed from tsarism to the Soviet system.

It is time we did something about it. We must show sound skepticism for too rapid progress, for boastfulness, etc. We must give thought to testing the steps forward we proclaim every hour, take every minute and then prove every second that they are flimsy, superficial, and misunderstood. The most harmful thing here would be haste. The most harmful thing would be to rely on the assumption that we know at least something, or that we have any considerable number of elements necessary for the building of a really new state apparatus, one really worthy to be called socialist, Soviet, etc.

No, we are ridiculously deficient of such an apparatus, and even

1. Lenin, CW, vol. 33, pp. 487–502.

First published in Pravda, March 4, 1923. In an October 23, 1923, letter, Trotsky informed the Central Committee that the majority of the Political Bureau had been initially opposed to publishing this article at all. At first, only Trotsky and Kamenev favored printing Lenin's views, but the others finally gave way. V.V. Kuibyshev, head of the Control Commission, went so far as to propose initially that the article be printed only in a special single copy of Pravda, published solely to deceive Lenin. See Trotsky, "Second Letter to the CC" in The Challenge of the Left Opposition (1923–25) (New York: Pathfinder, 1975), p. 62.

of the elements of it, and we must remember that we should not stint time on building it, and that it will take many, many years.

What elements have we for building this apparatus? Only two. First, the workers who are absorbed in the struggle for socialism. These elements are not sufficiently educated. They would like to build a better apparatus for us, but they do not know how. They cannot build one. They have not yet developed the culture required for this, and it is culture that is required. Nothing will be achieved in this by doing things in a rush, by assault, by vim or vigor, or in general, by any of the best human qualities. Second, we have elements of knowledge, education, and training, but they are ridiculously inadequate compared with all other countries.

Here we must not forget that we are too prone to compensate (or imagine that we can compensate) our lack of knowledge by zeal, haste, etc.

In order to renovate our state apparatus we must at all costs set out, first, to learn, second, to learn, and third, to learn, and then see to it that learning shall not remain a dead letter or a fashionable catchphrase (and we should admit in all frankness that this happens very often with us), that learning shall really become part of our very being, that it shall actually and fully become a constituent element of our social life. In short, we must not make the demands that are made by bourgeois western Europe, but demands that are fit and proper for a country which has set out to develop into a socialist country.

The conclusions to be drawn from the above are the following: we must make the Workers and Peasants Inspection a really exemplary institution, an instrument to improve our state apparatus.

In order that it may attain the desired high level, we must follow the rule: "Measure your cloth seven times before you cut."

For this purpose, we must utilize the very best of what there is in our social system and utilize it with the greatest caution, thoughtfulness, and knowledge to build up the new people's commissariat.

For this purpose, the best elements that we have in our social system—such as, first, the advanced workers and second, the really enlightened elements for whom we can vouch that they will not take the word for the deed and will not utter a single word that goes against their conscience—should not shrink from admitting any difficulty and should not shrink from any struggle in order to achieve the object they have seriously set themselves.

We have been bustling for five years trying to improve our state apparatus, but it has been mere bustle, which has proved useless in these five years, or even futile, or even harmful. This bustle created the impression that we were doing something, but in effect it was only clogging up our institutions and our brains.

It is high time things were changed.

We must follow the rule: Better fewer, but better. We must follow the rule: Better get good human material in two or even three years than work in haste without hope of getting any at all.

I know that it will be hard to keep to this rule and apply it under our conditions. I know that the opposite rule will force its way through a thousand loopholes. I know that enormous resistance will have to be put up, that devilish persistence will be required, that in the first few years at least work in this field will be hellishly hard. Nevertheless, I am convinced that only by such effort shall we be able to achieve our aim, and that only by achieving this aim shall we create a republic that is really worthy of the name of Soviet, social-ist, and so on and so forth.

Many readers probably thought that the figures I quoted by way of illustration in my first article were too small.[2] I am sure that many calculations may be made to prove that they are. But I think that we must put one thing above all such and other calculations, i.e., our desire to obtain really exemplary quality.

I think that the time has at last come when we must work in real earnest to improve our state apparatus and in this there can scarcely be anything more harmful than haste. That is why I would sound a strong warning against inflating the figures. In my opinion, we

2. Lenin refers here to the proposal in his article printed in chapter 8 that the staff of the Workers and Peasants Inspection be reduced to 300–400 from 1,200.

should, on the contrary, be especially sparing with figures in this matter.

Let us say frankly that the People's Commissariat of the Workers and Peasants Inspection does not at present enjoy the slightest authority. Everybody knows that no other institutions are worse organized than those of our Workers and Peasants Inspection, and that under present conditions nothing can be expected from this people's commissariat. We must have this firmly fixed in our minds if we really want to create within a few years an institution that will, first, be an exemplary institution, second, win everybody's absolute confidence, and, thirdly, prove to all and sundry that we have really justified the work of such a highly placed institution as the Central Control Commission.

In my opinion, we must immediately and irrevocably reject all overall figures for the size of office staffs. We must select employees for the Workers and Peasants Inspection with particular care and only on the basis of the strictest test. Indeed, what is the use of establishing a people's commissariat which carries on anyhow, which does not enjoy the slightest confidence, and whose word carries scarcely any weight? I think that our main object in launching the work of reconstruction that we now have in mind is to avoid all this.

The workers whom we are enlisting as members of the Central Control Commission must be irreproachable Communists, and I think that a great deal has yet to be done to teach them the methods and objects of their work. Furthermore, there must be a definite number of secretaries to assist in this work, who must be tested thrice over before they are appointed to their posts. Lastly, the officials whom in exceptional cases we shall accept directly as employees of the Workers and Peasants Inspection must conform to the following requirements:

First, they must be recommended by several Communists.

Second, they must pass a test for knowledge of our state apparatus.

Third, they must pass a test in the fundamentals of the theory of our state apparatus, in the fundamentals of management, office routine, etc.

Fourth, they must work in such close harmony with the members of the Central Control Commission and with their own secretariat that we could vouch for the work of the whole apparatus.

I know that these requirements are extraordinarily strict, and I am very much afraid that the majority of the "practical" workers in the Workers and Peasants Inspection will say that these requirements are impracticable or will scoff at them. But I ask any of the present chiefs of the Workers and Peasants Inspection, or anyone associated with that body, whether they can honestly tell me the practical purpose of a people's commissariat like the Workers and Peasants Inspection. I think this question will help them recover their sense of proportion. Either it is not worth while having another of the numerous reorganizations that we have had of this hopeless affair, the Workers and Peasants Inspection, or we must really set to work by slow, difficult, and unusual methods and by testing these methods over and over again to create something really exemplary, something that will win the respect of all and sundry for its merits, and not only because of its rank and title.

If we do not arm ourselves with patience, if we do not devote several years to this task, we had better not tackle it at all.

In my opinion we ought to select a minimum number of the higher labor research institutes, etc., which we have baked so hastily, see whether they are organized properly, and allow them to continue working, but only in a way that conforms to the high standards of modern science and gives us all its benefits. If we do that it will not be utopian to hope that within a few years we shall have an institution that will be able to perform its functions, to work systematically and steadily on improving our state apparatus, an institution backed by the trust of the working class, of the Russian Communist Party, and the whole population of our republic.

The spadework for this could be begun at once. If the People's Commissariat of the Workers and Peasants Inspection accepted the present plan of reorganization, it could now take preparatory steps and work methodically until the task is completed, without haste, and not hesitating to alter what has already been done.

Any halfhearted solution would be extremely harmful in this matter. A measure for the size of the staff of the Workers and Peasants Inspection based on any other consideration would, in fact, be based on the old bureaucratic considerations, on old prejudices, on what has already been condemned, universally ridiculed, etc.

In substance, the matter is as follows:

Either we prove now that we have really learned something about state organization (we ought to have learned something in five years), or we prove that we are not sufficiently mature for it. If the latter is the case, we had better not tackle the task.

I think that with the available human material it will not be immodest to assume that we have learned enough to be able systematically to rebuild at least one people's commissariat. True, this one people's commissariat will have to be the model for our entire state apparatus.

We ought at once to announce a contest in the compilation of two or more textbooks on the organization of labor in general and on management in particular. We can take as a basis the book already published by Yermansky, although it should be said in parentheses that he obviously sympathizes with Menshevism and is unfit to compile textbooks for the Soviet system. We can also take as a basis the recent book by Kerzhentsev, and some of the other partial textbooks available may be useful too.

We ought to send several qualified and conscientious people to Germany or to Britain to collect literature and to study this question. I mention Britain in case it is found impossible to send people to the USA or Canada.

We ought to appoint a commission to draw up the preliminary program of examinations for prospective employees of the Workers and Peasants Inspection; ditto for candidates to the Central Control Commission.

These and similar measures will not, of course, cause any difficulties for the people's commissar or the collegium of the Workers and Peasants Inspection, or for the Presidium of the Central Control Commission.

Simultaneously, a preparatory commission should be appointed to select candidates for membership of the Central Control Commission. I hope that we shall now be able to find more than enough candidates for this post among the experienced workers in all departments, as well as among the students of our Soviet higher schools. It would hardly be right to exclude one or another category beforehand. Probably preference will have to be given to a mixed composition for this institution, which should combine many qualities and dissimilar merits. Consequently, the task of drawing up the list of candidates will entail a considerable amount of work. For example, it would be least desirable for the staff of the new people's commissariat to consist of people of one type, only of officials, say, or for it to exclude people of the propagandist type or people whose principal quality is sociability or the ability to penetrate into circles that are not altogether customary for officials in this field, etc.

*   *   *

I think I shall be able to express my idea best if I compare my plan with that of academic institutions. Under the guidance of their presidium, the members of the Central Control Commission should systematically examine all the papers and documents of the Political Bureau. Moreover, they should divide their time correctly between various jobs in investigating the routine in our institutions, from the very small and privately owned offices to the highest state institutions. And lastly, their functions should include the study of theory, i.e., the theory of organization of the work they intend to devote themselves to, and practical work under the guidance either of older comrades or of teachers in the higher institutes for the organization of labor.

I do not think, however, that they will be able to confine themselves to this sort of academic work. In addition, they will have to prepare themselves for work which I would not hesitate to call training to catch—I will not say rogues, but something like that, and working out special ruses to screen their movements, their approach, etc.

If such proposals were made in western European government institutions, they would rouse frightful resentment, a feeling of moral
indignation, etc., but I trust that we have not become so bureaucratic as to be capable of that. NEP has not yet succeeded in gaining
such respect as to cause any of us to be shocked at the idea that
somebody may be caught. Our Soviet republic is of such recent construction and there are such heaps of the old lumber still lying
around that it would hardly occur to anyone to be shocked at the
idea that we should delve into them by means of ruses, by means of
investigations sometimes directed to rather remote sources or in a
roundabout way. And even if it did occur to anyone to be shocked
by this, we may be sure that such a person would make himself a
laughingstock.

Let us hope that our new Workers and Peasants Inspection will
abandon what the French call *pruderie,* which we may call ridiculous primness, or ridiculous swank, and which plays entirely into the
hands of our Soviet and party bureaucracy. Let it be said in parentheses that we have bureaucrats in our party offices as well as in
Soviet offices.

When I said above that we must study and study hard in institutes
for the higher organization of labor, etc., I did not by any means
imply "studying" in the schoolroom way, nor did I confine myself
to the idea of studying only in the schoolroom way. I hope that not
a single genuine revolutionary will suspect me of refusing, in this
case, to understand "studies" to include resorting to some semihumorous trick, cunning device, piece of trickery, or something of that
sort. I know that in the staid and earnest states of western Europe
such an idea would horrify people and that not a single decent
official would even entertain it. I hope, however, that we have not
yet become as bureaucratic as all that and that in our midst the discussion of this idea will give rise to nothing more than amusement.

Indeed, why not combine pleasure with utility? Why not resort to
some humorous or semihumorous trick to expose something ridiculous, something harmful, something semiridiculous, semiharmful, etc.?

It seems to me that our Workers and Peasants Inspection will gain a great deal if it undertakes to examine these ideas, and that the list of cases in which our Central Control Commission and its colleagues in the Workers and Peasants Inspection achieved a few of their most brilliant victories will be enriched by not a few exploits of our future Workers and Peasants Inspection and Central Control Commission members in places not quite mentionable in prim and staid textbooks.

*   *   *

How can a party institution be amalgamated with a Soviet institution? Is there not something improper in this suggestion?

I do not ask these questions on my own behalf, but on behalf of those I hinted at above when I said that we have bureaucrats in our party institutions as well as in the Soviet institutions.

But why, indeed, should we not amalgamate the two if this is in the interests of our work? Do we not all see that such an amalgamation has been very beneficial in the case of the People's Commissariat of Foreign Affairs, where it was brought about at the very beginning? Does not the Political Bureau discuss from the party point of view many questions, both minor and important, concerning the "moves" we should make in reply to the "moves" of foreign powers in order to forestall their, say, "cunning," if we are not to use a less respectable term? Is not this flexible amalgamation of a Soviet institution with a party institution a source of great strength in our politics? I think that what has proved its usefulness, what has been definitely adopted in our foreign politics and has become so customary that it no longer calls forth any doubt in this field, will be at least as appropriate (in fact, I think it will be much more appropriate) for our state apparatus as a whole. The functions of the Workers and Peasants Inspection cover our state apparatus as a whole, and its activities should affect all and every state institution without exception: local, central, commercial, purely administrative, educational, archive, theatrical, etc.—in short, all without any exception.

Why then should not an institution, whose activities have such wide scope and which moreover requires such extraordinary flexibility of forms, be permitted to adopt this peculiar amalgamation of a party control institution with a Soviet control institution?

I see no obstacles to this. What is more, I think that such an amalgamation is the only guarantee of success in our work. I think that all doubts on this score arise in the dustiest corners of our government offices and that they deserve to be treated with nothing but ridicule.

*   *   *

Another doubt: Is it expedient to combine educational activities with official activities? I think that it is not only expedient, but necessary. Generally speaking, in spite of our revolutionary attitude towards the western European form of state, we have allowed ourselves to become infected with a number of its most harmful and ridiculous prejudices; to some extent we have been deliberately infected with them by our dear bureaucrats, who counted on being able again and again to fish in the muddy waters of these prejudices. And they did fish in these muddy waters to so great an extent that only the blind among us failed to see how extensively this fishing was practiced.

In all spheres of social, economic, and political relationships we are "frightfully" revolutionary. But as regards precedence, the observance of the forms and rites of office management, our "revolutionariness" often gives way to the mustiest routine. On more than one occasion, we have witnessed the very interesting phenomenon of a great leap forward in social life being accompanied by amazing timidity whenever the slightest changes are proposed.

This is natural, for the boldest steps forward were taken in a field which was long reserved for theoretical study, which was promoted mainly and even almost exclusively in theory. The Russian, when away from work, found solace from bleak bureaucratic realities in unusually bold theoretical constructions, and that is why in our country these unusually bold theoretical constructions assumed an unusually lopsided character. Theoretical audacity in general constructions went hand in hand with amazing timidity as regards certain very minor reforms in office routine. Some great universal agrarian revolution was worked out with an audacity unexampled in any other country, and at the same time the imagination failed when it came to working out a tenth-rate reform in office routine; the imagination, or patience, was lacking to apply to this reform the general propositions that produced such brilliant results when applied to general problems.

That is why in our present life reckless audacity goes hand in hand, to an astonishing degree, with timidity of thought even when it comes to very minor changes.

I think that this has happened in all really great revolutions, for really great revolutions grow out of the contradictions between the old, between what is directed towards developing the old and the very abstract striving for the new, which must be so new as not to contain the tiniest particle of the old.

And the more abrupt the revolution, the longer will many of these contradictions last.

*   *   *

The general feature of our present life is the following: we have destroyed capitalist industry and have done our best to raze to the ground the medieval institutions and landed proprietorship, and thus created a small and very small peasantry, which is following the lead of the proletariat because it has confidence in the results of its revolutionary work.

It is not easy for us, however, on the basis of this confidence alone, to hold out until the socialist revolution is victorious in more developed countries, because economic necessity, especially under NEP, keeps the productivity of labor of the small and very small peasants at an extremely low level. Moreover, the international situation, too, threw Russia back and, by and large, reduced the labor productivity of the people to a level considerably below prewar. The western European capitalist powers, partly deliberately and partly unconsciously, did everything they could to throw us back, to utilize the elements of the civil war in Russia in order to spread as much ruin in the country as possible. It was precisely this way out of the imperialist war that seemed to have many advantages.

They argued somewhat as follows: "If we fail to overthrow the revolutionary system in Russia, we shall, at all events, hinder its progress towards socialism." And from their point of view they could argue in no other way. In the end, their problem was half-solved. They failed to overthrow the new system created by the revolution, but they did prevent it from at once taking the step forward that would have justified the forecasts of the socialists, that would have enabled the latter to develop the productive forces with enormous speed, to develop all the potentialities which, taken together, would have produced socialism; socialists would thus have proved to all and sundry that socialism contains within itself gigantic forces and that mankind had now entered into a new stage of development of extraordinarily brilliant prospects.

The system of international relationships which has now taken shape is one in which a European state, Germany, is enslaved by the victor countries. Furthermore, owing to their victory, a number of states, the oldest states in the West, are in a position to make some insignificant concessions to their oppressed classes—concessions which, insignificant though they are, nevertheless retard the revolutionary movement in those countries and create some semblance of "class truce."[3]

At the same time, as a result of the last imperialist war, a number of countries of the East, India, China, etc., have been completely jolted out of the rut. Their development has definitely shifted to general European capitalist lines. The general European ferment has begun to affect them, and it is now clear to the whole world that they have been drawn into a process of development that must lead to a crisis in the whole of world capitalism.

Thus, at the present time we are confronted with the question—

---

3. Lenin detailed the evolution of the postwar situation of world capitalism and its relationship to the tactics of the Soviet Communist Party in theses and reports to the Third Congress of the Communist International in June and July 1921. See Lenin, CW, vol. 32, pp. 453–96.

shall we be able to hold on with our small and very small peasant production, and in our present state of ruin, until the western European capitalist countries consummate their development towards socialism? But they are consummating it not as we formerly expected. They are consummating it not through the gradual "maturing" of socialism but through the exploitation of some countries by others, through the exploitation of the first of the countries vanquished in the imperialist war combined with the exploitation of the whole of the East. On the other hand, precisely as a result of the first imperialist war, the East has been definitely drawn into the revolutionary movement, has been definitely drawn into the general maelstrom of the world revolutionary movement.

What tactics does this situation prescribe for our country? Obviously the following: we must display extreme caution so as to preserve our workers government and to retain our small and very small peasantry under its leadership and authority. We have the advantage that the whole world is now passing to a movement that must give rise to a world socialist revolution. But we are laboring under the disadvantage that the imperialists have succeeded in splitting the world into two camps, and this split is made more complicated by the fact that it is extremely difficult for Germany—which is really a land of advanced, cultured, capitalist development—to rise to her feet. All the capitalist powers of what is called the West are pecking at her and preventing her from rising. On the other hand, the entire East—with its hundreds of millions of exploited working people, reduced to the last degree of human suffering—has been forced into a position where its physical and material strength cannot possibly be compared with the physical, material, and military strength of any of the much smaller western European states.

Can we save ourselves from the impending conflict with these imperialist countries? May we hope that the internal antagonisms and conflicts between the thriving imperialist countries of the West and the thriving imperialist countries of the East will give us a second respite as they did the first time, when the campaign of the western European counterrevolution in support of the Russian counterrevolution broke down owing to the antagonisms in the camp of the counterrevolutionaries of the West and the East, in the camp of the eastern and western exploiters, in the camp of Japan and the USA?

I think the reply to this question should be that the issue depends upon too many factors, and that the outcome of the struggle as a whole can be forecast only because in the long run capitalism itself is educating and training the vast majority of the population of the globe for the struggle.

In the last analysis, the outcome of the struggle will be determined by the fact that Russia, India, China, etc., account for the overwhelming majority of the population of the globe. And during the past few years, it is this majority that has been drawn into the struggle for emancipation with extraordinary rapidity, so that in this respect there cannot be the slightest doubt what the final outcome of the world struggle will be. In this sense, the complete victory of socialism is fully and absolutely assured.

But what interests us is not the inevitability of this complete victory of socialism, but the tactics which we, the Russian Communist Party, we, the Russian Soviet government, should pursue to prevent the western European counterrevolutionary states from crushing us. To ensure our existence until the next military conflict between the counterrevolutionary imperialist West and the revolutionary and nationalist East, between the most civilized countries of the world and the orientally backward countries which, however, comprise the majority, this majority must become civilized. We, too, lack enough civilization to enable us to pass straight on to socialism, although we do have the political requisites for it. We should adopt the following tactics, or pursue the following policy, to save ourselves.

We must strive to build up a state in which the workers retain the leadership of the peasants, in which they retain the confidence of the peasants, and by exercising the greatest economy remove every trace of extravagance from our social relations.

We must reduce our state apparatus to the utmost degree of economy. We must banish from it all traces of extravagance, of which so much has been left over from tsarist Russia, from its bureaucratic capitalist state machine.

Will not this be a reign of peasant limitations?

No. If we see to it that the working class retains its leadership over the peasantry, we shall be able, by exercising the greatest possible thrift in the economic life of our state, to use every saving we make to develop our large-scale machine industry, to develop electrification, the hydraulic extraction of peat, to complete the Volkhov Power Project, etc.[4]

In this and in this alone lies our hope. Only when we have done this shall we, speaking figuratively, be able to change horses, to change from the peasant, muzhik horse of poverty, from the horse of an economy designed for a ruined peasant country, to the horse which the proletariat is seeking and must seek—the horse of large-scale machine industry, of electrification, of the Volkhov Power Station, etc.

That is how I link up in my mind the general plan of our work, of our policy, of our tactics, of our strategy, with the functions of the reorganized Workers and Peasants Inspection. This is what, in my opinion, justifies the exceptional care, the exceptional attention that we must devote to the Workers and Peasants Inspection in raising it to an exceptionally high level, in giving it a leadership with Central Committee rights, etc., etc.

And this justification is that only by thoroughly purging our government machine, by reducing to the utmost everything that is not absolutely essential in it, shall we be certain of being able to keep going. Moreover, we shall be able to keep going not on the level of a small peasant country, not on the level of universal limitation, but on a level steadily advancing to large-scale machine industry.

These are the lofty tasks that I dream of for our Workers and Peasants Inspection. That is why I am planning for it the amalgamation of the most authoritative party body with an "ordinary" people's commissariat.

4. The hydroelectric power station on the Volkhov River was the first of the large electric power construction projects in the Soviet Union. It was completed in 1926.

To Leon Trotsky

MARCH 5, 1923

Top secret

Personal

Dear Comrade Trotsky,

It is my earnest request that you should undertake the defense of the Georgian case in the party CC.[5] This case is now under "persecution" by Stalin and Dzerzhinsky, and I cannot rely on their impartiality. Quite to the contrary. I would feel at ease if you agreed to undertake its defense. If you should refuse to do so for any reason, return the whole case to me. I shall consider it a sign that you do not accept.

With best comradely greetings,

Lenin[6]

5. Lenin, *CW*, vol. 45, p. 607. This and the following two letters were published in the fifth Russian edition of Lenin's works, their first inclusion in a collection of his works. The letters to Trotsky and the Georgian Communists were included by Trotsky in 1927 in his "Letter to the Bureau of Party History." See Trotsky, *Stalin School of Falsification*, p. 69.

Lenin's March 5 letter to Trotsky followed a report to Lenin two days earlier from the confidential committee he had organized among his personal staff to review the Dzerzhinsky commission's investigation on Georgia. The conclusion from his staff's report appears in appendix 1 of this volume. With his note to Trotsky, Lenin enclosed a copy of "The Question of Nationalities or 'Autonomization'" (printed in chapter 5)—the first time he had shown it to another member of the Political Bureau. Lenin also received Trotsky's reply, agreeing to defend the Georgian Communists.

6. A separate sheet, appended to the letter, contains this note by one of Lenin's secretaries: "Comrade Trotsky, To the letter communicated to you by phone, Vladimir Ilyich asked to add for your information that Comrade Kamenev is going to Georgia on Wednesday, and wants to know whether you wish to send anything there yourself. March 5, '23." (Lenin, *CW*, vol. 45, p. 607.)

In a Central Committee meeting in late March 1923, Trotsky presented a motion that sharply criticized the Transcaucasian Federation as excessively centralized, denied that the dissident Communists in Georgia had advanced an incorrect policy on the national question, and proposed Ordzhonikidze's recall from the Caucasus. The motion was defeated.

See appendix 3 for a March 19, 1923, article by Trotsky on the national question and an April 16, 1923, letter by Lenin's secretary Fotieva stressing the importance Lenin had attached to his article on the national question and noting that Lenin had mandated Trotsky to defend his views on this matter.

To Joseph Stalin

MARCH 5, 1923

Top secret

Personal

Copy to Comrades Kamenev and Zinoviev

Dear Comrade Stalin,

You have been so rude as to summon my wife to the telephone and abuse her.[7] Although she had told you that she was prepared to forget this, the fact nevertheless became known through her to Zinoviev and Kamenev. I have no intention of forgetting so easily what has been done against me, and it goes without saying that what has been done against my wife I consider having been done against me as well. I ask you, therefore, to think it over whether you are prepared to withdraw what you have said and to make your apologies, or whether you prefer that relations between us should be broken off.

Respectfully yours,

Lenin

7. Lenin, CW, vol. 45, pp. 607–8.

To P.G. Mdivani, F.Y. Makharadze, and others

MARCH 6, 1923

Top secret
Comrades Mdivani, Makharadze, and others
Copy to Comrades Trotsky and Kamenev
Dear comrades,

I am following your case with all my heart.[8] I am indignant over Ordzhonikidze's rudeness and the connivance of Stalin and Dzerzhinsky. I am preparing for you notes and a speech.

Respectfully yours,

Lenin

---

8. Lenin, *CW*, vol. 45, p. 608.

Lenin on the Fight for Soviet Republics in Georgia and the Transcaucasus (1921, 1923)

Letter to G.K. Ordzhonikidze

MARCH 2, 1921

Sergo Ordzhonikidze,

Please convey to the Georgian Communists, and in particular to all members of the Georgian Revolutionary Committee, my warm greetings to Soviet Georgia.[1] My special request to them is to inform me whether or not we are in complete agreement on the following three questions:

First, immediate arming of the workers and poor peasants and formation of a strong Georgian Red Army.

Second, there is need for a special policy of concessions with regard to the Georgian intelligentsia and small merchants. It should be realized that it is not only imprudent to nationalize them, but that there is even need for certain sacrifices in order to improve their position and enable them to continue their small trade.

Third, it is of tremendous importance to devise an acceptable compromise for a bloc with Zhordania or similar Georgian Mensheviks, who before the uprising had not been absolutely opposed to the idea of Soviet power in Georgia on certain terms.

Please bear in mind that Georgia's domestic and international positions both require that her Communists should avoid any mechanical copying of the Russian pattern. They must skillfully work out their own flexible tactics based on bigger concessions to all the petty-bourgeois elements.

Please reply,

Lenin

1. Lenin, *CW*, vol. 32, p. 160.

To the Communists of Azerbaijan, Georgia, Armenia, Dagestan, and the Mountaineer Republic

APRIL 14, 1921

I send my warmest greetings to the Soviet republics of the Caucasus and would like to express the hope that their close alliance will serve as a model of national peace, unprecedented under the bourgeoisie and impossible under the capitalist system.[2]

But important as national peace among the workers and peasants of the Caucasian nationalities is, it is even more important to maintain and develop Soviet power as the transition to socialism. The task is difficult but fully feasible. The most important thing for its successful fulfillment is that the Communists of the Transcaucasus should be fully alive to the *singularity* of their position and of the position of their republics, as distinct from the position and conditions of the RSFSR; that they should appreciate the need to refrain from copying our tactics, but thoughtfully vary them in adaptation to the differing concrete conditions.

The Soviet republic of Russia had no outside political or military assistance. On the contrary, for years and years it fought the Entente military invasions and blockade.

The Soviet republics of the Caucasus have had political and some military assistance from the RSFSR. This alone has made a vast difference.

Footnotes start on next page

Second, there is now no cause to fear any Entente invasion or military assistance to the Georgian, Azerbaijan, Armenian, Dagestan, and Mountaineer White Guards. The Entente "burnt their fingers" in Russia and that will probably compel them to be more cautious for some time.

Third, the Caucasian republics have an even more pronounced peasant character than Russia.

Fourth, Russia has been, and to a considerable extent still is, economically isolated from the advanced capitalist countries. The Caucasus is in a position to start trading and "living together" with the capitalist West sooner and with greater ease.

These are not all the differences, but they are sufficient to demonstrate the need for different tactics.

You will need to practice more moderation and caution and show more readiness to make concessions to the petty bourgeoisie, the intelligentsia, and particularly the peasantry. You must make economic use of the capitalist West swiftly, intensely, and in every possible way through a policy of concessions and trade. Oil, manganese, coal (Tkvarcheli mines), and copper are some of your immense mineral resources. You have every possibility to develop an extensive policy of concessions and trade with foreign countries.

This must be done on a wide scale, with firmness, skill, and circumspection, and it must be utilized to the utmost for improving the condition of the workers and peasants and for enlisting the intelligentsia in the work of economic construction. Through trade with Italy, America, and other countries, you must exert every effort to develop the productive forces of your rich land, your water resources, and irrigation, which is especially important as a means of advancing agriculture and livestock farming.

What the republics of the Caucasus can and must do, as distinct from the RSFSR, is to effect a slower, more cautious, and more sys-

2. Excerpted from Lenin, *CW*, vol. 32, pp. 316–18. The Mountaineer Republic included what is known today as North Ossetia, Chechnya, and Dagestan.

tematic transition to socialism. That is what you must understand and what you must be able to carry out, as distinct from our own tactics.

We fought to make the first breach in the wall of world capitalism. The breach has been made. We have maintained our positions in a fierce and superhuman war against the Whites, the Socialist Revolutionaries, and the Mensheviks, who were supported by the Entente countries, their blockade and military assistance.

You, comrade Communists of the Caucasus, have no need to force a breach. You must take advantage of the favorable international situation in 1921 and learn to build the new with greater caution and more method. In 1921 Europe and the world are not what they were in 1917 and 1918.

Do not copy our tactics but analyze the reasons for their peculiar features, the conditions that gave rise to them, and their results; go beyond the letter and apply the spirit, the essence, and the lessons of the 1917–21 experience. You must make trade with the capitalist countries your economic foundation right away. The cost should be no object even if it means letting them have tens of millions' worth of valuable minerals.

You must make immediate efforts to improve the condition of the peasants and start on extensive electrification and irrigation projects. What you need most is irrigation, for more than anything else it will revive the area and regenerate it, bury the past, and make the transition to socialism more certain.

I hope you will pardon my slipshod style: I have had to write the letter at very short notice, so as to send it along with Comrade Myasnikov. Once again I send my best greetings and wishes to the workers and peasants of the Soviet republics of the Caucasus.

N. Lenin

On the Federation of Transcaucasian Republics

MEMO TO STALIN

NOVEMBER 28, 1921

Comrade Stalin, in the main I agree with you, but I feel that the wording should be somewhat amended.[3]

1. While a federation of Transcaucasian republics is absolutely correct in principle and should be implemented without fail, its immediate practical realization must be regarded as premature, i.e., a certain period of time will be required for its discussion, propagation, and adoption by lower Soviet bodies;

2. The Central Committees of Georgia, Armenia, and Azerbaijan shall be instructed (through the Caucasian Bureau) to submit the federation question for broad discussion in the party and by the *worker and peasant masses,* conduct vigorous propaganda *in favor* of a federation and secure *decisions* to that effect by the congresses of soviets in each of these republics. Should serious opposition arise, the Political Bureau of the CC, RCP must be informed accurately and in good time.

Lenin

3. Lenin, CW, vol. 33, p. 127. This memo was first published in 1923 as part of the materials for the Twelfth Congress of the Russian Communist Party.

Regarding the conclusions of the Dzerzhinsky commission

MARCH 3, 1923

1. The Dzerzhinsky commission came to the following conclusion:[4]

"The political line carried out by the Caucasian Bureau, initially, and then by the Transcaucasian Regional Committee, and by Comrade Ordzhonikidze in particular, corresponded fully to the instructions of the RCP Central Committee and were entirely correct."

It is necessary to distinguish between two lines: first, the line of the RCP CC up to the middle of 1922, which was elaborated, as we know, in Comrade Lenin's letter; and, second, the line after the middle of 1922, which comes through in the following words of the executive secretary of the new Central Committee of Georgia (see his report to the

> "The line of Comrade Ordzhonikidze corresponded fully to the instructions of the RCP Central Committee."

4. This document, not previously published in any language, is the concluding section of a report drawn up for Lenin by three of his secretaries in February and March 1923. It followed the report back from the commission headed by Dzerzhinsky, charged with investigating recent events in Georgia.

The quotes that appear in the right hand column summarize findings of

264

November 22, 1922, plenum of the CC of Georgia):

"Comrades in Georgia fetishized a tactic of concessions, even though this is not a time for political
concessions, but rather, as in Russia, for a political
offensive. The class struggle is sharpening over the
national question, but a large part of the party and
the former CC persist in their policy, not wanting to
accept this fact."

---

the Dzerzhinsky commission. Alongside these, Lenin's secretaries set out
their conclusions.

One of the incidents the commission had uncovered was the physical attack
by Ordzhonikidze against Kobakhidze, one of the dissenting CP leaders in Georgia. (See footnote 12, chapter 5.) These facts had been summarized on December
12 by Dzerzhinsky to Lenin, who in the meantime had fallen seriously ill.

Lenin charged his secretaries with thoroughly reviewing Dzerzhinsky's
report. According to instructions dictated to his secretaries, they were to
find out:

"1. Why was the former Georgian CC accused of deviationism?

"2. Why were they accused of breaking party discipline?

"3. Why was the Zakkraykom [the regional leadership of the Transcaucasian Federation] accused of repressing the Georgian CC?

"4. Physical means of oppression (the 'biomechanics').

"5. The line adopted by the CC of the RCP in the absence and in the
presence of Vladimir Ilyich.

"6. With whom did the commission come into contact in the course of
its work? Did it inquire only into the accusations made against the Georgian CC, or also into those made against the Zakkraykom? Did it study
the affair of the 'biomechanics'?

"7. The present situation: the electoral campaign, the Mensheviks, oppression, the national quarrel."

"Biomechanics" refers to the physical attack on Kobakhidze by Ordzhonikidze.

On February 14 Lenin gave the secretaries further instructions:

"Three elements: (1) it is not permitted to strike someone; (2) concessions
are indispensable; (3) one cannot compare a small state with a large one.

"Did Stalin know (of the incident)? Why didn't he do something about it?"

After receiving the report Lenin sent his March 5 message to Trotsky,
and on March 6 his letter of support to the dissenting Georgian CP leaders (see chapter 9).

"Regarding the Conclusions of the Dzerzhinsky Commission" is
printed by permission of the Russian Institute for the Preservation and
Study of Documents of Contemporary History.

The conclusion of the Dzerzhinsky commission is accurate only with regard to the second period, when the RCP CC supported without fail the Transcaucasian Regional Committee.

2. In its conclusions, the Dzerzhinsky commission writes:

"The Transcaucasian Regional Committee, and Comrade Ordzhonikidze in particular, are accused of carrying out a war communist policy from the top down, with excessive haste, and without the slightest regard for local party organizations, while failing to prepare public opinion for its measures. They are accused of carrying out a line often in contradiction with that of the RCP CC or with failure to advance a line. These charges are without foundation. The commission concludes that on all the fundamental questions, and especially that of federation of the Transcaucasus, the Regional Committee always campaigned along party and soviet lines. It did so despite the resistance of the former CC of Georgia, whose conduct unquestionably weakened this campaign."

This conclusion does not entirely correspond to the facts assembled by the Dzerzhinsky commission itself "on all the fundamental questions, and especially that of federation of the Trzanscaucasus." Precisely on the question of federation, the Caucasus Bureau took its decision without any preparatory discussion in the party, publishing it the following day in the newspaper. And on this very question the RCP CC supported the line of the CC of Georgia, giving instructions for a campaign along party and soviet lines. The commission, as is evident from the conclusion quoted above, ignores this fact. As for resistance to the campaign by the CC of Georgia, no evidence of this is found in the documents of the commission.

As for the Regional Commission's use of a war communist policy, the following quotation from the

> "The charge that the Transcaucasian Regional Committee was carrying out a policy of war communism has no foundation in reality."

executive secretary of the new CC of Georgia shows that war communism has still not been completely overcome. Reproaching the old CC for the absence of a firm dictatorial line at a November 8, 1922, meeting of district and regional secretaries, he said, "Here you don't see a firm Chekist regime.[5] Everybody moves about freely. And there is not that fear that characterizes a proletarian dictatorship." (From the letter of the Makharadze and Mdivani group to the RCP CC.)

3. According to the Dzerzhinsky commission:

"Charges that the Transcaucasian Regional Committee and the new CC of Georgia displayed 'Russian obstructionism,' paid insufficient attention to the national question in Georgia, and discriminated along national lines, are without foundation. The commission maintains that the Regional Committee gave close attention to all conflicts rooted in 'Russian obstructionism' and 'colonialist tendencies' and took energetic measures against them."

"Accusations against the Regional Committee of Russian obstructionism are unfounded."

The commission artificially narrows the question of "great powerism" by posing it on a formal plane: when disputes were brought to the attention of the Regional Committee, they say, the committee examined them carefully. The commission did not pose in their full scope the questions:

a) Did the policies of the Regional Committee contribute to the overall growth of "Russian obstructionism," creating conditions that aggravated it?

b) Did the struggle within the party against the so-called deviationists, once it had been carried into the soviets and had become the property of the masses, become transformed into a legal method of great-power repression?

c) When the line of the former CC was declared to be a nationalist deviation in the Georgian party, was

5. The Cheka was the Russian abbreviation for the security police. In January 1922 the Cheka was replaced by the State Political Administration (GPU).

this not in itself a manifestation of great-powerism?

d) Was not the very slogan "deviationists" and its utilization tendentious?

4. The Dzerzhinsky commission states in its conclusions:

"The Caucasian Bureau and the Transcaucasian Regional Committee, following the directives of the RCP CC, and of Lenin in particular, and taking into account the particular conditions of the Transcaucasian republics, and especially of Georgia, quite consciously made concessions to the nationalist sentiments of the masses and the intelligentsia."

How these concessions were expressed concretely is not evident from the materials of the commission. On the contrary, what is evident from these materials is that the Central Committee of Georgia's demands for concessions and for a policy of concessions were seen as being a nationalist deviation in the party, one that must be fought without mercy.

"The Regional Committee consciously granted certain concessions."

5. During a session of the commission, Comrade Dzerzhinsky stated:

"They ['the deviationists'] are not Communists to the marrow of their bones. They are unable to substantiate with facts the existence of nationalism in the peasantry. They themselves are creating the conditions for nationalism; and for that reason they are very dangerous for the party." (From the commission minutes.)

It thus follows that it is not objective conditions that create nationalism in Georgia, but rather a small group of Communists, who in the opinion of the commission have broken with us. From this Comrade Manuilsky draws the logical conclusion:

"The continued presence here of Comrade Makharadze and others at the top is destructive to our party. The removal of these top-rung figures is essential to restore the Georgian party's health and give it

"The 'deviationists' are only a small group that has broken with the masses."

the opportunity to overcome atamanism, this cult of personality."

The assertion that the "deviationists" represent a small upper layer cut off from the masses also finds expression in a letter of the RCP CC to the provincial committees:

"The above-mentioned group of Georgian Communists (Mdivani, Makharadze, Kavtaradze, Tsintsadze, Toroshelidze) represent an insignificant minority of the Communist Party of Georgia."

However, the materials of the Dzerzhinsky commission contain no convincing proof of this. On the contrary, the materials contain a petition to the CC of the RCP from five hundred workers in defense of the former Central Committee of Georgia.

After the resignation of the former CC, votes were held at numerous meetings of the CP of Georgia that favored the new Central Committee. This voting, however, provides no more than formal evidence supporting the findings of the Dzerzhinsky commission, since it was carried out under great pressure in an atmosphere of baiting, intimidation, and repression.

6. The Dzerzhinsky commission recognizes that:

"The Transcaucasian Regional Committee is by and large acting correctly in carrying out a struggle against the line of the former CC of Georgia."

But the commission did not address *how* and by what methods this struggle was conducted. As early as August 1921 the Caucasian Bureau spoke about the methods of struggle, indicating the necessity to "combat the nationalist deviation mercilessly" and to "burn out the nationalist survivals with a red-hot iron." Addressing a November 21 party meeting in Tiflis, Comrade Ordzhonikidze underscored this still more vigorously and broadly: "We believe the number one task of our party, *and of Soviet power,* is to wage a merciless struggle against the remnants of the

"The Regional Committee acted correctly in conducting a struggle against the CC of Georgia."

shameful past, to burn out with a red-hot iron, to use the words of Comrade Stalin, the remnants of nationalism."

In the process of this struggle, the group of Mdivani and Makharadze, a majority of the Central Committee, and significant layers of the party in Georgia were accused of "deviationism." The tactic of the red-hot iron, in its extreme manifestations, descended to foul abuse at party meetings, defamation, baiting, and intimidation. The commission did not examine and verify the numerous statements on hand in this regard and did not attach to them cardinal importance. The commission did not get down to the question of whether these methods of struggle were correct, and whether they played a decisive role in reducing the Communist Party of Georgia to its present condition.

The Dzerzhinsky commission confirms that this entire intraparty struggle found a vivid reverberation in the masses, and that the Mensheviks amplified it in their interests and carried on a definite nationalist agitation to the effect that the CC of Georgia, which had tried to carry through a line of concessions, had run up against the great-power ambitions of the representatives of Moscow.

Signed: L. Fotieva, N. Gorbunov, M. Glyasser

The Workers and Peasants Inspection
(1919–20, 1923)

Note on the reorganization of state control

TO JOSEPH STALIN

MARCH 8, 1919

To J.V. Stalin:

I think the following should be added to the decree on control:[1]

1. formation of central (and local) bodies for workers' participation;

2. introduction by law of the systematic participation of voluntary inspectors from among the workers, with compulsory participation of up to two-thirds women;

3. giving immediate priority to the following as our urgent tasks:

a) lightning inquiries into citizens' complaints

b) combating red tape

c) revolutionary measures to combat abuses and red tape

d) special attention to boosting labor productivity, and

e) to increasing the quantity of production, etc.

1. Lenin, *CW*, vol. 28, p. 486. See also vol. 36, p. 504.

Political Bureau directives on a workers inspection

JANUARY 23, 1920

The Presidium of the All-Russia Central Executive Committee and the State Control Commissariat to be asked to be guided by the following directives of the CC, RCP:[2]

1. No new bodies to be set up in any field of state administration, and the existing commissariats to be improved.

2. The Workers and Peasants Inspection to be developed, strengthened, and extended in every way, all work being directed toward ensuring complete numerical predominance of workers and peasants in State Control.

3. No skilled workers, only unskilled workers, mainly women, to be enlisted in the Workers Inspection.

4. A new draft of Workers and Peasants Inspection under the State Control Commissariat to be drawn up immediately with the cooperation of Avanesov and submitted to the Politburo not later than 1/28/1920.

2. Lenin, *CW*, vol. 42, p. 160.

Remarks on and addenda to drafts for 'Rules for the Workers and Peasants Inspection'

JANUARY 24, 1920

To Comrade Stalin. Copies to Avanesov and Tomsky, and also to Kiselyov, member of the Presidium of the All-Russia Central Executive Committee.

On the basis of directive given by the Central Committee the three drafts should, in my opinion, be worked up into one.[3]

I think you should add:

1. The "Department" of the Workers and Peasants Inspection at the State Control Commissariat should be a temporary one for the purpose of involving the Workers and Peasants Inspection *in all* departments of the State Control Commissariat, and should then disappear as a special department.

2. Purpose: *all* working people, both men and *particularly women*, should serve in the Workers and Peasants Inspection.

3. For this draw up lists in the localities (in accordance with the constitution), excluding clerks, etc.

—all others *in turn* to participate in the Workers and Peasants Inspection.

4. Participation to vary according to the degree of development of the participants—beginning with the role of "listener," or witness, or

Footnotes start on next page

learner for the illiterate and completely undeveloped workers and peasants, and ending with the granting of all rights (or almost all) to the literate and developed who have been *tested* in some way or another.

5. Pay special attention to (and make strictly precise rules for), and *extend* control by the Workers and Peasants Inspection over accounting for food, *goods*, warehouses, tools, materials, fuel, etc., etc. (in dining rooms, etc., especially).

Women, literally *every woman, must* be drawn into this work.

6. So as not to get into a mess with the involvement of masses of participants they must be drawn into the work gradually, in turn, etc. The ways in which they participate must also be carefully planned (two or three at a time, rarely, in special cases, more, so that they will not waste the working time of the clerks).

7. Detailed instructions must be compiled.

8. Officials of the State Control Commissariat must (in accordance with a special instruction), first, invite representatives of the Workers and Peasants Inspection to all their operations, and secondly, deliver lectures to *nonparty* conferences of workers and peasants (popular lectures according to a specially approved program on the principles of the State Control Commissariat and its methods; perhaps the lectures could be replaced by the reading of a pamphlet that we shall publish—that is, the State Control Commissariat, Stalin and Avanesov, will publish it with the special participation of the party—and commenting on that pamphlet).

9. *Gradually* summon peasants from the localities (they must be nonparty peasants) to participate in the State Control Commissariat at the center; begin with at least (if it is impossible to do more) one or two from each province and then, depending on transport and other conditions, *increase the number.* The same thing for nonparty workers.

10. Gradually introduce the verification of the participation of working people in the State Control Commissariat by the party and the trade unions, i.e., through these organizations verify whether everyone participates and what results come from the participation insofar as learning the business of state administration is concerned.

Lenin

Plan of an article:
'What should we do with the WPI?'

DICTATED NOT LATER THAN JANUARY 9, 1923

1. Our state apparatus as a whole is most closely tied, most imbued with the old spirit.[4]

In this way we may better renovate it.

2. Such a type of apparatus as that directly connected with the Central Committee makes for the greatest mobility.

3. It enjoys greatest authority.

4. Won't that make for too many CC members?

5. The conference nature of the CC plenums has already grown out of our previous party building.

6. A ruling is possible limiting attendance of CC members at meetings of higher government bodies (the CPC, CLD, All-Russia Central Executive Committee, etc.).

7. It is possible to arrange their taking turns in attending these meetings.

8. It is possible to arrange their taking turns at the meetings of the board of the Workers and Peasants Inspection.

9. Possible objections to this plan: too many inspectors, too much supervision, too many chiefs having the right to demand an immediate reply and tearing the staff away from their direct duties, etc.

10. Answer: we propose an unusual type of personnel for the WPI.

11. How account for the fact that the Commissariat of Foreign Affairs has a better type of staff? And what are the conditions for making a similar renovated apparatus out of the WPI?

12. The WPI should start right away organizing the work on new lines, guided by five years' experience.

13. New organization of work on the part of the CC Secretariat (training new members of the CC in all the details of administration).

14. Better organization of Politburo meetings will come about in the course of the work itself.

15. Important gain from increasing the number of CC members—lessening the personal and casual element in its decisions, etc.

4. Lenin, *CW*, vol. 42, pp. 433–34.

What should we do with the Workers and Peasants Inspection? (First draft)

JANUARY 9, 1923

Without a doubt, the Workers and Peasants Inspection is an enormous difficulty for us.[5] So far nothing has come of it, and the question remains of its organization and even its expediency.

I think that those who doubt the need for it are wrong. At the same time, however, I do not deny that the problem presented by our state machinery and the task of improving it is very difficult and far from being solved.

With the exception of the People's Commissariat of Foreign Affairs, our state apparatus is largely a survival of the past, and scarcely affected by any drastic change. It has only been slightly touched up on the surface. In all other respects, in order to get it to work properly, it has always been necessary for the workers and peasants state—a state built entirely on new lines—to concentrate members of the party in it throughout the hierarchical framework.

In order to confirm what has been said, it is worth remembering how we acted in the critical moments of the civil war, how we concentrated our best party forces in the Red Army, how we resorted to the mobilization of the advanced workers from among the party ranks.

And so, I believe, as a result of all our attempts to reorganize the Workers and Peasants Inspection, the conclusion follows that we have not made one more attempt. Namely, we have not tried to put this matter into the hands of our workers and peasants, by placing them at the head of our party as members of the Central Committee.

I visualize this reform of the WPI in the following manner: some fifty to seventy-five workers and peasants, fully tried and trusted as to conscientiousness and devotion, will be elected to the CC of the party in addition to the other CC members. At the same time, the staff of the WPI should be reduced at last (at long last!) to several hundred, consisting, on the one hand, of persons with the most experience in the WPI work in general—i.e., persons who are most familiar with the general supervision of our apparatus of highly skilled specialists and who have a knowledge of both our apparatus and of the principles and problems of office work organization, methods of verification and investigation—and, on the other hand, of persons of the purely secretarial, auxiliary staff.

The task of the new members of the CC, who have fully equal rights with the other members of the CC, is, by long, hard work, to make a study of and improve our state machinery. All the other members of the WPI staff are to help them in this, some as persons most familiar with this machinery and with the work of the WPI, others as employees of the secretarial type.

At the same time the People's Commissariat of the Workers and Peasants Inspection could remain the same commissariat it has been up till now. The new members of the CC could be considered temporarily attached to it. The people's commissar of the WPI could retain his present rank, position, and rights along with the members of his board.

What do we stand to gain from such an organization? First of all, we would drop once and for all the practice of new reorganizations undertaken on the basis of an inadequate study of our apparatus. Second, we would enhance the authority of this commissariat both

5. Lenin, *CW*, vol. 42, pp. 435–40. The final version of this article appears in chapter 8.

by means of enlisting members of the CC to it and by reducing its staff to a few hundred members. From the present position, under which the members of the People's Commissariat of the WPI as a general rule live on sops from the inspected institutions, we would pass immediately to a position under which the maximum independence of the WPI employees would be guaranteed either by a very high salary (this could be achieved by reducing the number of the staff to a few hundred very highly skilled and tested top-level workers), or by those assistants of a purely secretarial type, who would be under the constant control and supervision of both the above-mentioned members of the CC and of the few specialists left by us after careful screening of the commissariat's staff.

The new members of the Central Committee would be assigned the task of making a closer and more careful study of our machinery of state in all its ramifications, including, incidentally, the state trusts.

This job cannot be done quickly. No definite time limit, therefore, would be set for them. On the other hand, they could reckon several years' work by alternating members of the CC working on the same assignment, i.e., by a decision of a party congress, we would guarantee to members of the CC the possibility of working at this job for several years and then returning to their former jobs.

TAKEN DOWN BY M.V.

JANUARY 13, 1923

I foresee that this plan will evoke no end of objections, most of which will be prompted by the vicious howl of the worst of the old elements in our state apparatus, who have remained really old, that is, prerevolutionary. They will say that this will lead to nothing but complete chaos in the work, that the CC members, not knowing what to do, will loiter about the commissariats and government offices, interfering everywhere with the work, demanding explanations, etc., etc.

I think that the nature of these objections clearly betrays the source they come from and are hardly worth answering. Obviously, if we had in mind an ordinary type of staff, some of these objections might be warranted. But the thing is, we do not have in mind the usual type of staff for this commissariat, but single out for it the best workers who, on verification by the party congress, deserve to be elected to the CC. In this way, I believe, we guarantee that the staff of the People's Commissariat of the WPI will be as good as the best of our commissariats, namely, the People's Commissariat of Foreign Affairs.

How do we account for the Commissariat of Foreign Affairs having the best staff of employees? In the first place, because diplomats of the old stamp could not remain there to any noticeable degree; second, because we selected people there anew, selected them by entirely new standards, by their fitness for the new tasks; third, because there, in the foreign commissariat, we do not have (as in other commissariats) that plethora of haphazardly selected employees who, practically speaking, have inherited all the old qualities of officialdom; and fourth, because the foreign commissariat is working under the direct guidance of our Central Committee. This, as a matter of fact, is the only one of our commissariats that has been fully renovated and that is really working for the workers and peasants government and in the spirit of that government and not merely giving the impression of working for it, while actually, in the main, working against it or in the wrong spirit.

Now what conditions are we faced with in our attempt to make a truly renovated apparatus out of the WPI? The first condition—conscientiousness, will be fully ensured by selection; the second condition is the high qualities of the staff members as regards their devotion to the cause and their abilities; the third condition is their closeness to the highest party body and their equal rights with those who lead our party and, through it, the whole of our state apparatus.

It may be said that no amount of conscientiousness or party author-itativeness can make up for what, in this case, is the most important thing, namely, knowledge of one's business, knowledge of our state apparatus, and knowledge of the way it should be remodeled.

My reply to this is that one of the essential conditions of my pro-posal is that we are not to expect quick results in the work of the new commissariat and anticipate that this work will go on for many years. The question then boils down to organizing the work of the new commissariat.

And here I feel justified in presuming that both our party workers and the people now in charge of the WPI have accumulated sufficient experience, sufficient knowledge, sufficient ability, and other qualities to properly organize the training of the new CC members, and a practical training at that, i.e., by combining their familiarization with all the details of our state apparatus with a study of what modern science has achieved in the bourgeois states as regards efficient organization of every kind of staff work.

TAKEN DOWN BY L.F.

JANUARY 13, 1923

I assume that it goes without saying that the WPI will start at once, on the basis of five years' experience, organizing the work on new lines. It will divide the new workers into a number of groups and assign the work among these groups systematically. It will di-vide these groups into periodically employed people with a practical knowledge of foreign experience and people engaged in theoretical work with knowledge of the results of modern science in the field of organization of labor generally and managerial work in particular. It will arrange for all the WPI workers to go through the jobs assigned to them, systematically working from the bottom upwards, perform-

ing varied functions in varied fields of administration, in varied localities, in varied conditions of work as regards nationalities, and so
on.

In short, I assume that the comrades in the WPI have learned
something during these five years and will be able to apply the
knowledge they have gained to the new organization of the commissariat. Moreover, it should not be forgotten that we have, I believe,
three scientific institutions carrying out research into problems of
work organization (the Central Institute of Labor, a special group
under the WPI, and a group under the Military Commissariat). A
meeting of these three groups was held recently,[6] and it is to be
hoped that their work will now proceed in a more efficient manner
and in a better team spirit than heretofore.

What is the new work organization that I propose for the Secretariat of our CC? Naturally, the increased number of CC members
will require a new organization of the work. I must point out, however, that actually we have already passed to a form of organization
of our CC plenums similar to that of the highest conferences. The
thing now is to organize the training of these new CC members in
all Central Committee work and familiarize them with the work of
the leading state institutions. If we are late with this, we shall not be
fulfilling one of our main duties, namely, that of taking advantage of
our being in power in order to teach the best elements of the working people all the details of administration. Such measures as making better arrangements for the meetings of our Politburo, holding
them twice a week and reducing the length of sittings, better preparation of all the documents for these meetings and arranging for
these documents to be at the disposal of all the members of the CC
in good time. These measures now follow from the entire course of
the work and are essential, so much so that any kind of objection to
this is hardly conceivable. Naturally, this will call for an increase in
expenditure on secretarial-type personnel, but to grudge the money

6. A conference on the organization of management was held in September 1922 in Moscow.

for these expenses would be most unwise.

Besides, speaking frankly to comrades, I consider an important advantage in increasing the number of CC members to be a reduction of the chances of a personal, incidental element being introduced in its decisions. These decisions will be better prepared, the endorsements made at such meetings will be more thoroughly verified, and as a result there will be greater stability in our CC, both as regards the continuity of its work and its power to resist splits that might arise from insufficient contact of this body with the masses.

Lenin

Toward the Party Congress
(1923)

Thoughts on the party:
The national question and the education of the party youth
by Leon Trotsky

MARCH 19, 1923

Goethe said long ago that old truths have to be won afresh again and again.[1] This applies to individuals, to parties, and to entire classes. Our party must win for itself afresh, that is, must think out anew, its national program, and consciously check it in actual experience.

Both the domestic policy and the international policy of our party are determined by two fundamental lines—the revolutionary class movement of the Western proletariat and the national-revolutionary movement of the East. We have said before how important it is for us to forge strong living ties between the education of our youth—indeed, of the whole party—and the actual course of the proletarian movement throughout the world. (The education of the party, like that of the individual, is never finished; as long as you live, you learn.) Here we must say that not the least useful political exercise for the orientation and self-education of the party is a clear understanding of the national question.

In saying "not the least," we may risk being misunderstood. After all, what we have in the West is the proletariat, the struggle for power, while in the East, "all in all," it is only a matter of liberating pre-

Footnotes start on next page

289

dominantly peasant nations from an alien yoke. Of course, considered abstractly, these two movements belong to different epochs of social development; but historically they are linked together, directed from two sides against one and the same mighty foe: imperialism. And if we should fail to understand the colossal importance of the national-revolutionary factor, its immeasurable explosive power, we would risk hopelessly compromising the revolutionary movement of the West, and ourselves along with it, for many years if not forever.

From the experience of our revolution we have firmly mastered the importance of correct relations between the proletariat and the peasantry, that is, relations corresponding to their class forces and the course of development of the revolutionary movement throughout the world. We have learned to decline the word *smychka* in all its cases,[2] and that is not accidental—it must be admitted that sometimes we even bring this word in where it is quite irrelevant! But we have thoroughly mastered the basic question. Our government is not called a workers and peasants government for nothing. If the success of our revolution depends on correct collaboration between the proletariat and the peasantry, the success of the world revolution depends, above all, on correct collaboration between the West European proletariat and the peasant, national-revolutionary East. Russia is a gigantic junction of the proletarian West and the peasant East; a junction and at the same time a proving ground.

In Russia itself, however, the question of relations between the

1. This article was first published in a 1923 pamphlet entitled *The Tasks of the Twelfth Party Congress.* An English translation of the main article in that pamphlet, from which it took its name, is available in *Leon Trotsky Speaks* (New York: Pathfinder, 1972), pp. 134–73.

2. The term *smychka,* meaning link or bond, was used to describe the alliance between the working class and the peasantry that was the foundation of the Soviet state. In Russian, to decline a word in all its cases means to list each of the six forms it may take to indicate different grammatical roles in a sentence.

proletariat and the peasantry is not at all homogeneous. One part of the question is the relations between the Great Russian proletariat and the Great Russian peasantry. Here the question stands in its purely class content. This strips and simplifies the task, thereby rendering it easier to solve.

The relations between the Great Russian proletariat, which plays first fiddle in our union state, and the Azerbaijani, Turkestani, Georgian, or Ukrainian peasantry, however, are something else again. There, in the formerly oppressed "borderlands," all social class, economic, administrative, and cultural questions are sharply refracted through a national prism. There, misunderstandings between proletariat and peasantry (and we have seen not a few in these last few years) inevitably assume a national coloring. This also applies to a considerable extent to the proletariat of the formerly oppressed nations.

What in Moscow or Petrograd will be understood as a simple practical conflict between the center and the localities, town and country, textile workers and metal workers, can easily assume in Georgia, Azerbaijan, and even in the Ukraine, the form of a conflict between "great power" Moscow and the demands of small and weaker nations. In certain cases this is the truth of the matter; in others it can appear to be true. Our task consists, first, in preventing it from being true, and, second, in preventing it from seeming true. And this is a very big task, which we must accomplish at all costs, by both constitutional and administrative methods, and above all by party methods.

In what does the danger consist as regards an incorrect policy toward the peasantry? In the fact that the peasantry may cease to be led by the proletariat and fall under the leadership of the bourgeoisie. But this danger is ten times greater when it is a question of the peasant masses—and to a considerable extent also, the young and numerically weak proletariat—of *the small and backward nations that were oppressed by tsarism.* The national link between classes is also a *smychka*, one that has often shown itself in history to be a very strong and tenacious bond. The Georgian Mensheviks, the

Ukrainian Petlyurists, the Armenian Dashnaks, the Azerbaijani Musavatists,[3] and the rest were condemned to insignificance by our correct, that is, attentive and courteous, attitude toward the national demands of those people whose ancient historical resentments were being exploited by those parties.

Conversely, a lack of understanding or an insufficient understanding on our part of the enormous historical importance of winning the complete and unconditional trust of the formerly oppressed nations would inevitably lend each and every demand, every resentment, every discontent of the indigenous working masses a *national*-oppositional coloring. On that basis a nationalist ideology would create, or more exactly, would re-create, a strong "link" between the bourgeoisie and the toilers, wholly directed against the revolution.

The dictatorship of the working class has opened up for the first time in history the possibility of a correct solution to the national question. The Soviet system establishes a completely favorable state framework for this: elastic, resilient, and at the same time always capable of giving expression both to the centripetal tendencies of the revolution, surrounded as it is by innumerable and irreconcilable enemies, and to the planning requirements of a socialist economy. But we should fall into crude self-delusion if we conceitedly supposed that we have already solved the national question. Actually, great-power chauvinism is often hidden under this complacency (and it can be found even in the ranks of our party). It is not of the aggressive kind, but slumbering and not liking to be disturbed.

A "solution" to the national question can be secured only by ensuring to every nation completely unconstrained access to world cul-

3. The Petlyurists were followers of S.V. Petlyura, a bourgeois nationalist who headed an anti-Soviet regime in the Ukraine in 1918–19 and fought together with the Polish army that invaded the Ukraine in 1920. The Dashnaks belonged to the Dashnaktsutiun, a petty-bourgeois party that headed an anti-Soviet government in Armenia in 1918–20. The Musavat Party, a bourgeois party in Azerbaijan, headed an anti-Soviet government there 1918–20.

ture in the language the given nation considers to be its mother tongue. This presumes a great material and cultural advance by our entire union, and we are still far away from that. It is beyond our power to arbitrarily shorten the time that such an advance must take. But one thing *is* in our power: to show and prove to all the small, weak, and backward nations and nationalities formerly oppressed by tsarism that if very important and considerable demands of theirs are not satisfied, this is due to objective conditions common to the whole union, and not at all to inattention, and not at all to great-power partiality. This must be done not in the programmatic declarations, but in our day-to-day state work. And this task, the winning of the complete and unconditional trust of the small and weak nations, confirmed by all their experience, is a paramount party task.

The civil war cut the deepest and clearest channel in the consciousness of the millions of people living in the Soviet Union. In the motives and aims of this war, so far as our party was concerned, there was not an atom of nationalism or "imperialism." The war was essentially a class revolutionary war and in this form it embraced the entire territory of the old tsarist empire, even at moments overflowing the old frontiers. The civil war intersected national groupings in different directions and at different angles, and often bore heavily on certain parts of the present union. During this very severe struggle to save the revolution, the laws of war took precedence over all other laws. Bridges were blown up regardless of what damage would result to economic life. Buildings were taken over for headquarters and barracks from which schoolchildren and their teachers had to be evicted. A harsh military regime cannot but bear heavily on cultural life in general and national culture in particular. Contributing to this was the fact that in particular cases the backwardness of a Red Army unit, the ill will of certain elements in the Communist organization in such a unit, and the inadequate efforts of the political commissars concerned gave rise to ignoring and even roughly trampling upon national feelings and moods. But these were all isolated and passing phenomena.

The civil war welded together with blood the working people of all nationalities in struggle against their class oppressors. But in general, by its very essence, it could not be a school of everyday coexistence and cooperation. It could not go beyond formal and "constitutional" principles to practical, material, and moral equality of the citizens of small and backward nationalities with citizens of the former ruling nationality in *enjoying all those benefits, tangible and intangible, which can and must be ensured by belonging to the Soviet Union.* A feeling of national resentment has been accumulated in the formerly oppressed nations over decades and centuries. And this heritage, as with the oppressed position of women it should be said, cannot be disposed of merely by declarations, however sincere they may be and even if they are given legislative character.

It is necessary that a woman should feel, in ordinary life, in everyday experience, that there are no external restrictions and constraints upon her and no contemptuous or condescending attitude is being taken toward her. On the contrary, she must feel that she not only has her "rights" but is being given fraternal collaboration directed toward helping her to rise to a higher level.

It is necessary that a small nation should feel that a radical and irreversible change has taken place in the consciousness of the former "ruling" nation. It should feel that all departures by members of this nation from practical and moral equality, from actual, living national fraternity will be punished as strikebreaking and treason by the "ruling" nation itself, that is, by its ruling class. Precisely now, with the onset of more organic work, both economic and cultural, the small nations will observe with watchful attention how they are affected by the general economic, political, juridical, and cultural measures of the government of the Soviet Union, that is, primarily what line our party is carrying out in these questions.

Our enemies seek and will continue to seek opportunities for themselves in this sphere. What a rabid international campaign the Social Democrats waged and are still waging around the Georgian question, depicting the eviction of the Mensheviks from Georgia as the suppression of the Georgian nation! We have shown, and with complete justification, that the purging of the Menshevik agents of imperialism from Georgia was a question of life and death for our entire revolution. For us it is beyond question that the proletarian revolution wholly coincides in its aims and consequences with the interests of the small and oppressed peoples. But the living, struggling, as yet uncompleted revolution may in its advance clash with and, without wishing to, inflict blows upon national interests and sentiments. It is not to be doubted that the invasion of Georgia by the Red Army, going to the aid of the Georgian insurgents, not only was interpreted by the charlatans of international Menshevism as "predatory" policy on the part of the Soviet power, but could also be understood in that sense, and was in fact so understood, by a certain section of the Georgian peasantry and even of the Georgian workers.

In struggling against this mood and these views it is absolutely insufficient to show, even with documentation, that the Georgian Mensheviks had deliberately provided an opening for world imperialism that was of the greatest danger to the revolution. The backward section of the Georgian working people that was gripped by national mistrust of the Red Army is distinguished by this fact: it cannot grasp the significance of revolutionary events in their European and worldwide setting. The only convincing policy for us can be a policy that in deeds shows the Georgian peasantry that its national-cultural interests, its national feelings, its national self-respect, which in the past has too often been insulted, find today all the satisfaction that is possible under the objective circumstances.

It is very possible that we can expect a certain exacerbation of national sensitivity and even national mistrust among those nationalities which formerly were oppressed and which, of course, demand of the revolution, and quite rightly, that it guarantee them against any sort of relapse into national inequality in the future. On this basis it is quite possible that a penetration or intensification of nationalistic tendencies (predominantly *defensive*-nationalistic) may take place even among the Communists of the small nations. Such phenomena, however, as a general rule, are not of an independent nature but are reflexive, symptomatic. Just as anarchist-adventurist tendencies in working-class circles are usually a sign and result of the opportunist character of the leaders of the labor organizations, so nationalist tendencies among the Communists of the small nations are a sign that the aims of great-powerism are not yet everywhere eradicated in the general state machine or even in some corners of the ruling party itself.

The danger in this direction is all the greater because the young generation of party members have not, on the whole, come up against the national question in politics. In tsarist Russia this question inescapably confronted the revolutionary party in the form of national oppression and played an outstanding role in our day-to-day agitation. Party theory accorded a big place to the national question. The "old men" passed through all this—although even here cases of recidivism have not been rare. The youth were born to politics in a country without national oppression. They know about the question of military defense of the republic; they went on to questions of the economy. The national question hardly faced them in any real way. For this reason it sometimes seems to them that it is something already settled, like religion, for instance. Is there really, they ask, anything to be said or thought about such a matter?

Among the small or backward nations themselves there is often to be observed insufficient attention to the national question on the part of the more revolutionary elements, including the proletarians. Having adhered to the Russian Communist Party and at once enlarged their own horizons, these young, sincere, ardent revolutionists are sometimes inclined to look upon the national question on their own doorstep not as a problem to be solved but as a mere obstacle to be jumped over. It is certainly the case that a struggle against their own domestic nationalism, even if it has grown out of former oppression, is an important task for revolutionary elements everywhere. But on soil that has been plowed by the old oppression, this struggle must assume a patient, propagandist character and must rely on thoughtfully meeting national demands, not on ignoring them.

A brushing aside of the national question is sometimes found in the case of quite old comrades on the grounds that it is, they say, a temporary "concession," something like our "Narodnik" agrarian program,[4] or the NEP. Well, this comparison can be accepted, conditionally. It would of course be easier to build socialism if there were no need to make national "concessions"; that is, if there had not been oppression in the past, and if in the present there were not differences in language and national culture. It would also be easier to build socialism if we did not have millions of peasants. One can go even further and say: It would be better for the proletarian revolution if Asia constituted a capitalist arena of class struggle like Europe. But putting the question like that is utterly remote from life. Essentially, inattention or a contemptuous attitude to the national question often conceals a lifeless, confused, rationalistic attitude toward history. The mighty revolutionary realism of our party, on the contrary, consists in taking facts as they are and combining them practically in the interests of the revolution.

If, on the eve of October, we had closed our eyes to the peasantry we would, of course, not have been any nearer to socialism today, and indeed we should not have got so far as Soviet power. Only in these years since October has our party fully understood the significance of the peasantry: the "old men" understood in practice what previously they had only known in theory, and the youth, having come up against the question in practice, are now comprehending its experience theoretically. *In the field of the national question the party as a whole undoubtedly needs a refresher course, and*

4. The Narodniks, a revolutionary movement in Russia in the late nineteenth century, demanded distribution of the landed estates to the peasantry as the key to opening the road to socialist development. Before 1917, the Bolshevik program, while demanding confiscation of the landlords' estates, did not call for the division of the land among the peasants. The Decree on Land adopted by the Bolshevik-led government in November 1917 expropriated and nationalized the land from these estates but empowered the peasantry to distribute this land and farm it on a family basis.

the youth a beginners' course. And this course must be undertaken in good time and according to a very stiff program, for whoever ignores the national question risks getting bogged down in it.

An attentive attitude toward national demands does not mean at all, of course, the cultivation of economic separation. That could only be of advantage to the local ("national") bureaucracy but certainly not to the masses. It is quite obvious that a centralized administration of the railways throughout the union does not at all exclude the use of national languages on the railways. And when evaluating demands and programs for autonomy it is proper to strictly and attentively distinguish between the purely bureaucratic, "prestige and precedence" pretensions of the administrative upper circles and the genuine, everyday, vital interests and demands of the masses. The former are sometimes extremely Russified in relation to the local population, and at the same time separatist in relation to the center.

The widest independence in the national-cultural sphere is in principle fully compatible with economic centralization, insofar as centralization is required by national and production-technique conditions. But state coordination of economic centralization with national-cultural decentralization—in life, in practice—is a big and complex task. Its implementation requires prudence, thoughtfulness, and self-control. Undoubtedly, the nationalities that formerly suffered oppression and that still bear the marks of it may show themselves inclined to uphold their autonomy also in those fields that could be essentially centralized without any loss to national independence and with great administrative or economic benefit to all. But even in such doubtful matters it is necessary first of all to do everything that can be done so that at least the leading circles of the small or backward nation may appreciate the advantages and benefits of centralization. They can then help the masses to appreciate the measure in question, not as some sort of pressure from the center but as a measure that meets the interests of all and is being put into effect by consent. In politics it is impossible to think rationalistically, and in the national question less than anywhere else.

Two more words in conclusion. Not long ago I had occasion to hear from a certain not-so-young Communist that to bring forward the importance of the national factor in the revolution is—it is embarrassing but it must be confessed—Menshevism and liberalism. Here already we see what it really means to turn things and concepts upside down! The position of Menshevism on the national question is this: While Menshevism is in opposition, it is nationally sentimental and given to democratic appeals, never daring to put the question sharply, that is, on the plane of calling on the oppressed to revolt. When the national bourgeoisie is in danger, or when Menshevism itself is in power, it is filled to the brim with awareness of the importance and responsibility of the great-power mission entrusted to it by the bourgeoisie and continues the centralizing oppressive policy, dressing it up with charges of nationalism against— the oppressed nations. Bolshevism showed its revolutionary farsightedness in the fact that it knew how to appreciate from the class point of view the enormous revolutionary importance of the national factor. And in this spirit and direction Bolshevism will continue in the future to educate the youth.

Letter to L.B. Kamenev on Lenin's article on the national question for the twelfth party congress

by L.A. Fotieva

APRIL 16, 1923

To Comrade Kamenev (copy to Comrade Trotsky)

Lev Borisovich:

To round out our telephone conversation, I am informing you, as acting chairman of the Political Bureau, of the following:[5]

As I already told you, on December 31, 1922, Vladimir Ilyich dictated an article on the national question.

This question has worried him extremely and he was preparing to speak on it at the party congress. Not long before his last illness he told me that he would publish this article, but later. After that he took sick without giving final instructions.[6]

---

5. Printed in Trotsky, "Letter to the Bureau of Party History," in *Stalin School of Falsification*, p. 70.

6. The article referred to is the section of Lenin's "Letter to the Party Congress" written on December 30–31, 1922 (see chapter 5). When the twelfth party congress opened on April 17, 1923, its presiding committee decided against publishing this article. It did make the article known among congress delegates, but with the proviso that it not be quoted or discussed in the congress sessions. The attitude to it of forces led by Stalin was voiced by A.S. Yenukidze, secretary of the Soviet Central Executive Committee, who explained that Lenin had been the victim of one-sided, inaccurate information.

The resolution on the national question presented by Stalin at the Twelfth Congress affirmed many general principles of communism on this question, including the need to combat Great Russian chauvinism. Yet in his report Sta-

Vladimir Ilyich considered this article to be a guiding one and extremely important. At his direction it was communicated to Comrade Trotsky, whom Vladimir Ilyich authorized to defend his point of view upon the given question at the party congress in view of their solidarity upon it.

The only copy of the article in my possession is preserved at Vladimir Ilyich's instructions in his secret archive.

I bring the above facts to your attention.

I could not do it earlier since I returned to work only today after a sickness.

L. Fotieva

Personal secretary of Comrade Lenin

---

lin implicitly rejected Lenin's position, warning against "bowing and scraping before the representatives" of minority nationalities. The "political basis of the dictatorship of the proletariat is primarily and chiefly the central, industrial [i.e., Russian] regions," Stalin added, not in the "peasant border regions." In contrast to Lenin's call for special measures to help overcome the legacy of centuries of oppression, Stalin warned against "a new theory to the effect that the Great Russian proletariat must be placed in a position of inequality in relation to the former oppressed nations."

When the dissenting leaders in Georgia criticized the policies of Stalin and Ordzhonikidze, they received little backing from the party's central leaders. Mdivani was prevented by the chair from quoting Lenin's letter pledging support to him. The views of his current were rejected by spokesmen for the official policy as a "nationalist deviation." Among Political Bureau members, only Bukharin spoke in their defense. Trotsky was not present at the session.

No action was taken on any of Lenin's proposals, including those addressing errors of leadership in the dispute in Georgia. Christian Rakovsky, head of state of the Ukraine, called for revision of the terms of the Soviet republics' unification, asking that nine-tenths of the commissariats be left to the national republics. His proposals were whittled down in committee to a motion to give the non-Russian Soviet republics a slight majority in the Soviet of Nationalities, one of the two supreme bodies of the Soviet system. This was then defeated.

Glossary

Avanesov, Varlaam Aleksandrovich (1884–1930) – joined RSDLP 1903; secretary and member of presidium of All-Russia Soviet Central Executive Committee 1917–19; deputy chairman of Workers and Peasants Inspection.

Bauer, Otto (1881–1938) – leader of Austrian Social Democratic Party and theoretician of Austro-Marxism; Austrian foreign minister 1918–19; opposed Comintern and helped found centrist Two-and-a-Half International.

Bolshevik Party. *See* RSDLP

Bordiga, Amadeo (1889–1970) – Italian revolutionary; head of Italian CP and member of Comintern Control Commission from 1921; member of Comintern Executive Committee presidium 1922–28; replaced as Italian CP leader 1926; expelled for "Trotskyism" 1930.

Bukharin, Nikolai (1888–1938) – joined Bolsheviks 1906; Central Committee member from 1917; editor of *Pravda* 1919–29; head of Comintern 1926–29; headed Right Opposition 1928–29; expelled from Russian CP 1929; executed after Stalin's frame-up trials.

Central Control Commission – body within RCP, formed September 1920; mandated to investigate complaints and violations of discipline and of comradely relations, and combat bureaucratic abuses within the party.

Central Executive Committee – executive body elected by
  Congress of Soviets.

Cheka. *See* State Political Administration

Comintern (Communist or Third International) – world
  organization of Communist movement founded in 1919 as
  revolutionary alternative to class-collaborationist Socialist
  (Second) International.

Constitutional Democrats – also known as Cadets (from the
  Russian pronunciation of the party's initials); principal
  bourgeois party in Russia; founded 1905; supported
  constitutional monarchy; participated in Provisional
  Government in 1917; after October revolution, worked for
  overthrow of Soviet government.

Council of Labor and Defense – coordinating body for defense
  and economic activities; a permanent commission of the
  Council of People's Commissars.

Council of People's Commissars – chief executive agency of Soviet
  government.

Denikin, Anton Ivanovich (1872–1947) – tsarist general; White
  army commander in chief in southern Russia in civil war
  1918–20.

Dzerzhinsky, Feliks (1877–1926) – Polish-born revolutionary;
  Bolshevik Party Central Committee member from 1917;
  headed Cheka (security police) from 1917.

Fotieva, Lydia Aleksandrovna (1881–1969) – Bolshevik from
  1904; worked as secretary in Council of People's
  Commissars and as Lenin's personal secretary.

Frumkin, Moisei Ilyich (1878–1939) – joined RSDLP 1898;
  deputy people's commissar of food until 1922, then deputy
  commissar of foreign trade; supported Right Opposition led
  by Bukharin 1928–29; expelled during purges 1937.

Glyasser, Maria Ignatievna (1890–1951) – joined Bolshevik Party
  1917; secretary in Council of People's Commissars 1918–
  24; one of Lenin's personal secretaries.

Gorbunov, Nikolai Petrovich (1892–1938) – joined Bolshevik
Party 1917; Lenin's assistant in Council of People's
Commissars secretariat; served as council's business
manager.

Haskell, William (1878–1952) – U.S. army officer; representative
in Russia of American Relief Administration 1921–23.

Hoover, Herbert (1874–1964) – after World War I headed
American Relief Administration, which provided medicine
and supplies to famine- and disease-ridden areas of Europe
and particularly served counterrevolutionary forces in
Russian civil war; Republican president of United States
1929–33.

Kamenev, Lev Borisovich (1883–1936) – joined RSDLP 1901;
Bolshevik from 1903; Bolshevik Central Committee and
Political Bureau member from 1917; chairman of Moscow
Soviet 1919–26; deputy chairman of Council of People's
Commissars 1922; aligned with Stalin and Zinoviev 1923–
25; joined Trotsky and Zinoviev in United Opposition to
bureaucratic current led by Stalin 1926–27; executed
during Stalin's frame-up trials.

Kautsky, Karl (1854–1938) – leader of German Social Democratic
Party; apologist for chauvinist SPD majority during World
War I; vehement opponent of Russian October revolution.

Kavtaradze, Sergei Ivanovich (1885–1971) – joined RSDLP 1903;
opposed Stalin in Georgian dispute 1922–23; chairman of
Georgian Council of People's Commissars 1922–23;
supported communist opposition led by Trotsky; expelled
from Russian CP 1927.

Kerzhentsev, Platon Mikhailovich (1881–1940) – Bolshevik from
1904; Soviet ambassador to Sweden 1921–23; head of
Institute for the Scientific Organization of Labor (a division
of Workers and Peasants Inspection) 1923–24.

Khodorovsky, Iosif Isayevich (1885–1940) – joined RSDLP 1903;
secretary of Bolshevik Central Committee Siberian bureau
1921–22; later deputy commissar of education.

Kolchak, Aleksandr Vasiliyevich (1873–1920) – tsarist admiral;
head of White armies in Siberia and "supreme ruler" of
Russian White forces 1918–19; defeated by Red Army;
tried and executed.

Krasin, Leonid Borisovich (1870–1926) – joined RSDLP in 1890s;
politically inactive 1908–17; rejoined Bolsheviks in 1917;
commissar of foreign trade 1922–24.

Krestinsky, Nikolai Nikolayevich (1883–1938) – joined RSDLP
1903; secretary of Bolshevik Central Committee 1919–21;
ambassador to Germany from 1921; supported communist
opposition led by Trotsky 1923–27; executed during
Stalin's frame-up trials.

Krupskaya, Nadezhda Konstantinovna (1869–1939) – joined
RSDLP 1898; collaborator and wife of Lenin; member
Bolshevik Party Central Control Commission from 1924;
briefly supported United Opposition led by Trotsky and
Zinoviev 1926.

Krzhizhanovsky, Gleb Maximilianovich (1872–1959) – joined
Marxist movement 1893; headed Commission for the
Electrification of Russia from 1920; headed State Planning
Commission 1921–30; victim of frame-up purges in 1930s.

Kuibyshev, Valerian Vladimirovich (1888–1935) – joined RSDLP
1904; Bolshevik; secretary of Communist Party Central
Committee April 1922; aligned with Stalin; head of Central
Control Commission and Workers and Peasants Inspection
from May 1923 to 1926.

Lenin, Vladimir Ilyich (1870–1924) – born Vladimir Ilyich
Ulyanov; founder of St. Petersburg League for Emancipation
of the Working Class 1895; exiled to Siberia 1896; escaped
abroad and helped publish Iskra 1990-1903; central leader
of Bolsheviks from 1903; exiled 1907; issued call for new,
revolutionary International 1914; returned to Russia and led
Bolsheviks in struggle for Soviet power 1917; chairman of
Council of People's Commissars 1917–24; central leader of
Comintern; used pen name N. Lenin.

Makharadze, Filipp Yeseyevich (1868–1941) – joined Bolsheviks 1903; party leader in Georgia; Georgian Soviet Central Executive Committee chairman from 1922; opposed Stalin in Georgian dispute 1922–23.

Manuilsky, Dmitri (1883–1952) – with Trotsky, a member of group that fused with Bolsheviks in 1917; supporter of Stalin in 1920s; secretary of Comintern 1931–43.

Mdivani, Polikarp Gurgenovich (Budu) (1877–1937) – head of Georgian revolutionary government 1921; opposed Stalin in Georgian dispute 1922–23; member of Georgian Central Committee until October 1922; supporter of communist opposition led by Trotsky; expelled from party 1928; executed in 1937.

Menshevik Party. *See* RSDLP

Miroshnikov, Ivan Ivanovich (1894–1939) – joined Bolshevik Party 1917; deputy business manager of Council of People's Commissars 1921–37.

Molotov, Vyacheslav Mikhailovich (1890–1986) – joined Bolsheviks 1906; became Political Bureau candidate member and a Central Committee secretary 1921; prominent leader of party and government under Stalin.

Münzenberg, Willi (1889–1940) – German revolutionary; secretary of Communist Youth International 1919–21; headed Workers' International Relief, which sent material aid to Soviet republic, from 1921; German CP Central Committee member from 1927; broke with Stalinism and was expelled 1938.

Orakhelashvili, Mamia Dmitrevich (1881–1937) – Bolshevik from 1903; leader of Georgian Bolshevik Party and Soviet government; secretary of Transcaucasian committee of Central Committee 1922; chairman of Transcaucasian Soviet government 1922–23; Russian CP Central Committee candidate member 1923; full member 1927; executed during Stalin frame-up trials.

Ordzhonikidze, Grigory Konstantinovich (Sergo) (1886–1937) –

joined Bolsheviks 1903; Central Committee member 1912;
chairman of Caucasian Bureau 1921–26; president
Transcaucasian committee of Central Committee;
supported Stalin in Georgian dispute and thereafter;
commissar of heavy industry from 1932; sought to limit
scope of purges 1937; was shot or committed suicide.

Owen, Robert (1771–1858) – English industrialist, social reformer,
and utopian socialist; advocated a system of communist
producers' cooperatives.

Poincaré, Raymond (1860–1934) – president of France 1913–20
and prime minister 1922–24.

Pyatakov, Georgi Leonidovich (1890–1937) – joined Bolsheviks
1910; headed first Soviet Ukrainian government 1919;
candidate Central Committee member 1921; held leading
posts in Soviet industry; supporter of communist opposition
led by Trotsky; expelled from party 1927; executed during
frame-up trials.

Radek, Karl (1885–1939) – Polish-born revolutionary, joined
Bolsheviks 1917; Bolshevik Central Committee member
1919–24; played leading role in Comintern; supporter of
communist opposition led by Trotsky 1923–29; expelled
from CP 1927; arrested during frame-up trials and died in
prison.

Rákosi, Mátyás (1892–1971) – member of Hungarian CP from
1918; member of Hungarian revolutionary government
1919; worked in Comintern Executive Committee 1920–
24 and was its secretary from 1921; headed Hungarian CP
1945–56.

Rakovsky, Christian (1873–1941) – Romanian-born
revolutionary; Bolshevik Central Committee member
1919–27; headed Soviet Ukrainian government 1919–23;
supporter of communist opposition led by Trotsky 1923–
34; died in prison following Moscow frame-up trials.

RSDLP (Russian Social Democratic Labor Party) – founded 1898;
divided at 1903 congress into Bolshevik (majority) and

Menshevik (minority) factions. Bolsheviks changed name to
    Russian Communist Party (Bolsheviks) in March 1918.

Russian Communist Party. *See* RSDLP

Rykov, Aleksey Ivanovich (1881–1938) – joined RSDLP 1899;
    Political Bureau member from 1922; deputy chairman of
    Council of People's Commissars 1921; succeeded Lenin as
    chairman of this body 1924; leader of Right Opposition
    1928–29; executed during frame-up trials.

Second International – founded 1889 as international association
    of workers parties; collapsed at outbreak of World War I
    when leaders of most member parties supported interests of
    own bourgeoisies; revolutionary left wing founded
    Communist International 1919; right wing formed Bern
    International on procapitalist basis 1919 and Labor and
    Socialist International based in London 1923.

Sklyansky, Efraim Markovich (1892–1925) – joined Bolshevik
    Party 1913; deputy commissar of military affairs and
    deputy chairman of Revolutionary Military Council of the
    Republic 1918–24.

Smena vekh (Changing landmarks) – published in Prague and Paris
    1921–22; represented wing of Russian bourgeoisie that
    advocated collaborating with NEP, hoping it would
    regenerate capitalism.

Socialist Revolutionary Party (SR) – formed 1901–2 by rightward-
    moving currents from populist Narodnik tradition; split
    between supporters and opponents of Soviet power on eve of
    October revolution; subsequently, Right SRs opposed
    October revolution and took up arms against Soviet
    government. Left SRs backed October revolution and Soviet
    power; joined Bolsheviks in coalition government November
    28, 1917; broke from Soviet government and organized
    attempted insurrection July 1918; minority currents split
    away and eventually joined Russian CP.

Sokolnikov, Grigory Yakovlevich (1888–1939) – joined
    Bolsheviks 1905; Bolshevik Central Committee member

1917–19, 1922–30; commissar of finance 1922–26; briefly
supported communist opposition led by Trotsky and
Zinoviev; shot after Moscow frame-up trial.

Stalin, Joseph (1879–1953) – joined RSDLP 1898; Bolshevik from
1903; member of Central Committee from 1912;
commissar of nationalities 1917–23; head of Workers and
Peasants Inspection 1919–22; general secretary of Central
Committee from 1922; after Lenin's death presided over
bureaucratic degeneration of Russian CP and Comintern
and their rejection of revolutionary internationalist course;
organized frame-up trials in 1930s and execution of
majority of Bolshevik leaders of Lenin's time.

State Planning Commission (Gosplan) – highest economic
planning body in Russia, established 1921.

State Political Administration – also known by its Russian initials
(GPU); state security police, established February 1922; a
division of Commissariat of Internal Affairs (NKVD);
successor to the Cheka—Russian abbreviation for All-
Russia Extraordinary Commission for Combating
Counterrevolution, Speculation, and Delinquency in Office.

Stomonyakov, Boris Spiridonovich (1882–1941) – Bulgarian-
born revolutionary; joined RSDLP 1902; in Bulgarian
diplomatic service 1917; Soviet trade representative in
Berlin 1920–25.

Sukhanov, Nikolai Nikolayevich (1882–1940) – joined
Mensheviks 1909; quit Mensheviks 1919; worked in Soviet
economic apparatus; wrote seven-volume *Notes on the
Revolution;* jailed 1931 for "sabotage" and "espionage";
shot.

Todorsky, Aleksandr (b. 1894) – joined Bolshevik Party 1918;
prominent Red Army commander during civil war;
imprisoned during frame-up purges of 1930s.

Trotsky, Leon (1879–1940) – aligned with Mensheviks 1903–4;
took intermediate position between Bolsheviks and
Mensheviks 1904–17; joined Bolsheviks and elected to

Central Committee 1917; commissar of foreign affairs
1917–18; organized and led Red Army 1918–25;
prominent leader of Comintern; from 1923 led opposition
in Russian CP and Comintern to the retreat from Leninist
policies; expelled from party 1927; exiled abroad 1929;
assassinated by agent of Stalin.

Tsintsadze, Kote Maksimovich (1887–1930) – joined Bolsheviks
1904; chairman of Georgian Cheka 1921; member
Georgian CP Central Committee and Central Executive
Committee of Georgian Soviet republic; opposed Stalin in
Georgian dispute 1922–23; expelled from party as
supporter of communist opposition led by Trotsky 1927;
deported to Siberia 1928.

Tsyurupa, Aleksandr Dmitriyevich (1870–1928) – joined RSDLP
1898; commissar of food from 1918; deputy chairman of
Council of People's Commissars from 1921; commissar of
Workers and Peasants Inspection 1922–23; Central
Committee member from 1923; chairman of State Planning
Commission 1923–25.

Two-and-a-Half International – derogatory name applied to
International Association of Socialist Parties; formed 1921
by centrist parties that opposed Soviet power but had left
Second International, with which it reunited 1923.

Urquhart, Leslie (1874–1933) – British capitalist with large
investments in Russia before 1917 October revolution;
helped organize intervention and blockade against Soviet
Russia; negotiated unsuccessfully to obtain concession to
operate Soviet mines 1922.

Ustryalov, N.V. (b. 1890) – prominent Cadet leader; served in
Kolchak White Guard regime; after Kolchak's fall,
emigrated to China; leading collaborator of *Smena vekh*
1921–22; favored cooperation with Soviet government;
returned to Soviet Union 1935; imprisoned for "anti-Soviet
activity" 1937.

Varga, Eugen (1879–1964) – Hungarian Communist; chairman of

Hungarian revolutionary government's Supreme Economic
Council 1919; exiled to Russia and joined Russian CP
1920.

Volodicheva, Maria Akimovna (b. 1881) – joined RSDLP 1917;
assistant secretary to Council of People's Commissars and
of Labor and Defense; one of Lenin's secretaries during his
last illness.

White Guards – (also known as Whites); general designation for
Russian counterrevolutionary forces following October
Revolution.

Workers and Peasants Inspection – body established in early 1920
that organized workers and peasants, both members and
nonmembers of Communist Party, in observation and
control of operations of state and Communist Party
apparatus.

Workers Opposition – syndicalist current formed within Russian
Communist Party in 1920; demanded transfer of
management of Soviet economy to trade unions; many of
its leaders later strongly criticized measures enacted to
introduce NEP.

Yenukidze, Avel' Sofronovich (1877–1937) – joined RSDLP
1898; Bolshevik; All-Russia Soviet Central Executive
Committee secretary 1918–35; expelled from CP June
1936; executed.

Zhordania, Noy Nikolayevich (1870–1953) – headed Georgian
Menshevik government 1918–21.

Zinoviev, Gregory (1883–1936) – joined RSDLP 1901; Political
Bureau full member 1921–27; president of Comintern
1919–26; aligned with Stalin and Kamenev 1923–25;
joined Trotsky and Kamenev in United Opposition to
bureaucratic current led by Stalin 1926–27; executed
following first frame-up trial.

Index

The Communist International in Lenin's Time

To See the Dawn

Baku, 1920—First Congress of the Peoples of the East
How can peasants and workers in the colonial world achieve freedom from imperialist exploitation? By what means can working people overcome divisions incited by their national ruling classes and act together for their common class interests? These questions were addressed by 2,000 delegates to the 1920 Congress of the Peoples of the East. $19.95

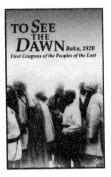

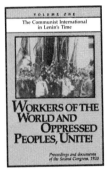

Workers of the World and Oppressed Peoples, Unite!

Proceedings and Documents of the Second Congress, 1920
The debate among delegates from 37 countries takes up key questions of working-class strategy and program and offers a vivid portrait of social struggles in the era of the October revolution.
2 vols., set $65.00

Lenin's Struggle for a Revolutionary International

Documents, 1907-1916; The Preparatory Years
The debate among revolutionary working-class leaders, including V.I. Lenin and Leon Trotsky, on a socialist response to World War I. $32.95

Other volumes in the series:
The German Revolution and the Debate on Soviet Power (1918-1919)
Founding the Communist International (March 1919)

Available from Pathfinder

The Russian revolution

Collected Works of V.I. Lenin

Writings of V.I. Lenin (1870-1924), the central
leader of the Bolshevik Party, the October 1917
Russian revolution, the young Soviet republic, and
the early Communist International. 45 vols. plus
2-vol. index, $500.00

Selected Works of V.I. Lenin

Three-volume selection includes "State and Revolution,"
"Imperialism, the Highest Stage of Capitalism," "One Step
Forward, Two Steps Back," "The April Theses," "The Tax in
Kind," and more. 3-vol. set, $50

Speeches at Party Congresses (1918-1922)

V.I. Lenin
The most pressing questions facing the Russian revolution, taken
up in speeches by the central leader of the Bolshevik Party. $17.95

Alliance of the Working Class and the Peasantry

V.I. Lenin
From the early years of the Marxist movement in Russia, Lenin
fought to forge an alliance between the working class and the
toiling peasantry. Such an alliance was needed to make possible
working-class leadership of the democratic revolution and, on that
basis, the opening of the socialist revolution. $17.95

The History of the Russian Revolution

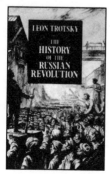

Leon Trotsky
The social, economic, and political dynamics of
the first socialist revolution. The story is told by
one of the revolution's principal leaders writing
from exile in the early 1930s, with these historic
events still fresh in his mind. $35.95

The Revolution Betrayed
WHAT IS THE SOVIET UNION AND
WHERE IS IT GOING?
Leon Trotsky
Classic study of the Soviet workers state and its
degeneration under the brutal domination of the
privileged social caste whose spokesman was Stalin.
Illuminates the roots of the Russian crisis of the
1990s. Also available in Russian and Spanish.
$19.95

The Challenge of the Left Opposition
Leon Trotsky
Documents the fight of the communist opposition
from 1923 to 1929 against the reactionary political
and economic policies of the rising bureaucratic
caste in the Soviet Union. Volume 1 (1923-25),
$27.95. Volume 2 (1926-27), $30.95. Volume 3
(1928-29), $27.95

The Stalin School of Falsification
Leon Trotsky
Reprinting authentic documents from the
Bolshevik archives, Trotsky demonstrates how the
Stalinist bureaucracy falsified history to serve its
own interests and preserve its caste privileges.
$25.95

Questions of National Policy and
Proletarian Internationalism
V.I. Lenin
Why uniting working people the world over in the fight for socialism
requires unconditional support for the right of self-determination of
oppressed nations and nationalities. $12.95

Pathfinder
See addresses at front of book.

Also from Pathfinder

The Changing Face of U.S. Politics
Working-Class Politics and the Trade Unions
Jack Barnes
A handbook for workers coming into the factories, mines, and mills, as they react to the uncertain life, ceaseless turmoil, and brutality of capitalism in the closing years of the twentieth century. It shows how millions of workers, as political resistance grows, will revolutionize themselves, their unions, and all of society. $19.95

The Bolivian Diary of Ernesto Che Guevara
Guevara's account, newly translated, of the 1966-67 guerrilla struggle in Bolivia. A day-by-day chronicle by one of the central leaders of the Cuban revolution of the campaign to forge a continent-wide revolutionary movement of workers and peasants capable of contending for power. Includes excerpts from the diaries and accounts of other combatants. Introduction by Mary-Alice Waters. $21.95

To Speak the Truth
Why Washington's 'Cold War' against Cuba Doesn't End
Fidel Castro and Che Guevara
In historic speeches before the United Nations and its bodies, Guevara and Castro address the workers of the world, explaining why the U.S. government is determined to destroy the example set by the socialist revolution in Cuba and why its effort will fail. $16.95

Nelson Mandela Speaks
Forging a Democratic, Nonracial South Africa
Mandela's speeches from 1990 through 1993 recount the course of struggle that put an end to apartheid and opened the fight for a deep-going political, economic, and social transformation in South Africa. $18.95

Revolutionary Continuity
Marxist Leadership in the United States
Farrell Dobbs
How successive generations of fighters took part in the
struggles of the U.S. labor movement, seeking to build
a leadership that could advance the class interests of
workers and small farmers and link up with fellow
toilers around the world. 2 vols., $16.95 each

Cosmetics, Fashions, and the Exploitation of Women
Joseph Hansen, Evelyn Reed, and Mary-Alice Waters
How big business promotes cosmetics to generate
profits and perpetuate the oppression of women. In
her introduction, Mary-Alice Waters explains how
the entry of millions of women into the workforce
during and after World War II irreversibly changed
U.S. society and laid the basis for a renewed rise of
struggles for women's equality. $12.95

The Struggle for a Proletarian Party
James P. Cannon
In a political struggle in the late 1930s with a petty-bourgeois current in
the Socialist Workers Party, Cannon and other SWP leaders defended
the political and organizational principles of Marxism. The debate
unfolded as Washington prepared to drag U.S. working people into the
slaughter of World War II. A companion to *In Defense of Marxism* by
Leon Trotsky. $19.95

February 1965: The Final Speeches
Malcolm X
Speeches from the last three weeks of Malcolm X's life, presenting the
accelerating evolution of his political views. A large part is material
previously unavailable, with some in print for the first time. The
inaugural volume in Pathfinder's selected works of Malcolm X. $17.95

Write for a free catalog.

Available from Pathfinder

Collected Works of Karl Marx and Frederick Engels
The writings, in 50 volumes, of the founders of the modern revolutionary working-class movement. Vols. 1-34, 38-46 available. Still to be published are vols. 35-37 (Capital) and vols. 47-50 (Engels's final correspondence, 1883-95). $1,075 for 43-vol. set, $25 per volume.

The Communist Manifesto
Karl Marx and Frederick Engels
Founding document of the modern working-class movement published in 1848. Explains how capitalism arose as a specific stage in the economic development of class society and how it will be superseded by socialism through worldwide revolutionary action by the working class. Booklet, $2.50

Genesis of Capital
Karl Marx
The starting point of capitalism, of the development that created both the wage-laborer and the capitalist, was the "servitude of the laborer," Marx writes. This series of events, in which the peasants were driven from the land and deprived of the tools of production "is written in the annals of mankind in letters of blood and fire." Booklet, $3.00

Selected Correspondence
Karl Marx and Frederick Engels
In their correspondence, "Marx and Engels return again and again to the most diverse aspects of their doctrine, emphasizing and explaining—at times discussing and debating—what is newest (in relation to earlier views), most important, and most diffcult."—V.I. Lenin, 1913. $19.95

The Teamster series:
Lessons from
the labor battles of the 1930s
Farrell Dobbs

Four books on the 1930s strikes and organizing drive that transformed the Teamsters union in Minnesota and much of the Midwest into a fighting industrial union movement. Written by a leader of the communist movement in the U.S. and organizer of the Teamsters union during the rise of the CIO.

Teamster Rebellion $16.95
Teamster Power $17.95
Teamster Politics $17.95
Teamster Bureaucracy $18.95

In Defense of Marxism
THE SOCIAL AND POLITICAL CONTRADICTIONS OF
THE SOVIET UNION
Leon Trotsky

During the buildup toward U.S. entry in World War II, Trotsky explains why workers have a stake in opposing imperialist war and in combating assaults on the degenerated Soviet workers state by either the fascist or "democratic" capitalist powers.
$24.95

La revolución traicionada
¿QUÉ ES Y ADÓNDE SE DIRIGE LA UNIÓN
SOVIÉTICA?
Leon Trotsky

Spanish edition of the Revolution Betrayed: What is the Soviet Union and Where Is It Going? $18.95

OTHER TITLES ALSO AVAILABLE IN SPANISH.

WRITE FOR A CATALOG.

New International

A MAGAZINE OF MARXIST POLITICS AND THEORY

New International no. 10
Imperialism's March toward Fascism and War *by Jack Barnes* • What the 1987 Stock Market Crash Foretold • Defending Cuba, Defending Cuba's Socialist Revolution *by Mary-Alice Waters* • The Curve of Capitalist Development *by Leon Trotsky* $14.00

New International no. 9
The Triumph of the Nicaraguan Revolution • Washington's Contra War and the Challenge of Forging Proletarian Leadership • The Political Degeneration of the FSLN and the Demise of the Workers and Farmers Government $14.00

New International no. 8
The Politics of Economics: Che Guevara and Marxist Continuity *by Steve Clark and Jack Barnes* • Che's Contribution to the Cuban Economy *by Carlos Rafael Rodríguez* • On the Concept of Value *and* The Meaning of Socialist Planning *two articles by Ernesto Che Guevara* $10.00

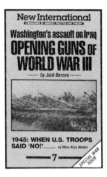

New International no. 7

Opening Guns of World War III:
Washington's Assault on Iraq *by Jack Barnes*
• Communist Policy in Wartime as well as in
Peacetime *by Mary-Alice Waters* • Lessons
from the Iran-Iraq War *by Samad Sharif*
$12.00

New International no. 6

The Second Assassination of Maurice Bishop
by Steve Clark • Washington's 50-year
Domestic Contra Operation *by Larry Seigle*
• Land, Labor, and the Canadian Revolution
by Michel Dugré • Renewal or Death: Cuba's
Rectification Process *two speeches*
by Fidel Castro $10.00

New International no. 5

The Coming Revolution in South Africa *by Jack
Barnes* • The Future Belongs to the Majority *by
Oliver Tambo* • Why Cuban Volunteers Are in
Angola *two speeches by Fidel Castro* $9.00

New International no. 4

The Fight for a Workers and Farmers
Government in the United States *by Jack
Barnes* • The Crisis Facing Working
Farmers *by Doug Jenness* • Land Reform
and Farm Cooperatives in Cuba *two
speeches by Fidel Castro* $9.00

New International no. 3

Communism and the Fight for a Popular Revolutionary Government: 1848 to Today *by Mary-Alice Waters* • 'A Nose for Power': Preparing the Nicaraguan Revolution *by Tomás Borge* • National Liberation and Socialism in the Americas *by Manuel Piñeiro* $8.00

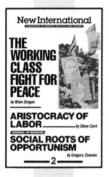

New International no. 2

The Aristocracy of Labor: Development of the Marxist Position *by Steve Clark* • The Working-Class Fight for Peace *by Brian Grogan* • The Social Roots of Opportunism *by Gregory Zinoviev* $8.00

New International no. 1

Their Trotsky and Ours: Communist Continuity Today *by Jack Barnes* • Lenin and the Colonial Question *by Carlos Rafael Rodríguez* • The 1916 Easter Rebellion in Ireland: Two Views *by V.I. Lenin and Leon Trotsky* $8.00